The Competitiveness of G20 Nations

Report on the Group of Twenty (G20) National Innovation Competitiveness Development (2001-2010)

Chief Editors: Li Jianping, Li Minrong & Zhao Xinli

Deputy Chief Editors: Li Jianjian, Huang Maoxing & Su Hongwen

Paths International Ltd

社 会 科 学 文 献 出 版 社
SOCIAL SCIENCES ACADEMIC PRESS (CHINA)

Acclaim for the Book

2012 Key Research Project of National Research Center of Comprehensive Economic Competitiveness

2012-2013 phased research result of the first Young Talents Development Program jointly launched by the Organization Department and Propaganda Department of CPC Central Committee

2011-2012 Major Research Results of "Innovation Team of the Research Center of Comprehensive Industrial and Regional Economic Competitiveness in Fujian Normal University," a Local University Special Project Supported by Central Finance

2011-2012 Research Results of "Fujian Normal University Regional Economic Overall Competitiveness Lab" supported by the project of University Featured Dominant Discipline Labs Co-funded by Central and Local Government

Phased Research Result of General Project (No. 10BJL046) of 2010 National Social Science Fund

Phased Research Result of Youth Project (No. 10CJL006) of 2010 National Social Science Fund

Phased Research Result of Project (No. NCET-10-0017) Supported by 2010 Program for New Century Excellent Talents in University of Ministry of Education

Final Research Result of 2011-2012 Key Research Project of FJNU Political Economics as Fujian Provincial Key Discipline & Key Project Supporting WTSEZ by Fujian Provincial Universities

Phased Research Result of Project funded by 2011 Fujian Provincial University Sci-Tech Innovation Team Incubation Program

Phased Research Result of Project (No. JA10074S) supported by Program for New CenturyExcellent Talents in University of Fujian Province

Phased research result 2012-2013 of FJNU Innovation Team Building Program

Editorial Committee

For Report on the Group of Twenty (G20) National Innovation Competitiveness Development

Editorial Committee

Directors: Lu Zhongyuan, Li Shenming, Li Jianping
Deputy Directors: Gao Yanjing, Xie Shouguang, Li Minrong, Zhao Xinli
Members: Li Jianjian, Huang Maoxing, Su Hongwen

List of Compilers

Chief Editors: Li Jianping, Li Minrong, Zhao Xinli
Deputy Editors: Li Jianjian, Huang Maoxing, Su Hongwen
Editors: Huang Maoxing, Li Junjun, Ye Qi, Lin Shoufu, Chen Hongzhao, Wang Zhenzhen, Zheng Wei, Zhou Limei, Liu Xiaofeng, Chen Weixiong, Shen Neng ,Chen Ling, Lin Qian, Zhang Baoying, Wu Yuning, Yang Xuexing, Yang Ting, Lei Xiaoqiu, Chen Xianlong, Guo Shaokang, Wu Qimian,Xiao Lei

Introduction of the Main Editors

Mr. Li Jianping was born in 1946 in Wenzhou of Zhejiang Province. He is a former President of Fujian Normal University, Director of FJNU Branch of National Research Center of Comprehensive Economic Competitiveness, professor, PhD supervisor, an expert of Fujian Province, receiver of the State Council Special Allowance and National Young & Mid-aged Expert with Outstanding Contribution. He is also an academic leader of Fujian university key discipline "Political Economics," a PhD program in the discipline of Theoretical Economics and sub-discipline of Fundamentals of Marxism. He is Vice Chairman of China Association of Capital Studies, the National Association of Marxist Economics History, China Association of Historic Materialism, Fujian Province Association of Social Sciences, and Fujian Province Association for Science and Technology, as well as economic adviser of the People's Government of Fujian Province. Li Jianping has been doing research on Marxist economic ideological history, capital and socialist market economy, economic reform methodology, and regional economic development. He has taken charge of over 20 national and provincial/ministerial key research projects, compiled/wrote more than 60 such academic books (including those he coauthored) such as *Dialectic Exploration on Volume I of Capital* and *A Report of Overall Competitiveness of China's Provincial Economy* and published over 100 academic papers in periodicals like *People's Daily* and *Economics Information*. He is receiver of seven first prizes and two second prizes in Fujian Province Excellent Philosophy and Social Sciences Research Result Award, as well as the Excellent Theoretical Paper Award in the 7th National "Five-One" Project.

Mr. Li Minrong was born in 1955 in Anze of Shanxi Province; he holds a PhD in Economics. He is Director of Development Research Center of the People's Government of Fujian Province, adjunct professor of Fujian Normal University, doctoral supervisor and Vice President of China Regional Economics Society. Li Minrong has been researching macroeconomics, regional economic competitiveness, and modern logistics, and has published more than 20 books (including those he coauthored), such as *A Study of the Overall Competitiveness of China's Provincial Economy (1998-2004)*, *Annual Report on Competitiveness of China's Provincial Agriculture*, *Annual Report on Competitiveness of China's Provincial Forestry*, and *West Shore of Taiwan Straits and Taiwan* published in Taiwan; he has also contributed more than 240 academic papers in periodicals like *People's*

Daily, Qiushi Journal, Management World, and *Economics Information.* Recently he has taken charge of several provincial key research projects, including the National Social Science Fund project, A *Research of Forecasting and Evaluation of Overall Competitiveness of China's Provincial Economy, Application of the Empirical Economics Theories and Methodology in Regional Economy,* and A *Study on the Several Key Issues in Constructing Western Taiwan Straits Economic Zone* during the "Eleventh Five-year" period. His research achievements include more than 10 provincial/ministerial awards, including third prizes of the second and third Excellent Achievements in Social Sciences award of Xinjiang Uygur Autonomous Region, as well as first prize of Provincial Prize for Progress in Science and Technology (third place), first prizes of the 7th and 8th Excellent Achievements in Social Sciences, second prize of the 6th Excellent Achievements in Social Sciences, and third prize of the 7th Excellent Achievements in Social Sciences in Fujian Province; over another 20 papers and research reports have won him provincial awards.

Mr. Zhao Xinli was born in 1961 in Shenyang of Liaoning Province; he holds a PhD in aviation and aerospace engineering and a post doc in system engineering. He is currently a counselor of Permanent Mission of China to the UN, adjunct professor and doctoral supervisor at Harbin Institute of Technology. He is the receiver of the State Council Special Allowance, academician of the International Eurasian Academy of Sciences (IEAS), and advisor of the People's Government of Fujian Province; he also successively worked as a member of National Coordination Group on Patent Work, Executive Director of China Information Industry Association, Senior Consultant of China Consulting Association, and Vice President of Chinese Society for the History of Local Science and Technology. He has taken charge of and completed dozens of national-level research projects funded by 863 Program, Natural Science Foundation, Social Science Foundation, Postdoctoral Foundation, etc.; he is a major participant of several national projects funded by Soft Science and 973 Program and is in charge of dozens of provincial and/or ministerial projects, and has been awarded multiple prizes at the provincial and/or ministerial level; he has published over 100 papers and 10 books. He has once studied or worked at Beijing University of Aeronautics and Astronautics, Shenyang Aircraft Corporation, Lockheed Aircraft Corporation of US, Tsinghua University, the Ministry of Science and Technology of China, Economic Department of the Liaison Office of Chinese Central Government to Macao SAR, Institute of Science and Technology Information of China (ISTIC), and China Science and Technology Exchange Center (CSTEC); he holds concurrent posts as Chairperson of the Chinese side of Sino-Europe Advanced Manufacturing Technological Cooperation Committee, Executive Deputy Chief Librarian of National Engineering Library,

Deputy Director General of the Sino-Japan Technical Cooperation Affairs Center, and Deputy Director General of China-Europe Sci-tech Cooperation Office.

Mr. Li Jianjian, Doctor of Economics, was born in 1954 in Xianyou of Fujian Province. He is now Dean of the School of Economics at Fujian Normal University, doctoral supervisor, and an expert receiving the State Council Special Allowance and one of the academic pacesetters in political economics in Fujian Normal University. His major fields of academic research are capital and socialist market economy, history of economic thought, and urban land economy; he successively has taken charge of or participated in over 20 research projects supported by the Natural Science Foundation of China, Fujian Province Social Science Planning Fund, Fujian Province Development and Reformation Commission, and Fujian Provincial Department of Education, as well as other international cooperation projects; he has also published more than 10 monographic and/or co-authored books including *Studies on China's Urban Land Market Structure*, *Application and Development of Capital in Socialist Market Economy* and *Socialist Market Economy and the Reform & Opening up*, compiled multiple textbooks such as *Textbook for Selected Readings on Capital*, *Political Economics*, *Discourse on Development Economics and Chinese Economic Development*, and published over 70 papers in periodicals like *Economic Research Journal*, *Contemporary Economic Research*, and *China Real Estate*. He was honored as Excellent CPC Member in Fujian Provincial Universities, Outstanding Teacher of Fujian Province, and Advanced Teaching & Research Worker; his research results won many provincial and ministerial awards, including second prize of Excellent Teaching Achievement of the State Education Commission (collaborate), first prize of Fujian Province Excellent Philosophy and Social Science Research Result Award (collaborate), second prize and third prize of Fujian Province Excellent Social Science Research Result, and first prize of Fujian Normal University Excellent Teaching Achievement Award.

Mr. Huang Maoxing was born in 1976 in Putian City, Fujian Province of China, a holds a PhD in economics and is a professor. He is Vice President of the School of Economics in Fujian Normal University, and Executive Deputy Director of the FJNU Branch of National Research Center of Comprehensive Economic Competitiveness. He was a candidate of the 2011 Program for New Century Excellent Talents in University of Ministry of Education of China, the 2008 New Century Million Talent Project, and the 2010 Program for New Century Excellent Talents in University of Fujian Province, awarded the Seventh Fujian Youth 54 Medal in 2010, honored as the Sixth Excellent Young Social Science Expert of Fujian Province in 2010, and won the honorary title of the Fourth

Top 10 Young Teachers of Fujian Normal University. Huang Maoxing is the author or coauthor of over 19 books including, *Technical Choice and Upgrading Industrial Structure, Research on Technique Choice and Economic Growth*, and *Report of Predictive Study on the Overall Competitiveness of China's Provincial Economy*. He has published more than 90 academic papers in key periodicals such as *Economic Study, Management World, Economics Information*, and *Xinhua Digest*, and taken charge of more than 30 research projects at the national and/or ministerial level. His research achievements have won over 10 awards of different levels, including one first prize (coauthor) in the First National Excellent Papers on Economic Census Award of the State Council, four first prizes (coauthor) in the 7th-9th Fujian Excellent Social Science Researches Award, two second prizes in the 8th-9th Fujian Excellent Social Science Researches Award, and one first/second/third prize (coauthor) in Excellent Surveying Study Award of the CPC Fujian Provincial Committee and the People's Government of Fujian Province.

Abstract

Nowadays, international competition has become fiercer than ever. Restrictions form the population, resource, and environment is harsh and thus sci-tech innovation is much more important than any time in human history, especially under the backdrop of the global financial crisis and in the eve of a new technological revolution. Only the country that does well in sci-tech innovation can hold developmental initiative and reach the peak of prosperity. Innovation has become the main force to drive our society forward and national innovation competitiveness (NIC) has become the key element of national competitiveness.

Since War World II, the international political and economic structure has changed drastically. A new international relationship was shaped through dialogue between developed countries and emerging market economies, and exchange and cooperation began. Under this background, the Group of Twenty (G20) nations emerged because of demand and became an important international platform to solve international political and economic problems.

This book uses the G20 as the object of study and probes into the national innovation competitiveness (NIC) level of development, characteristics of change, underlying reason and strategic trend of each G20 nation in the first decade of the 21st century, so as to provide valuable theoretical and practical solutions for countries of the world to enhance innovation competitiveness. This book is composed of three main parts. The first part is theory and method, which comprehensively expounds the important significance, the main contents, and the technical route of national innovation competitiveness research; based on that, the G20 national innovation competitiveness evaluation indicator system and the mathematic model were constructed according to the characteristics of national innovation competitive, which has formed a relatively comprehensive national innovation competitive analysis framework. The second part is a general report to analyze the evaluation of G20 nations, revealing the strengths and weaknesses of each nation's innovation competitiveness and providing the basic paths and strategies for enhancing the competitiveness level. It will provide valuable analysis foundation for all countries in the world to speed up enhancement of innovation competitiveness. The third part is a sub report, which the purpose is to reveal the characteristics and differences of national innovation competitiveness of different types and at different levels of development through in-depth comparative analysis and evaluation of the 19 countries of G20 and to provide an empirical basis for the countries to enhance innovation competitiveness. The book is finally attached with the national innovation competitiveness evaluation scores of the G20 nations and also the list of changes from 2001 to 2009 for readers' information.

Preface

Innovation is the eternal theme in human and social development; it is the soul for a nation to advance and an inexhaustible driving power for a country to thrive. Since the Industrial Revolution, humankind has created material wealth that is more than the sum of the wealth made in the thousands of years before, and innovation is undoubtedly the biggest driving force in this process. The modern history of the world has shown that industrialization and modernization and following a path of innovation and development are the universal laws for national development. Developed countries have achieved industrialization by relying on technological revolution. For example, in the mid- and late 18th century, Great Britain achieved great progress in productivity by inventing the steamer; in the mid-19th century, Germany also realized industrialization; in the late 19th century, the US became a great power in electric power, automobile, aviation, oil extraction, and communication industries by encouraging creativity and innovation. In other words, innovation has become the major driving force of a nation's socioeconomic development and innovation competitiveness is the key element of national competitiveness.

The world now is suffering from the most serious global economic crisis since World War II and the economic recession that has hit the main economies of the world has not stopped. A look at the five technological revolutions over the 200 years of human history shows that whether it is the appearance of the steamer, or railways and canals, or electric power and heavy industries, or IC technology and information technology, they have all formed under an environment of crisis. Historical experience tells us that very often, economic crisis foreshadows new technological revolution. It is the great sci-tech breakthroughs and innovations that pushed significant adjustment in economic structure and provided new growth engine for economy to regain balance and to reach a higher level. Whoever can take dominance in sci-tech innovation would seize the priority in development and take the lead in recovery and the economic boom. Confronted with the backlash of the global crisis, all the major economies of the world have put their hope for economic revival through sci-tech innovation. In a sense, a new technological revolution of great significance is quietly brewing. In view of this, innovation is an urgent task for all countries of the world today. On one hand, we are faced with unprecedented challenges since the Industrial Revolution and serious problems such as resource depletion, environmental deterioration, global warming, food shortage, and spread of infectious diseases, are waiting for breakthroughs in sci-tech innovation; on the other hand, the world economic pattern and order formed after World War II is experiencing serious crisis; weak growth, heavy debts and high unemployment in advanced economies, intensified inflation in emerging economies, as well as deep contradictions causing global economic imbalances, are all in need of system innovation in the fields of global governance, financial supervision, and social administration. It can be said that innovation is the only way for us to face the challenges, to walk out from the crisis and realize sustainable development.

Research on national innovation competitiveness (NIC) and research on innovation can be traced back to the same point. The results from over hundred years of innovation studies have provided preconditions and a foundation for NIC research, while NIC integrates innovation and competitiveness, thus breaking the limitation of sole innovation studies. NIC research includes in-depth discussion from multiple disciplines and multiple dimensions, such as economics, management science, statistics, econometrics, human geography, operation research, and sociology. It focuses more on the exploration of innovation ability and leads to a brand-new economic model, development pattern, and lifestyle. To study NIC is not only to further the advancement of innovation ability and competitiveness theories, but also to match the trends in both international and China's technological innovation; it is of important theoretical and practical significance. Research on NIC not only follows the trends and requirements that China is faced with the historic opportunity of welcoming a world revolution of science and technology and that China is accelerating the construction of an innovative nation; it also explains from the unique angle of competition the meaning of contents such as innovation base, innovation environment, innovation input, innovation output, and innovation sustainability that are inherent within the national innovation system, so that the national strategy of constructing an innovative nation is deepened to concrete and meticulous evaluation. At the same time, such research also endows the concept of innovation ability with new connotation and conception.

In view of such and for the purpose of participation in the development of international competitiveness and as response to the new round of technological revolution, the FJNU Branch Center of National Research Center of Comprehensive Economic Competitiveness took charge of the project *Report on the Group of Twenty (G20) National Innovation Competitiveness Development (2001-2011)* yellow book; the book aims for comprehensive evaluation and analysis of the NIC of G20 nations during the first decade of the 21st century as well as provides reliable analytical and decision-making reference for all countries to foster new advantage, enhance the ability to participate, offer guidance, and occupy the commanding point for the strategy of scientific and technological development in the eve of new international technological revolution era. The Branch Center has annually released in the 1st Lecture Hall of Chinese Academy of Social Sciences the blue book series *A Report of Overall Competitiveness of China's Provincial Economy* during the period of China's NPC & CPPPCC from 2007 to 2011 (5 volumes released successively), and 2 volumes of the green book series *Report on China's Provincial Environment Competitiveness Development*. The book series have attracted coverage from both the Chinese new media as well as the international news media, and has led to widespread discussion amongst academic and theoretic circles. It is worth mentioning that when the Social Science Academic Press of Chinese Academy of Social Sciences held the Award Presentation Ceremony for China Excellent Book Series Award in Hefei of Anhui Province on August 26-27, 2011, there were more than 160 types of book series for appraisal and 10 types, including the blue book series *A Report of Overall Competitiveness of China's Provincial Economy,* the only one completed by a local university, which won the honor of China Excellent Book Series. In order to further the study on competitiveness and national competitiveness and meanwhile follow the trend in research on international development of science and technology, the Branch Center launched the research project for *Report on the Group of Twenty (G20) National Innovation Competitiveness Development (2001-2011)* Yellow Book at the end of 2009. The project received strong support from multiple authorities, including Management World Magazine of the Development Research Center of the State Council, the Social Sciences Academic Press of Chinese Academy of Social Sciences, the Development Research Center of People's Government of Fujian Province, and Fujian Provincial Administration of Press and Publication (Fujian Provincial Copyright Administration); it also received help from Mr. Zhao Xinli, Counselor of China's Permanent Mission to the UN and academician of International Eurasian Academy of Sciences (IEAS). The yellow book *Report on G20 National Innovation Competitiveness Development (2001-2011)* is a frontier research report newly released in the year 2011, in which we hope to go further on the research of NIC, add connotations to the concept and discuss the issue of developing and building NIC of G20 nations from theoretical, methodological, and experimental dimensions.

Based on adequate reference to results of related researches both in China and other countries, this report offers an in-depth analysis on the development, behavior, intrinsic motivation and future trends of G20 nations' NIC in the first decade of the 21st century, while giving close attention to research developments in multiple disciplines such as technological economics, competitiveness economics, management science, econometrics, and statistics. We also constructed an indicator system and mathematical model for G20 nations' NIC and completed a comprehensive and scientific comparative analysis and evaluation on the NIC of 19 countries of G20 (Note: Only G20 nations are selected for research and EU as a consortium is excluded from the scope of evaluation.) during the period of 2001-2009 (Note: As there is usually a two- year delay in international statistical data of science and technology, the latest data available for collection is up to 2009.); the research reveals the characteristics and relative differences in innovation competitiveness of countries of different types and different levels of development, identifies the internal competitive advantage and weaknesses of respective countries and reveals the evolutionary track and path of growth of G20 nations' NIC, which will provide valuable theoretical guidance and practical countermeasure for all countries to enhance NIC. The whole book is composed of three parts and appendices; its structure is as follows:

Part 1: Theory and Methodology, gives theoretical analysis and introduces the research methodology of this book. This part elaborates on the purpose and significance of the research, explains the theoretical connotations of NIC and provides detailed description of the indicator evaluation system and mathematical model for NIC. In addition, this part also introduces the roadmap and analytical approach of the research and expands on the scope of contents covered by the research.

Part 2: General Report, is a general report of evaluation and comparative analysis on G20 national innovation competitiveness. The general report is an evaluation analysis on NIC of 19 countries of G20 during 2001-2009, according to the constructed evaluation system consisting of 1 primary indicator, 5 secondary indicators and 35 tertiary indicators. Based on comprehensive analysis on the trends of G20 nations' NIC during 2001-2009, the report presents the regional distribution and development status of the NIC of all countries, reveals the strengths and/or weaknesses and relative position of each country. Changes in characteristics and development of NIC that occurred during the evaluation period are also to give development inspiration. As a result, strategic principles, orientation and measures to enhance NIC are proposed, so as to provide valuable reference in decision analysis of how to accelerate enhancement of NIC for all countries.

Part 3: Sub Report, is a NIC analysis by country. This part is a series of special country reports that give comprehensive and scientific comparative analysis and evaluation on NIC of the 19 countries of G20 including China and the US (all country reports are arranged alphabetically by country name). The reports shows the characteristics and relative differences in innovation competitiveness of countries of different types and different levels of development, identifies respective internal competitive advantages and weaknesses, and reveals the evolutionary track and path of growth of innovation competitiveness in each country.

This report draws from previous research results both in China and internationally, and utilizes theoretical knowledge and analytical approach used in multiple disciplines such as political economics, technical economics, management science, statistics, econometrics, and human geography, and attempts to make innovation and breakthrough in NIC theory, method study, and practical evaluation. It is a research area across multiple disciplines, whereas due to objective constraints like knowledge structure and academic ability of the team as well as data available, the study in certain aspects is still far from being comprehensive; there are many other issues that are left untouched and need further study. Therefore, we will continue to further the research, continue to complete the theoretical system and analytical method, and start new exploration and reflection over the issue of what specific measures would be helpful for all countries of the world to enhance NIC. We hope to further the research on both the theory and methodology of NIC together with concerned governments and related scientific institutions of the world, to make the evaluation of NIC more objective and valuable in providing decision-making reference about technological innovation for China and the rest of the world.

Authors
January 2012

Contents

Part 1   Theory and Methodology

Chapter 1

Theory and Methodology

Innovation is a nation's spirit to be progressive and the inexhaustible drive to be prosperous. During the process of world civilization, mankind has never stopped the pace in pursuing innovation, from transforming nature to utilizing nature to exploring the unknown world; it is the accumulation of every small innovation that created the magnificent civilization in human history and also pushed the steps of time. The First Industrial Revolution marked by the invention and application of the steamer opened the prologue of world's modern civilization; thereafter the Second and Third Industrial Revolution continuously rewrote the world economic pattern and refreshed the imprints of global development of science and technology. The history of mankind is actually a history of innovation shining with sparkling wisdom and filled with exploration and competition; it represents a sort of dream, a sort of strength, a sort of breakthrough, and a sort of leap. A look at the different times in human history shows different interpretations and requirements for innovation, and the expressions of the innovation processes are also different, some expressed as invention, some as application of new knowledge, and some others as improvement of existing production mode; but the results of innovation are the same, it is closely integrated with the nation's power, and its core element is the nation's competitiveness.

Competition is a natural attribute and essential to the market economy; it is the inexhaustible force that drives the development of a market economy. Any market player or economic region that wants to secure a position in the fierce market competition must face up to the competition and take an active part in it. However, bravely facing competition and taking an active part in it alone is not the key to success; it is only the key to participation. The deciding factor for a market player to succeed is whether it is highly competitive. In particular, during the post financial crisis era, sci-tech innovation is increasingly becoming a driving power of socioeconomic development and a major source of wealth. Countries in the world are trying to seize the opportunities brought about by the new round of technological revolution and industrial revolution, accelerate transformation of economic growth mode and social development pattern, completely change the situation of being passive in international competition, strive for dominance in the long-term development of the economy, and form long-term competitive advantage; the important catch point for all this lies in enhancing the NIC of the country.

The nation is the superstructure established on and decided by a certain economic base, and the economically dominant class exercises dictatorship over the ruled class and maintains the benefits of the ruling class by means of the nation. Since the inception of nations, the struggle between nations has never ceased. Nations constitute an important unit of the world economy, and are an indispensable part of the world. Enhancing NIC has attracted more and more attention from theoretical and academic circles and strategic decision makers in all countries. NIC research and enhancement must not only use the rationale and methodology of international competitiveness, national competitiveness,[1] and regional competitiveness as reference, but also integrate the contents and practices of both technological capability and innovation system; it must not only do a good job evaluating NIC but also strengthen the predicative analysis on future change and development of NIC. In this way, the study can provide theoretical and practical guidance for the enhancement of NIC or even the progressive and fast development of the world economy. Throughout world history, considering the brilliancy of the four ancient civilizations shaped by innovation, or the unprecedented productivity brought about by innovation to the capitalist countries, or innovation as the big push in adjusting the international standing of all nations, innovation has become more and more tied to competition, and even the driving force of competition; to increase competitiveness with innovation and to innovate under competition will forever be integrated into a nation's socioeconomic development.[2]

NIC is the driving force that enhances the competitiveness of a nation; it plays the ultimate role in increasing national competitiveness. In the long run, if a nation maintains prolonged efforts in innovation and enhances its innovation competitiveness, it can keep the advantage in international competition; in a short time, this advantage cannot be readily obtained by other countries. Facts have proved that the reason developed countries possess such strong national competitiveness is because they possess strong NIC and can maintain a potential for innovation. In a sense, NIC is the important content of national competitiveness, the expression of national competitiveness at the link of innovation, and a valuable approach and instrument to increase national competitiveness. Hence, in order to greatly enhance national competitiveness there is an urgent need to strengthen the research on NIC evaluation. Michael Porter argued that "competition" is a piece of fertile land for research, in which

---

1 When a market player is a nation, national competitiveness is equivalent to the international competitiveness of the nation, as a nation cannot compete with itself; actually researches about national competitiveness started from the research on international competitiveness.

2 Michael Porter, "On Competition," Gao Dengdi et al Trans., (Beijing: China Citic Press, 2003).

NIC evaluation studies will open up a new garden to give a splendid and aromatic blossom of theory.

I. NIC Research Context

For a long time, the world's huge industrial production system was built up as driven by factor inputs and has pushed the process of human industrialization, but factor inputs also encountered a bottleneck of environmental protection and sustainable development; factor inputs as a major driving force came under a wider and wider range of accusations. Atmospheric pollution caused by the Meuse Valley Incident that happened in Belgium in the 1930s, the Los Angeles photochemical smog episode in the US in the early 1940s, "The Big Smoke" in London during the 1950s and the "Minamata Disease" that occurred in Japan during 1953-1956 are collectively referred to as the four big environmental pollution incidents. As the representatives of the countless environmental pollution incidents, they also represent the unrecoverable pains of economic society left by the traditional industrialization pattern relying on large quantities of factor inputs. When people started to wonder about the process of the transformation in development model, capital input as the engine quietly took the lead; relying on operation in the fictitious capital market, it triggered a popular wave and established a large following among vast investors and inflated the economic bubble, finally leading to borrowed prosperity in the market. The growing bubbles were destined to pop, which caused not only turmoil in the financial market, but impacted the entire world economy and caused long durations of recession. Whether it is the economic crisis during 1929-1933, or the Asian financial crisis in 1997, or the global financial crisis in 2008, there harm and destruction on the economy were in no way less than what a war might have done to human society. There is no doubt that the world economy is coming to the crossroads of development pattern transformation and it is no coincidence that most countries choose to take innovation as the driving force in this new round of world economic growth. Whether it is for walking out from the morass of financial crisis, or for developing the strategic emerging industries, or for technological change, humankind has shifted from the pattern of development focusing only on quantity towards the pattern that endeavors to mine for economic development potential. Compared with traditional factors like land, capital, or others, innovation is increasingly becoming the core driving force of national development and ultimately determines the international competitiveness of a country.

The law of international economic development tells us that each large economic crisis may spur new technological and industrial revolution and hence create new technology and new industries. At present, developed countries are taking advantage of technological superiority to maintain their status in the technological revolution, while developing countries, especially emerging countries, also press on with them to seize opportunities, so as to take initiative in the tide of global innovation. The competition of innovation is no longer just for a few countries, but all countries are participating in it. It is not just for a few industries or sectors, but a competition that has integrated into many industries and sectors, an event that requires entire nations to participate in. Therefore, innovation is not only a means or instrument; it has already advanced as the core competitiveness of a country or region. The research on national competitiveness will surely arouse a hot wave of research with innovation as the key subject. NIC research occurs in a profound context that can be traced far back; elaboration of the context is given below.

1. From the development of world history, innovation has always been the perpetual driving force for socioeconomic development. In the long history of human development, productivity has always been an important criterion to measure social development; the development of productivity promoted the change in relations of production and thus changed social relations, changing from an underdeveloped level to a higher level. Productivity, representing human ability to transform nature, was always the invisible power to push social development, and also the common goal of pursuit in different ages. Productivity is a complex mixture of multiple factors, ranging from improving the quality of workers, changing the means of production, and advancing the products of labor; they all push the advancement of productivity; such changes and advancements are surely the resulted accumulation of a series of big or small innovations, whether consciously or unconsciously. From the development of the Stone Age in primitive society to the appearance of animal husbandry, humankind has experienced agricultural revolution and, after consolidation of slave society and feudal society, has created a splendid era of agricultural civilization. From the 14th century to the first half of the 17th century, the handicraft workshops along the Mediterranean, the Renaissance, discovery of the new world and the early colonial expansion fostered the basic factors of capitalist society and pushed the world to strive towards integration; particularly, the First Industrial Revolution that began with the British textile industry, which opened an era of industrial civilization. Thereafter, mankind has had to jump on the express train of technological innovation to keep up with the ever-changing society. In the development process, innovation has always played the role as the driving force of social development; facts have also proved that

western powers who were one step ahead in innovation not only laid a solid material foundation, but also opened the gap with the eastern world, and has become leader and guiding power of current world economic development and technological advancement.

China's economic history is one that runs windingly from power to decline and then towards revival, in which innovation is the theme. In ancient times, since the Xia, Shang and Zhou Dynasties, the innovation achievements of the Chinese nation are world-famous: the Si Muwu Big Quadrate Vessel that witnessed bronze manufacturing process innovation of the Chinese people, the Great Wall that represented huge construction engineering innovation, the Silk Route that innovatively explored the passage for foreign trade, to name only a few. And there were Confucianism and Taoist theory that represented ideological and theoretical innovation, the laws and statutes of the Qin and Tang era that represented legal innovation, and the "Tang & Song poetry" that represented cultural innovation. Innovation from various fields not only created splendid Chinese civilization, but also made China a powerful and prosperous country of the world and other countries swore allegiance under its advanced technology and the immense amount of wealth. In the modern era, China's pace for innovation slowed down. While industrial revolution progressed in the capitalist countries who embarked on the road of industrialization by means of technological innovation, China followed a closed-door policy, and secluded themselves from the outside world, not only causing stagnation and recession of the economy but also throwing the country into semi-colonial and semi-feudal society; under the invasion and slavery of foreign countries, nothing of the once superior country was left. After the establishment of the New China, a new era of innovation started; relying on the support of innovation policy as well as the courage of innovation amidst the Chinese people, China has continued to narrow the gap with developed countries, and many technologies have already reached advanced international standards; innovation has become a powerful driving force for the revival of the Chinese people. The inflexion of China's national competitive strength has proved that innovation is the determinant of national competitiveness.

2. From the direction of world economic competition, innovation is the catalyst to convert potential productivity into practical productivity. The present world economic competition is becoming increasingly fierce; the strength of competitiveness determines to some extent the international standing of a nation or region. For a long time, different nations or regions have taken actual hard power as key competitiveness in competition, such as economic strength, military strength, and diplomatic influencing power, which are all built upon material basis. Therefore, the evaluation of national competitiveness focuses particularly on the examination of actual strength factors. For example, in the competitiveness

evaluation system of such well-known evaluation organizations such as World Economic Forum (WEF) and IMD Business School of Switzerland (IMD), nearly all indicators are designed on the basis of material strength and the ranking of national competitiveness is obtained via comprehensive evaluation on all indicators. Although such evaluation methodology can assess the strength and weakness of current national competitiveness, it can hardly reveal the nation's potential for future development. With a view to the long-term development of a nation or region, potential is far more important than actual strength. However, in the orientation of most competitiveness evaluation and due to the wish for quick gains in economic development by all countries and regions, for a long time, the majority of countries and regions were more concerned with the performance of actual strength, even at the expense of environmental pollution, excessive consumption of resources and policies that were constantly radically changed. Competitiveness based on such foundation is not sustainable, and after temporary boosting of economic development there will be continued economic downturn or even recession.

In the present age, more and more countries and regions are aware of the importance of the sustainability of international competitiveness and have begun to speculate on how to convert the competitive potential into actual strength, and innovation has become the bridge that connects competitive potential and actual strength. At present, many countries and regions are not only concerned about GDP growth rate as the main indicator of hard power, but care also about soft power that characterize cultural value, social formation, development patterns, and international relations; not only about the performance of competitive strength based on the physical, but also about the spiritual, cultural, and other invisible forces; not only about the comparison of actual competitiveness, but also about wielding of potential competitive advantage. These new factors in competition are where the potential of national competitiveness lies; it enriches the contents of competitiveness and also adds more instruments to national competitiveness. Technology innovation is the valuable means to convert national competitive potential into actual strength. After experiencing the backlash of the 2008 financial crisis and in order to revitalize native industries, the US has taken "Reindustrialization" as a grand strategy to reshape its competitive edge and put forward policies and measures aimed at reinforcing the development of emerging industries and encouraging sci-tech innovation, with an attempt to develop advanced manufacturing industry and realize economic recovery via innovation. The emerging nations, represented by China, India, Brazil, Russia and the later included South Africa, the so-called BRICS, have made extraordinary performance in confrontation with this financial crisis and have increased national competitiveness through continued innovation. They have continuously increased investment in R&D, and the ratios of R&D fund to GDP in BRICS have reached 1% or even more, except for South Africa, which is a little lower. Dedicated to developing high and new technology industries, these countries took the lead in innovation as the engine of economic development. For example, China released seven strategic emerging industry development programs; Brazil stands at the front rank in new energy industry development in the world. It is not too much to say that innovation created the BRICS, because only innovation can tap into the development potential of economies, continually nurture the competition between the economies and realize sustainability and persistence.

3. From the means of achieving economic growth, innovation is the strategic engine that triggers a new round of world economic growth. For a long time, all countries and regions were dedicated to pursuing economic growth, which has always been one of the hottest fields for research and discussion. The ways and pattern of economic growth in different times and different regions were taken as the subject of study by scholars who have summarized the various factors promoting economic growth. A representative result of such studies is Harrod-Domar Growth Model which emphasizes the priority of capital input; Solow Growth Model stresses the effects of technological improvement; North argues that system innovation pushes economic growth; the "Learning-by-doing" model of Arrow et al. stresses the effects of knowledge and human capital; and the "Knowledge Spillover Growth Model" of Romer, the "Growth Model of Accumulation of Specialized Human Capital" of Lucas, as well as many other theories proved the various factors of economic growth with solid evidence and offered instructive reference for mankind to explore the ways of economic growth. It is true that at the different stages of world economic growth, large-scale capital input, technological improvement, system reform, and knowledge accumulation all played a major or minor role. Each country or region also used its own suitable methods for economic growth suitable for itself. In spite of the focus on different factors, one thing in common with the vast majority of the countries and regions is that they all once used large-scale investment as means to extensive economic growth. During the process of industrialization, developed countries consumed large quantity of natural resources like coal, oil, iron and steel, and other natural resources, which has led to environmental pollution and destruction. From the Industrial Revolution of the West in the 18th century to 1950, about 95% of the total carbon dioxide emission due to burning of fossil fuel was done by developed countries. During the 50 years of 1950-2000, the discharge amount in developed world was still 77% of total discharge. Even today, the developed world, with about 22% of world population, still consumes over 70% of the

global energy and discharges over 50% greenhouse gas. Under the constraint of double bottleneck for economic growth in both environment and resource, many countries began to rethink the way of economic growth and have regarded technology innovation as the main battlefield for promotion of economic growth; they set off on the way of intensive economic growth mode. National innovation strength has already demonstrated its powerful effects as engine for growth in many countries and triggered among all countries both the competition of economic growth in innovation and the competition of innovation in economic growth.

Due to the weakening effects of the third technological revolution and the shock from the global financial crisis, the world is now in the eve of a new round of technological revolution, which is not only the engine for all countries to walk out from the shadow of the crisis and realize a new round of world economic growth, but also a penetration point for world economy to transform the mode of development. In the global arena of technology, high and new technologies, such as life science and technology, information science and technology, nanometer technology and aerospace engineering, there will be more mature with more breakthroughs, while emerging industries, like communication industry, computer industry, new material industry, new energy industry, and ocean industry that are led by such technologies, will take dominance in the industrial structure, thus showing far-reaching influence on the overall national strength, the socioeconomic structure, and people's livelihood and will act as the basis for a new arena of competition where all countries will try to take hold of the competitive advantage. The global revolution of science and technology is still growing and the competition in the area of innovation under the macro context of innovation as the direction of a new round of world economic growth will surely be the main battlefield of national competition.

4. From the changing pattern of international relations, innovation is an important leverage to maintain international standing. International competition goes far beyond the comparison of economic strength and ranking of competitiveness; the deeper underlying motive is the struggle for international standing and the right to have a say. After World War II, the US, on behalf of the capitalist camp, and the former USSR, on behalf of the socialist camp, fought a war for global supremacy. The contest for hegemony between the US and the USSR mainly involved strengthening of military equipment via technological means and thus strengthening military power via innovation based on respective economic strength. For example, in the 1970s, the USSR made breakthroughs in strategic missile and strategic nuclear power; in the late 1980s and early 1990s the US launched the "Star Wars Program" in connection with nuclear strategy and nuclear arrangement, hence dragging

down the economically weak former USSR through a new round of arms race focusing on high technology. After the collapse of the USSR, although the world economy was developing with a trend of multi-polarization, the US was still the number one power in terms of economy, military, and technology, relying on its superiority in technology, and thus the US had a big say in international affairs. With the rise of other developed countries and emerging developing countries, which narrowed the gap in economy and technology between them and the US, the status of US as the leader of the world's sci-tech innovation was threatened, though yet to be replaced. It is the waves of innovation one after another that opened the penetration point for adjustment of international standing and international pattern.

Whichever country[3] has become the synonym of emerging nations, as increased investment in sci-tech innovation and promotion of the establishment of a sci-tech innovation system have won good international reputation for confronting the financial crisis for these nations. For example, even before the outbreak of the global financial crisis, Brazil released the "Growth Acceleration Program"(PAC), in which clean energy, such as ethanol and biological diesel, are the key innovation projects supported by the country; meanwhile, Brazil also opened the first computer chip manufacturing company of Latin America. President Lula commented that, "it is the watershed in the history of Brazil's science and technology reform." India kept putting information industry as the first prioritized industry in technology innovation and released multiple measures including the National Broadband Network program, establishment of IT Investment Park, an electronic component and electronic material development plan and a biological technology industry partnership program. China proposed development of strategic emerging industries, establishment of a technology innovation federation and strengthened emphasis on independent innovation, which makes the country extraordinarily outstanding in confrontation of the global financial crisis. As is said, the future international competition will be more drastic. Under the context of a new round of technological revolution, no country would choose to let the opportunity go. Instead, innovation will be done at quicker pace and with strengthened support. As the precondition and foundation of economic status, innovation will not only directly enhance the international competitiveness of all countries, but also help emerging economies become stronger and further seek improvement of political status.

Whichever country has the advantage in sci-tech innovation will take the priority in future development. The world economy is developing towards diversification and the

---

3 Bangladesh, Egypt, Indonesia, Iran, Mexico, Nigeria, Pakistan, Philippines, Turkey, South Korea, and Vietnam.

international competition will be more and more drastic. In order to fight for their interests and actively improve their international status, all countries are accelerating the pace of innovation; command of key technologies has become a common method adopted by all countries. After the outbreak of the financial crisis, the US sought to make breakthroughs in the new energy sector; the EU announced a 105 billion Euros investment to develop the green economy... In response to the global financial crisis, a "racing" competition to occupy the commanding points for future economic development has quietly started on the globe, and international relations and standing are subject to readjustment, which constitute a valuable opportunity for the emerging developing countries. The BRICS, and Next Eleven or N-11.

5. From the challenge in socioeconomic development, innovation is the ultimate motive power to drive transformation of development mode. Since World War II, the world economy developed fast with rapid expansion of the overall economy and the economic structure continued to improve. However, while bringing about a better life for mankind, it also produced many new problems. Due to long-term negligence in reconciling contradictions, the contradictions were intensified. The more the pursuit for wealth and profit was, the more the problems came. Now, these problems no longer just generally exist, but they have become an obstacle for socioeconomic development or even a direct threat to the safety of human society. These problems are mainly resource and environmental issues. Fossil energy dependence has not only caused global ecological disaster, such as global warming, but scientists also predict that by around 2030, the worldwide fossil fuel will be depleted. Environmental pollution and destruction can be seen everywhere: global warming, damage to the ozone layer, reduction of biological diversity, overspread of acid rain, and atmospheric pollution. For the issue of industrial restructuring, as the majority of countries and regions relied on large-scale input and substantial resource consumption to realize economic growth, the extensive and low-level industrial structure was formed. For example, long-term resource consumption and demographic dividend in China has caused the country to be faced with painful industrial transformation. Poverty is another issue. According to the Multidimensional Poverty Index 2010, released by the UN, there were another 300 million people worldwide added to the group of people in poverty; the total population in poverty has exceeded 1.7 billion, an increase of 21%. The poverty problem is no longer just an economic issue, as it also involves the political issues of the world, advancement of human civilization, and the stabilized harmonious development worldwide. Regarding the wealth gap problem, there is a growing gap between the rich countries and the poor countries, as well as a growing gap between the rich people and the poor people within a

country. According to statistics, the proportion of the number of rich families in the US is 4.1%, 8.4% in Switzerland, and 0.2% in China. It is pointed out in the Global Wealth Report 2006 released in May 2007 by BCG, that 0.4% of China's households possess the 70% of the national wealth, while in mature markets like Japan and Australia, normally 5% of households control 50%-60% of the national wealth. Although the wealth distribution is not balanced throughout the world, the wealth gap problem is actually a common phenomenon. In addition, population issues, financial market security issues, peace and stabilization problems, etc., are "stumbling blocks" of sustainable development in the world economy and need to overcome the current economic development "bottleneck."

There have been many attempts to solve these problems, but the most fundamental and effective of these all is still innovation and transformation of economic development mode, including new ways of thinking, new policies, new technologies, and new management; such new methods are the way to fundamentally break out of the original development model, as well as pave the way for new economic development. Therefore, whether reinforcing the effort in emerging hi-tech industries, advocating low-carbon production, confronting the global climate change, spreading of "IOT" technologies, continuing production of new-energy automobile, training technical talents, or pressing forward with innovation to increase wealth of knowledge, these are all no doubt closely related to innovation; innovation is the key to solve the challenges facing human development. Economic globalization has sped up technological globalization, making independent innovation ability the deciding factor of key national competitiveness; technological competition is becoming the focus of inter-national competition. Through recruitment of talents worldwide, establishment of R&D branches and control of intellectual property rights, developed countries have constantly consolidated their competitive advantage; the majority of developing countries, particularly the emerging countries, should follow such the global trend and build up independent innovation ability, and finally open a smooth way of development using the weapon of innovation.

II. Significance of NIC Research

When rapid economic development encountered the "travail" of transforming the traditional development mode, and when it is difficult for the real economy to recovery under financial crisis, debt crisis, and credit crisis one after another, "innovation" has been taken by many countries as medicine in order to save the economy. It is foreseeable that the future competition between nations will focus more on the competition of the real economy, while enhancement of such competitive strength will turn to innovation as the driving force by common consent. For example, on February 4, 2011, the US released "Strategy for American Innovation" that gave a report of how the US would "win the future" and maintain long-term competitiveness; in March, 2010, European Commission put forward "Europe 2020," a strategy proposing the idea of constructing an "innovative EU," which is the second ten-year economic development program of EU following "The Lisbon Strategy;" in 2011, the Chinese Academy of Sciences submitted "Innovation 2020," a program with major efforts in solving key technology issues related to the long-term development of the country. Innovation has risen to the level of a long-term development strategy in many countries and regions; it is the only way to enhance national competitiveness. At present, there are already many international evaluation organizations that are working on national competitiveness, but most studies are simply opinions based on present status, focusing on events that have happened or are happening, which is a comparison of actual strength. But there are few studies on the potential national competitiveness or future change, not to mention a study that takes innovation competitiveness as the key object for evaluation. Change of national competitiveness is a dynamic process. On the world stage in the future, innovation will play an important role; therefore, NIC will become the most apparent expression of national competitiveness. To do NIC research is not only a breakthrough in innovation theory and competitiveness theory, but also the trend to respond to international competition, which carries important theoretical and practical significance.

1. Theoretical Significance of NIC Research

(1) It opens up a new area for national competitiveness research and further enriches and develops theoretical system of competitiveness. Research on competitiveness can be traced back to the times of classical economics. Adam Smith's absolute cost advantage theory and David Ricardo's comparative cost advantage theory are regarded as the origin of competitiveness theory. Thereafter, many scholars studied competitiveness from the angles of economics and management science and accumulated rich theories; researches were about a range of vertical subjects ranging from international competitiveness to national competitiveness to regional competitiveness, as well as a horizontal array of different trades and sectors ranging from agriculture, industry, enterprise, financial secretary, and finance; thus they have constructed a relatively complete system and framework for competitiveness research as well as multiple evaluation methodologies from both a qualitative and quantitative approach, and have established a systematic theoretical foundation and evaluation

methodology for the study of competitiveness. After the 1980s, competitiveness theory was utilized in the evaluation of national competitiveness by IMD and WEF. At the same time, the competitiveness index evaluation system was established with extensive influence, and in The Competitive Advantage of Nations, Porter applied domestic competitive advantage to the field of international competitiveness. Thus, a relatively sound theoretical system for national competitiveness was hence formed. Actually, the influencing factors and internal structure of national competitiveness is always in motion and changing; the change in dominant factors of actual economic development and competitive advantage also indicates continuous input of new contents into national competitiveness. NIC research has followed the trend of economic development and emphasized innovation as a new factor of national competitiveness. The all-inclusive analysis concludes that national innovation is not only a kind of ability but also a kind of competitiveness; researches also analyzed the past, the present, and the future of NIC from a dynamic angle. A complete NIC theoretical system has been constructed with a solid foundation of research. The constructed indicator system has fully considered the complexity of both the direct and indirect elements that influence NIC, as well as the dimensionality and diversity of each form of existence and manifestation; it gives comprehensive reflection and evaluation to each element from multiple aspects. It covers not only the actual influencing factors like innovation base, innovation environment, innovation input, and innovation output, but also the potential influencing factors like innovation sustainability; it complies with the law of development of national innovation. NIC research has opened up a new area for national competitiveness research, deepened the connotation of national competitiveness and strengthened the vitality of research in this regard.

(2) It inherits and breaks through the existing national innovation theory and widens the visual field for research on national innovation ability. The idea of innovation has existed for a long time, but the topic of national innovation has been excluded from the research field of economists and management scientists till the 1970s and 1980s. Many scholars and research organizations have studied the issue of national innovation from both theoretical and empirical evaluation levels, focusing on national innovation system, national innovation ability, and national innovation strategy, and thus formed an enriched national innovation theory system; such theories are obtained through contemplation over the entirety of the technology innovation process and with systematic theories and methodologies based on the results of researches on the systematic theory of national technology innovation. At the same time, the strength or weakness in national innovation ability is also considered, which is valuable in instructing a country or region to construct

and implement its innovation strategy. With existing national innovation theories as the foundation, NIC research integrates two theoretical systems, national innovation and national competitiveness, and analyzes national innovation from the perspective of competitiveness, not only being the first to give rich connotations to the term national innovation competitiveness (NIC), but also providing detailed explanation to the constituents and mechanism of the formation of the term; not only dynamically reflecting the laws of NIC, but also showing concern about the comparison of innovation ability and innovation potential between different countries and regions as well as the dynamic variation of innovation trends and adjustment of the innovation standing of different countries and regions. NIC is more than the furthering of current innovation theory; it is also an external manifestation of and criterion to weigh national innovation system and innovation ability. The constructed evaluation indicator system will provide a more scientific and objective international comparison of innovation ability. NIC theory is a synthesized result of existing innovation theories, inheriting and developing theories and enriching them.

(3) To construct NIC theory system is a way to provide reliable theoretical reference to the rapid developing innovation practice in all countries. Theory is the basis for practice; practical activity must be done within the framework of theory and the progress of practical activity certainly requires continued innovation and deepening of theory. As the world is under the dual pressure of the global financial crisis and global climate change, many countries are preparing for a new round of sci-tech innovation and industry transformation so as to lead world economic development and the trend of human society. Emerging industries will become the markers of the new round of technological revolution, such as new energy, new material, energy saving, environmental protection, biotechnology, and broadband network industries; these will be the focal areas of innovation competition. Developed countries represented by the US, Japan, and Europe have started fierce contest for the right to speak in emerging industries and to occupy the dominant position. They successively launched new national development strategies to increase the support to scientific and technological input and accelerate the conversion of key science and technology achievements. Meanwhile, emerging countries represented by BRICS also took the historical opportunity to encourage independent innovation and expedite the deployment of strategic emerging industries domestically while promoting cooperation of strategic emerging industries internationally, showing great potential to surpass developed countries. Innovation activities in both the developed and developing countries all reflected the keyword of "competition;" all countries strive to be the pacesetter of this new round of

international competition by means of core competitiveness in the area of innovation. NIC research is the natural occurrence following the trend of such competition; it provides strong theoretical support to innovation practice through innovation and development on the theories of innovation and competitiveness from a dynamic perspective. International innovation competition between countries is based on the special theory of national innovation and competitiveness, and NIC research answers the questions of what national innovation is, why innovation activities need to be conducted under new situations and how to conduct national innovation. This study has constructed the NIC theory system that breaks the bottleneck in current innovation theory research and will provide theoretical support for the countries or regions that are involved in competition focusing on innovation.

(4) It is a study that crosses multiple disciplines and promotes the breakthroughs and innovations in research methodology and perspective. The coming of key breakthroughs in the frontier of scientific research and significant original scientific achievements are mostly the result of integration of multiple disciplines. Whether in natural sciences or in humanities and social sciences, interdisciplinary integration is the inexorable trend of academic research and also blurs the boundaries of the disciplines. It offers a wider visual field and more methodologies for academic research. NIC research integrates multiple disciplines of knowledge and methodology including economics, management science, mathematics, sociology, and science and technology studies; it has tied the seemingly independent disciplines close together and built up a bridge for cross-disciplinary research. For a long time, the perspectives adopted by scholars doing research on national innovation were mainly national innovation system, national innovation ability, and national innovation strategy; their studies were mostly qualitative research with an analytical approach of management science. Competitiveness study itself is actually the products of research crossing management science and economics, but NIC research not only organically integrates management science and economics but also emphasizes comparison between countries using mathematical methodology. It constructed a congruent evaluation model and system and concretized and quantified the originally abstract and invisible innovation, producing not only rankings of innovation competitiveness of countries and regions but also defining the gap of specific fields of innovation competitiveness. NIC research also looks into the development of physical technology in agriculture and manufacturing industries, especially the technological changes in strategic emerging industrial sectors, and studies how such changes further changes the innovation competitiveness of different countries. Through different kinds of quantized indicators, NIC depicts the relationship

between innovation and economy, and society and national strength in an objective and direct way; it also provides an objective criteria and measurement for assessing innovation activities in various regions, which breaks the traditional framework for research ideas and stimulates innovation in research methodology and perspective.

2. Practical Significance of NIC Research

(1) Research on and enhancement of NIC is an urgent requirement of this tide of innovation in the post-financial crisis era. The well-known competition theory scholar and professor of Harvard University, Michael Porter, divided the development of a country or region into four stages: Initial Factor-Driven Stage, Investment-Driven Stage, Innovation-Driven Stage, and Wealth-Driven Stage. Developed countries have shifted the engine to drive economic growth from investment to innovation after industrialization and achieved the third industrial revolution led by hi-tech and the information revolution occurred thereafter, which has driven the developed countries towards world power and has generated a group of newly industrialized countries. The practice of innovation development has proved that innovation can not only change the traditional development mode relying on intensive material investment to maintain high economic growth, but can also overcome the constraint of resource and environmental "bottlenecks;" it is a powerful force to realize sustained economic growth and reach the inherent potential of economic growth. For the past few decades, competition between countries, focusing on innovation has never ended, which made innovation one of the key factors that indicate the strength of national competitiveness. In particular after the global financial crisis, all countries have rethought the transformation of development mode and made adjustment, emphasizing independent innovation, and highlighting the proactive layout of high technology, and intellectual property control and introduction of high-end talent; innovation was an important instrument to shake off the crisis, to reduce unemployment, and to increase competitive advantage and international standing. Currently, all countries have efforts aimed at fostering new engine via innovation for the economic growth after the financial crisis, such as countries placing emphasis on strategic emerging industries, such as low-carbon, information, biology, energy, environment, or green manufacturing, or innovation strategies released in many countries, such as "Europe 2020" and "A Strategy for American Innovation: Securing Our Economic Growth and Prosperity." Therefore, innovation represents the direction and trend of world economic development and also represents the core and focus of future international competition; NIC research is being conducted under a broad world context with distinct significance of the times.

(2) Research on and enhancement of NIC is the strategic need of national competitiveness enhancement. Since the birth of nation, there has never been a cease to international wars. In the age of a low productivity level, international contests were mainly in the military field and the rich military thoughts formed in the long history of mankind are also products of research on national military power. In modern era and together with the progress of industrial revolution, there is differentiation in the productivity level between different countries, which resulted in differences in economic development, and thereby influencing the fields of technology, culture, and education. After World War II, the world entered a period of relatively stable development but meanwhile has given new meaning and content to national competitiveness; the struggle between countries were no longer destructive struggles of military power, but constructive contest widely conducted in the fields of economy, society, culture, and technology, which led to the national competition in real meaning and thus attracted scholars' attention to the research on national competitiveness. The first country that started studies on national competitiveness is the US. As early as the 1970s-1980s and in order to face the challenge from Western Europe and Japan, the US attempted to enhance national competitiveness through legislation. With the support from government, private scientific institutions and scholars started researches on national competitiveness and constructed competitiveness theory system with empirical evaluation; they conducted research on national competitiveness from the perspective of industries, enterprises, and public finances, or from an integrated perspective. But so far such researches have been mostly comprehensive evaluation focusing mainly on the evaluation of actual strength while neglecting the research on competitive potential and competitive strength in specific aspects. Competition is a dynamic process, which means the contents of competitiveness are always changing. NIC is the comprehensive manifestation of both actual and potential strengths; it is the key factor of inter-national comparison of strength at present and for a longer time in the future. NIC research broke the thinking limitations on national competitiveness research and emphasized competitive potential and the source of competitiveness; it has opened a new area for comparison of strength between nations.

(3) Research on and enhancement of NIC is an important guideline for establishing future national development strategy. After years of development, the majority of developing countries, particularly emerging economies, have already formed a good foundation for development and entered the stage of fast economic development, and have joined the fierce international competition. According to the International Monetary Fun (IMF) data, the growth rate of emerging and developing economies is over 4 percentage points higher than those of advanced economies during 2003-2010, the widest gap being

5.6 percentage points. The outbreak of the global financial crisis in 2008 even intensified the tendency of development in emerging and developing countries; the rise of group of emerging economies represented by BRICS has become an important force for changing world economic pattern and order and shaping the new international order. Although currently, global economy recovery is apparent, the pace of recovery is not balanced. For example, emerging economies grew forcefully, together with other developing countries, having contributed nearly 60% of the global economic growth in the year 2010. The gap of economic development between emerging economies and developing countries on the one side and the advanced economies on the other side has been shrinking and the former will certainly strive for improvement in international standing. Under the macro context of global economic transformation, international pattern and status will face a new round of adjustment; future international competition will be fiercer and spread across the multiple fields of economy, politics, culture, and society, which will bring about unprecedented opportunity and challenge for China as one of the emerging economies. Innovation will be a powerful force to push each nation's economy towards continued high growth in international competition; it is a major force behind the transformation of economic development, and is the only way to consolidate and improve international standing. Considering the momentum of international innovation development and through the comparison of innovation competitiveness of emerging international bodies represented by G20 nations including the US, France, Germany, China and the EU, NIC research pointed out the advantages and weaknesses of innovation competitiveness of G20 nations including China and discovered where the weakness lies in each country's innovation ability. Starting from the national conditions of China, the research will provide theoretical and empirical reference for the scientific selection of innovation way and innovation technology system, as well as the unique innovation road with Chinese characteristics.

(4) Research on and enhancement of NIC is an important step to accelerate the transformation of the world economic development mode. A look into modern world history, and it is not difficult to find a country or region that wants to stand out in fierce international competition. It is evident that scientific and technological progress and innovation plays an important pushing role, and they can break the bondage of original development mode focusing on the breakthroughs in economic development thinking and reconstruction of competitive advantage, and push economic entities towards development. In the 1760s, Britain led the First Industrial Revolution with the utilization of the steamer and thus established "the Empire on which the sun never sets." During the last 3 decades of the 19th century, the US, Germany, and other countries played leading roles in the Second

Industrial Revolution with their dominance in invention and utilization of electrical equipments, internal combustion engines and airplanes, and hence surpassed the old capitalist nation in the field of economy and technology. Since the third technological revolution during the 1940s and 1950s, technology innovation has rapidly advanced and given birth to a group of emerging hi-tech industries, leading society into the information age; the US also became a superpower by virtue of a leading role in innovation. It can be observed from the three technological revolutions in the history of mankind that in the short history of 200 years, not only reform focusing mainly on innovation promoted the developed countries to realize industrialization, but the total of accumulated productivity has outclassed the total of productivity ever since the emergence of human beings; each technological reform creates great opportunities for the transformation of the development mode, reflects the power of innovation, produces a group of dominant countries with powerful technological strength, and opens a new era for world economic development. Since the financial crisis in 2008, a new round of industrial revolution represented by new energy is approaching; transformation of the world economic development mode is again becoming a common issue that has received widespread attention. Whether it is the "reindustrialization" in the US or the "scientific development, harmonious development" in China, they all put innovation on a position of vital importance in the socioeconomic development of a country; for the development of strategic emerging industries in particular, enhancement of innovation ability is an inexorable method. Looking to transform the economic development mode, NIC research made forecasting of leading innovative countries through comparison of innovation competitiveness between countries, and highlighted the vital role of dominant innovative countries in leading the new round of world economic growth; it is the loudest "call" for the transformation of the world economic development mode.

(5) Research on and enhancement of NIC is the only way to strengthen overall national strength and to step into the group of great powers. Today's international competition is presented as a contest of overall national strength based on the economy and technology. The stronger a country's overall national strength is, the more rights to speak the country has in international affairs; on the contrary, countries with weak overall national strength could only passively face the pressure from great powers. In order to find a seat in the international competition, all countries are devoted to enhancing overall national strength. The concept of overall national strength covers a wide range of aspects, including labor, material, financial, and military strengths, but the most fundamental and most important is NIC; without strong NIC, the country's economic power cannot possibly be strong, not to mention overall national strength. Hence, competition of overall national

strength is first of all the competition of NIC. The activities of developing economy, technology, culture, and education in all countries have all focused on enhancing overall national strength via enhancement of innovation competitiveness. NIC is standing on the cusp of the development of the times; it has focused on the roadblocks in market economic development and has inputted new contents for the market economic practice in all countries. National innovation not only includes sci-tech innovation, resource innovation, and management innovation, but also involves innovation of development theory and innovation of system; it takes a nation as a uniform innovation entity in showing the nation's overall strength in innovation. As the Chinese President, Hu Jintao pointed out in a speech delivered at the 15th Academician Assembly of Chinese Academy of Sciences and the 10th Academician Assembly of Chinese Academy of Engineering, "Great changes in the pattern of productivity, production mode, mode of life, and socioeconomic development are happening worldwide. The rapid development of science and technology is changing the economic development mode. Innovation has become an important approach to solve global problems such as energy resources, ecological environment, natural disaster, and population health; it has become the main driving force of socioeconomic development." It is obvious that innovation is the key factor to solve the various problems existing in all countries during economic development and an important method to extend world economic development. Today, peace and development are the themes of the time; if a country is to be one of the great powers, to be the champion in international competition, the country must not break international rules, neither can it turn to aggression; the only way is to increase overall economic competitiveness. Although the Chinese economy shows higher overall national strength over the accumulation of fast development, it is not powerful enough as a whole; compared with developed countries, there is still a wide gap in innovation ability. Enhancement of overall national strength requires enhancement of abilities in various directions and significant enhancement of the ability for science and technology to serve socioeconomic development. In this sense, the research on and enhancement of NIC is the only way to enhance overall national strength.

Chapter 2

Primary Coverage of NIC

Innovation competitiveness is to enhance the competitiveness of a country with fundamental function to improve national competitiveness. country maintain its international competition with long innovation and continuous innovation competitiveness. Moreover, this kind of advantage be obtained easily by other countries in a short time. Why developed countries hold strong national competitiveness lies that they have strong NIC and maintain this advantage. Based on this, NIC is the important approach and means to enhance the competitiveness of a country. NIC is the important content of national competitiveness and the concrete representation of the national competitiveness in innovation. In order to drive the world economy towe must research NIC profoundly and put forth effort to enhance NIC actively with research. more and more attention the theoretical circle, the academic circle and strategic decision makers of all countries.

I. Concept and Connotation of NIC

1. Conceptualization of NIC

international competitiveness has become the development hotspot of the world. NIC is important of international competitiveness and the development of international competitiveness. the comprehensive integration of competitiveness like the strength of sci-tech innovation, the sci-tech innovation system, the sci-tech innovation mechanism, the environment of sci-tech innovation, the base of sci-tech innovation and the potential of sci-tech innovation. World Economic Forum (WEF) and International Institute for Management Development, Lausanne of Switzerland (IMD) are two important international organizations development and the application promotion of international competitiveness. theory and measurement as well as analysis and study, WEF and IMD have attached much importance to the function of sci-tech innovation activities in the development of international competitiveness. Under the frame of international competitiveness, they have brought the concept of international competitiveness for national science and technology and designed the indicator system measuring international sci-tech competitiveness to be used for the yearly *Global Competitiveness Report* and *World Competitiveness Yearbook*. According to the independent connotative meaning of sci-tech competitivenessit contains: the competition base of education and science, the competition level of technology, the competition level of R&D, the competition level of scientists and technicians, the competition level of sci-tech management, the competition level of sci-tech system and sci-tech environment and the competition level of intellectual property right. This narrowed concept of sci-tech competitiveness is also asmall system.

globalization of economy and sci-tech as well as the sci-tech the sci-tech competition among countries (regions) is becoming more and more drastic and NIC will become the vital factor deciding the success of country. According to different competitive agents and levels, national competitiveness can be classified into national economic competitiveness, national industrial competitiveness, national cultural competitiveness, national resource competitiveness and NIC. As for a country, NIC is the basic factor deciding its overall competitiveness level, which reflect status as well as the technical and economic exchange of a country or region in world sci-tech system and the basic pattern of sci-tech industries in international division of labor. The study of NIC not only help to understand and grasp the strength and potential of a country to participate in international competition thus to further regulate and instruct its industries and businesses to participate in international technical exchange and international division of labor and cooperation, but also help to understand the developing direction and focus of world science and technology thus to provide scientific decision basis for national governments to make macro sci-tech policies and industrial policies.

2. Concept of NIC

NIC is a concept derived from national competitiveness. At present, there is no authoritative definition in the academic circleHowever, the relevant national competitiveness and national innovation theories bring up rich connotation for it. In this study, we believe that NIC should be defined from a broader sense. NIC refers to the attraction to innovative resources and the spreading force to innovation space of a country within the world, and the influence, the and the driving force of it to surrounding countries or regions (Fig. 2.1). It is represented specifically as follows: in an environment of sci-tech support, the efficiency and level as well as the potential sci-tech strength of a country in sci-tech input, output and sci-tech and economic integration reflected through the activities of R&D, technology innovation and technology transformation, which comprehensively indicate the capacity of sci-tech in promoting economic development, enhancing economic strength and driving the sustainable development of the society.

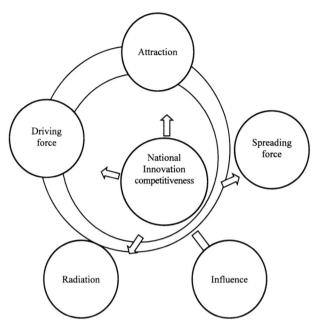

Fig. 2.1　Theoretical Model of NIC

3. Connotation of NIC

In this study, we believe that, to understand the scientific connotation of NIC correctly, we should pay close attention to the following aspects:

First, focus on global competition. Sci-tech globalization is background of sci-tech competition and we should emphasize that it is not international competition, but inexorable trend and immanent demand of global sci-tech development. The development history of world science and technology indicates that no country can develop without other countries and those in isolation washed out by further development of economy and sci-tech. As the global sci-tech value chain specialization rises, countries should find their own international status for their sci-tech in the global value chain, search their development advantage and thus participa in international competition. Therefore, the purpose to highlight the background of global competition is to express that NIC, i.e. the competitive agent, has a kind of active function.

Second, focus on the dynamics of innovative resource elements. The strength of NIC is closely connected with the innovative resources possessed by a country. seful recourses include not only domestic resources but also international resources, not only physical resources but also intangible resources. Furthermore, the connotation of available resources is changing and expanding. Modern sci-tech innovation and development enable those resources not useful in the past to become useful at present or in the future.

Third, focus on the utilization efficiency of innovative resources. NIC cannot go without innovative resources; however, the ultimate purpose to pursue the Possession of the most and best innovative resources does not mean strongest competitiveness. competition sci-tech innovation, it is of more practical significance for effective integration than the simple material possession of innovative resources. In other words, the strength of NIC depends more on the optimization and integration of the available innovative resources by the competitive agent as well as the innovation ability of the competitive agent.

Fourthly, focus on NIC is the competition capacity represented in international sci-tech competition. So, the strength of NIC is closely related to the competitive market. The characteristics of competitive market openness, internationalization degree and innovative culture will influence NIC. The arena of competition for NIC is international scientific and technological market, so, the higher degree of openness and freedom and competition reflect the real condition of NIC. If there are too many rules of protective and monopolistic competition and restrictive measures at the international market, there will be greater deviation between the result of NIC and the scientific and technological strength, which NIC.

Fifth, focus on the market expansion capacity of innovation output. The market expansion capacity is the comprehensive and ultimate representation of innovation competitiveness. To obtain stronger sci-tech output capacity, a country should have obvious advantage in the possession of innovative resources, R&D input, transformation of sci-tech achievements, sci-tech management level, organization and arrangement, sci-tech policies and environment etc. Market expansion is also the dynamic interactive process of all the links of the innovative activities. In competition with foreign countries, to obtain the competitive advantage, businesses and industries of a country will strengthen the technology innovation continuously amarket change and thus facilitate to enhance the competitive capacity. NIC is just market competition. t is operable.

Sixth, focus on the advantage elements of specific innovative activities. As the division boundary of labor of international science and technology transforms from industrial level to value chain, the sci-tech innovation of a country have strong international competitiveness in the whole innovation value chain; correspondingly, the competitive advantage of a countrybe represented in some specific innovative activity but at the link that it is located in the innovation value chain. Therefore, a country should only find the link in the global innovation value chain where its comparative advantage lies, domestic enterprises should, according to its core capacity and advantage resources, narrow its technical field to focus on certain link in the value chain, seize the favorable link to participate in international competition and position accurately in the global innovation value chain, thus, bring into play these advantage elements and enhance NIC.

Seventh, focus on the result of competition. The most purpose of participating in international competition is to beat the competitors and obtain more benefits. Since the competition is not unique in modes and diverse in approaches, the competitive result may also manifest in multiple forms, winning greater market share to obtain direct economic benefit like more innovative profits or indirect social benefit like better innovative brand effect. In the division pattern of global innovation value chain, the purpose of NIC is more characterized by macroeconomy and is embodied by the position of the innovative activities of a country in the global innovation value chain division. Specifically, it is the rise in the innovation value chain from low value-added link to high value-added link and from non-strategic link to strategic link.

To sum up, in this study we believe that under the background of sci-tech globalization, national innovation competition is the competition of value chain links, a selective competition, a two-way competition, a competition of comprehensive capacity and a competition of internalization fields. To understand NIC is favorable directly target the major goals of innovative nation-building, drive national sci-tech development, systematical establish the strategy to participate in international competition and elevate the national status in the global innovation value chain division.

4. and Difference of NIC and National Innovation Capacity.

ational innovation capacity represents the inner capacity of a country in innovative activities NIC contains not only the inner capacity of a country in innovation but also the innovation potential, innovation influence and innovation sustainability of a country in innovation. than national innovation capacity, national innovation capacity. ational innovation capacity is an important foundation for NIC. Then, what is the difference of NIC and national innovation capacity? It mainly includes: (1) the cope. The connotation and scope of NIC are relatively broad; the scope of national innovation capacity is smaller than (2) the overage. NIC is rich in content, including the attraction to sci-tech, radiation and the driving force of sci-tech; the content of national innovation capacity centers on innovative activities themselves, mainly involving the inner capacity showed in the process of innovative activities.

II. Factor Analysis of NIC

(I) Internal Factors of NIC

NIC is influenced by many direct indirect factors. Theoretically, analysis of various indirect influencing factors may involve all aspects of economy, society, culture and politics. In reality, this kind of cannot be completed with sufficient conditions and is also unnecessary. Therefore, scholars generally define the and build the analytical framework.

Technology Policy and Assessment Center (TPAC) of Georgia Institute of Technology the western academic institution research on the evaluation system of international sci-tech competitiveness. 1986, they established a conceptual model the key factors causing the changes of hi-tech industrial competitiveness of a country in the future. This model contains input indicators like national orientation, social and economic infrastructure, technical infrastructure and production capacity as well as output indicators like current technical conditions, attention to technique and technical growth rate. TPAC is committed to predict the new hi-tech industrial competition situation of developed and developing countries. In theory, they draw lessons from theoretical and empirical research literatures introduction, absorption and institutionalization of technical competence promoting competitiveness.

TPAC model Michael Porter diamond model or instance, both emphasi the importance of infrastructure feature rooted in the economic system of a country on competitiveness. The difference between the two models is that TPAC is designed to reveal the leading scientific and technological industrial indicators. In 15-year delay period for input indicators, that is to say, the technical absorption capacity and the institutionalization capacity of the input indicators will form competitiveness after 10 or 20 years. Nevertheless, according to the large frames of the models, the input indicators of TPACmodel too much stress on macro-factorsmicro-; Porter's diamond model particular stress on middle and micro-factors, regarding macro-factors including government policies as auxiliary.

TPAC's model and Porter's diamond model international competitive advantage have been scholars in the analysis of international competitiveness of different countries and regions. However, the competitive advantage models above are not perfect and final. characteristics of national sci-tech innovation competition as well as the reality of China, this study modifies Porter's diamond model from three aspects and thus ensureChina's innovation competition: the factors of NIC can be into five. competitiveness in innovation base, competitiveness in innovation environment, competitiveness in innovation input, competitiveness in innovation output and competitiveness in innovation sustainability. Of course, the five factors are also composed of a series of relevant factors, including resource factor, domestic market demand, innovation network system, competition structure and innovation strategy, national infrastructure, government policy, innovation environment of industrial cluster and connection between innovation cluster and infrastructure. The relationship of the factors and the effect of them on the immediate source factors and competition performance of NIC can be showed Fig. 2.2. The factors drive the innovation competition performance rising in interaction and thus drive the NIC. The innovation factors, domestic market demand, competition structure and innovation strategy as well as the innovation network system the immediate source factors of innovation; the other four dynamic factors like national infrastructure and government policy have influence on the immediate source factors of innovation and competition performance and innovation competitiveness.

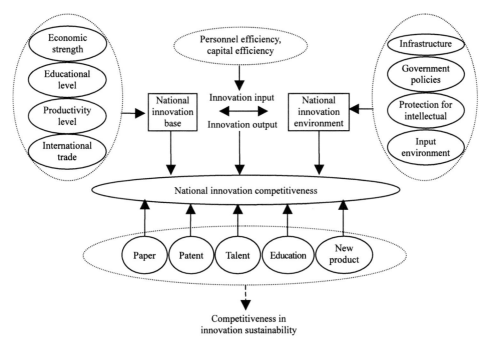

Fig. 2.2   Components of NIC

(II) Components of NIC and Internal Relation

NIC is a comprehensive concept with rich connotation, which integrates many aspects of national innovation and composes a comprehensive indicator. From the above eight internal factors of NIC, we plan to extract the five components as   NIC,competitiveness in innovation base, competitiveness in innovation environment, competitiveness in innovation input, competitiveness in innovation output and competitiveness in innovation sustainability The five components of NIC labor productivity,   resource consumption and production cost, and   sustainable development of economy and society and, by multiple economic and administrative means, comprehensively reflect and influenc the NIC.

1. Components of NIC

ompetitiveness in innovation base is the most basic element of NIC. Innovation base is the major factor   sci-tech input of country the creation of knowledge and the transformation and application of technology as well as the important factor   NIC. ompetitiveness in innovation base, on one, examines the impetus of national economic and social development basis and level to the innovation ability, and on the other, examines the internal demand of national innovation ability. It represent the national economic and social development basis and level, the input and contribution of the country to innovation development, and the degree of importance the country the enhancement of innovation ability, is the evaluation basis of NIC and the fundamental indicator weighing the strength of innovation competitiveness.

ompetitiveness in innovation environment is the primitive driving force for the formation of NIC and the necessity of NIC. Favorable innovation environment not only effectively gather innovation resources but also foster the innovation carrier with strong competitiveness (enterprise, college or university, and research institute). Meanwhile, superior innovation environment   marketization of innovation achievements, improve the innovation performance and accumulate progressive capacity of innovation, which is the important sign weighing the strength of innovation competitiveness.

ompetitiveness in innovation input is the and effective guarantee for the formation of NIC; without the input of innovation resource, innovation competitiveness will lose its material base. The scale, quality and structural optimization degree of innovation resource input determine The competitiveness in innovation input is the necessary guarantee for the formation of NIC, which comprehensively represents the contribution of the country to innovation input and is the key indicator weighing the strength of innovation competitiveness.

ompetitiveness in innovation output is the carrier for the formation of NIC. The result and quality of innovation output directly determine the level of innovation ability and represent the development and implementation dynamics of innovation activities. Of course, the innovation output be embodied through a series of complex and difficult steps. ompetitiveness in innovation output,capabilit, is the primary coverage to enhance NIC and the important indicator weighing the strength of innovation competitiveness.

ompetitiveness in innovation sustainability is important embodiment for the formation of NIC. It involves both the influence of innovation on national production and life and the influence of the country on innovation and activities, the evaluation the current of national innovation innovation development. innovation activities, the competitiveness in innovation sustainability does not influence the innovation competitiveness of country, but also influence the innovation competitiveness of other countries It is also one of the important indicators weighing the strength of innovation competitiveness.

2. Internal Relation among the Components of NIC

ompetitiveness in innovation base and competitiveness in innovation environment comprehensively reflect the innovative activities in structure pattern, which are the foundation and guarantee of competitiveness in innovation input, competitiveness in innovation output and competitiveness in innovation sustainability. Without the basic conditions of economic and social development as well as innovation environment necessary for innovative actions, there no effective support to human innovative ideas and activities and even impossible for problem-solving, invention, creation and utilization in science and technology. Whereas, through the promotion and reinforcement of various national administrative and economic policies, innovative systems and mechanisms innovative activities, the process and effectinnovation input and competitiveness in innovation output, and thus we make some adjustment and improvement based on the performance. The ultimate purpose innovation competitiveness is to enhance labor productivity, transform the production mode, sound and fast development of economy and society, improve people's living demand and meanwhile put forth effort to enhance the ability of the public in understanding and which is the fundamental content to be reflected by competitiveness in innovation sustainability and also the key of national competitive advantage., competitiveness in innovation base, competitiveness in innovation environment, competitiveness in innovation input, competitiveness in innovation output and competitiveness in innovation sustainability are not independent individuals but factor-structure-organization-function-optimization. rowth and coordination of competitiveness in innovation base, competitiveness in innovation environment, competitiveness in innovation input, competitiveness in innovation output and competitiveness in innovation sustainability.

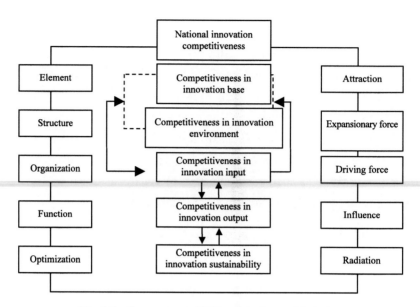

Fig. 2.3   Components of NIC and the Internal Relation

III. Model for the Formation of NIC

Xun Zi, the Chinese thinker of the Warring States (403-221 B.C.), "Yu Duo Er Wu Gua, Gua Ze Xin Zheng Yi" too many desires and scarce resources competition. NIC, at its root, is the scramble among countries for limited innovation resources. As a result, NIC is firstly embodied as the scrambling of countries for innovation resources, i.e. the collection or attraction capacity for innovation resources. Here the resources mainly involve high-class production factors R&D resources, human resources and knowledge resource, including both innovation resources within a country and the foreign innovation resources. nnovation resources are the requisite condition for a country to participate in sci-tech competition. However, the scramble among countries for innovation resources is just the means but not the purpose. Marx said that people for everything related to their benefit. It is perceived that the purpose for competition is to obtain more economic benefit and the countries' innovation competition is just to bring more value them. The creation process of value is also the production process of goods and service, embodied by the process of allocating and optimizing innovation resources collected by countries and then transforming them into innovative products. So, NIC is also represented as the allocation and transformation capacity for innovation resources. Finally, innovative products realize their value and when converted into currency. Meanwhile, production is for consumption and consumption is just the ultimate purpose of production. Therefore, the ultimate goal of national innovation competition is to improve overall national competitiveness. The collection (or attraction) capacity for innovation resources and the allocation capacity for innovation resource interact and influence each other. Between thethe collection (or attraction) capacity for innovation resources is the driving source of national innovation competition because innovation resources are the basic condition for a country in sci-tech operation and development. Without these innovation resources, national sci-tech activities cannot, it is impossible to allocate and process the innovation resources and produce innovative products. On the contrary, the allocation efficiency of national innovation resources directly influences the attraction of a country to collect innovation resources and tboth determine the overall national competitiveness.

Further, the collection (attraction) capacity and the allocation capacity of a country for innovation resources are formed through the synergy and interaction among the regions within the country. Based on the symbiotic relationship among the regions within the country, through the of competition and cooperation, the resources, market and production factors flow smoothly and achieve optimizreorganization within the country; the national science and technology be integrated and produce the effect "the whole is larger than the sum of the individuals" Obviously, the collection capacity and allocation capacity of a country for innovation resources are based on the integration capacity of the country for science and technology. Besides, the comprehensive and comparative advantage of a country in nature, economy, society, technology and is also the indispensable factor for the country to build NIC. The resources of a country nature, economy, society, technologyare the root or foundation of the country for sci-tech integration capacity, resource collection capacity and resource allocation capacity.

The foundation for the formation of NIC is determined by a variety of resource elements and the quality, quantity, and composition of the various resource elements used for innovation determine the innovation basis of a country. The formation of competitiveness in innovation base is not only limited to resources related to innovation. Apart from technique, labor and capital, all macro-economic activities and all kinds of micro-resources owned by individuals can also be converted into innovation resource. The economic scale and economic development determine the resources of the country and the capacity of it to convert them into innovation resource.

Possessing affluent innovation resources is just a comparative advantage and competitiveness. omparative advantage is just a relative advantage in resource possession and conversion, temporarily and ostensibly. To advantage it requires the ability to convert it into innovation resource. However, this ability cannot be imitated; it the competitive advantage formed by a country long-term efforts. Innovation environment is the environment presented through appropriate system and arrangement by a country for all kinds of principal innovation in infrastructure, policy design, regulatory framework, social organization and cultural atmosphere, including both the hard environment innovation process and the internal soft environment. Favorable innovation environment innovation resource, not only favorable to utilize domestic resources but also favorable to attract and allocate foreign resources, not only able to allocate present resources but also able to absorb and utilize future resources. Innovation environment determines whether a country can collect optimize and allocate innovation resources, arouse innovation enthusiasm and coordinate innovative activities.

NIC the input of all kinds of innovation elements; the scale, structure and strength of the innovation element in input restrict the formation of NIC. Although, in terms of the innovation system of a country, the innovation element input is diverse, it is generally classified into two categoriescapital input and human input. Human input should be the vital element of innovation input because the core of innovation is theoretical innovation, technology innovation and management innovation, all of which are achieved through human activities. in innovation activities. potential and improve the utilization efficiency of innovation element input.

The formation of NIC is embodied in various innovation achievements. Innovation output is the result and embodiment of competitiveness and also the important indicator the utilization efficiency of innovation elements. The quantity and quality of innovation output depend on input capacity as well as the optimization and allocation capacity of innovation elements. The relationship between innovation input and output is the direct representation of innovation efficiency. Innovation output is the achievement of former innovation and also the basis of follow-up innovation. nnovation achievements and should be converted into elements and basis further innovation, which is the innovation element of competitive advantage. Therefore, there is interactive relationship among innovation output, innovation base and innovation input and

The innovation process repeats in cycles and requires continuous. NIC represents not only the current competitive advantage but also the potential innovation ability and continuous capability. This capability is important embodiment of the competitive advantage of a country. The competitiveness in innovation sustainability is to achieve favorable and sustainable development of the innovation process. Thus we should guarantee the continuous collection and perpetual utilization of innovation resources and continually enhance the collection capacity for innovation resources; insist the continuous modification and improvement for innovation environment and arouse the and coordination of the innovation principal; promote steady growth of innovation input and continually enhance the optimization and allocation capacity for innovation resources; and achieve the continuous increase of innovation output and continually exert the scale effect of innovation output.

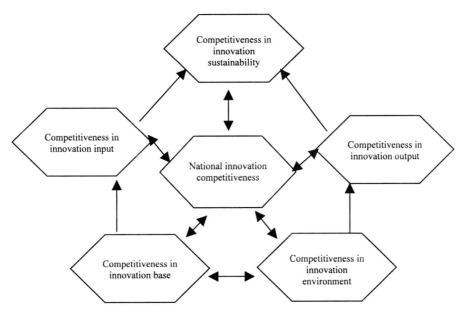

Fig. 2.4   Model for Enhancement Elements of NIC

Based on the above analysis on the conceptual model of NIC, we believe that the functions of NIC contain fivevariables, including competitiveness in innovation base, competitiveness in innovation environment, competitiveness in innovation input, competitiveness in innovation output and competitiveness in sustainability, with the model as follows:

$$NCC_{it} = A_i \bullet f(CB_{it}, CE_{it}, CI_{ti}, CO_{it}, CS_{it})$$

In the formula, NCC_{it} refers to the NIC of Country i in Year t; A_i refers to the innovation resource allocation capacity of Country i; CB_{it} refers to the competitiveness in innovation base of Country i in Year t; CE_{it} refers to the competitiveness in innovation environment of Country i in Year t; CI_{it} refers to the competitiveness in innovation input of Country i in Year t; CO_{it} refers to the competitiveness in innovation output of Country i in Year t; CS_{it} refers to the competitiveness in innovation sustainability of Country i in Year t. The above mathematical model for NIC includes the components NIC but does not define the relationship among the components. According to the study on the national innovation system, the relationship among the elements of NIC.

NIC is not a static state but a dynamic ascending process achiev the capacity (see Fig. 3.3). Due to the growth of innovation efficiency, the influence of national innovation increases. The dynamic of national innovation ability continually propels the economic and social prosperity of the country.

Consequently, the formation of NIC follows the evolving path of "resource element-organization and structure-function implement - innovation advantage" and the research paradigm of NIC also follows the thought of "innovation opportunity-innovation environment-innovation driving-innovation efficiency-innovation ability-innovation sustainability" (see Fig. 2.). By implementing the innovation strategies, we realize the competitive advantage of innovation and carry forward the strategic research of NIC.

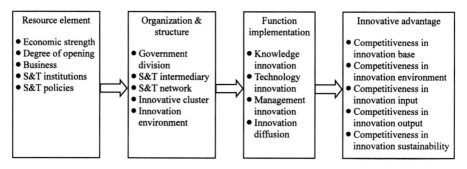

Fig. 2.5   Formation Path of NIC

Chapter 3

Establishment of the Evaluation System for NIC

In order to objectively and evaluate the level of NIC and comprehensively understand NIC as well as its inter mechanism, we overall evaluation NIC. Thus, such an indicator system is required to reflect all aspects involvNIC, take its internal structural characteristics into consideration, and make evaluation and analysis for it with scientific and mathematical model. Innovation everywhere, in each division of industries and businesses of every country as well as various fields of international trade and financial work, has become an important national competitiveness. As the foundation and source maintaining the competitive advantage of a country, it is also affected by many factors infrastructure, environment and input. Therefore, it is a highly complicated process to establish an indicator system and mathematical model for overall evaluation, analysis and research on NIC. This chapter is on the mechanism of NIC, innovation abilities, conditions and levels of G20 nations to establish with great efforts the scientific and prospective evaluation indicator system and mathematical model for national innovation competitiveness.

I. Characteristics and Building Principles for the Indicator System of NIC

In this report, we will make an overall evaluation on the innovation competitiveness of G20 nations either qualitative evaluation method or quantitative evaluation method. The qualitative evaluation is rather subjective and arbitrary and the evaluation result is. Thus, it and positioning and will greatly decrease the reference value for policies. Whereas, the quantitative evaluation overcome these problems determine important representative indicators to compose the evaluation indicator system of NICmeasure and evaluate the innovation competitiveness level of countries with mathematical model, and thus translate the innovation competitiveness into From the evaluation result, we primary indicators and weak link restricting and influencing the innovation competitiveness level of countries, and propose corresponding counter measures as the decision basis and reference for countries to enhance the innovation competitiveness level.

The most important link in quantitative evaluation is to establish an evaluation indicator system, which should reflect the level of NIC objectively and accuratelyscientific and reasonable mathematical evaluation model. It is the foundation and key for the overall evaluation, analysis and research of innovation competitiveness. cientific indicator system and mathematical model of innovation competitiveness should be established certain principle and based on the mechanism of innovation competitiveness.

1. In Mechanism of NIC

Historical development proves that innovation necessity for human progress, and the power supply for sustainable development of a country. countr should attach great importance to innovation and protect it, and providsatisfactory innovation ability and environment. A country will win in international competition only if it holds continuous competitive advantage in innovation.

Nowadays, national innovation ability has become the focus of international competition and NIC is the dynamic representation and the goal of national innovation ability., NIC and national innovation ability are derived from the same origin in the inner mechanism; the strength of a country in innovation ability directly determines the of the country in competitiveness.

According to the summary about the study of national innovation ability in Chapter 2, the influencing factors to national innovation ability include the quality of human resources; the efficiency of public policies; the public investment of innovation orientation (OECD, 1991-1998); the public innovation infrastructure, the innovation environment of industrial cluster and the connection between the both (Jeffrey L. Furman, Michael E. Porter, Scott Stern, 2002); the resources and systems supporting innovation and the sustainability in innovation (Mei-Chih Hu, John A. Mathews, 2005, 2007). It is observed from the above research that there are three aspects influence national innovation ability: the infrastructure supporting national innovation, innovation environment and innovation input, innovation input includes input in human resources and funds.

as for NIC, we believe that it is affected by three aspects innovation infrastructure, innovation environment and innovation inputwe believe that Therefore, NIC should cover five aspects competitiveness in innovation base, competitiveness in innovation environment, competitiveness in innovation input, competitiveness in innovation output and competitiveness in innovation sustainability. Thus, it can be seen that NIC involves o establish scientific and evaluation indicator system and mathematical model for environmental competitiveness, we should understand the abundant content and mechanism of NIC, and reflect them in the indicator system and mathematical model.

(1) NIC covers NIC covers five aspectscompetitiveness in innovation base, competitiveness in innovation environment, competitiveness in innovation input, competitiveness in innovation output and competitiveness in innovation sustainability, which comprehensively represents all the influencing factors of NIC. Therefore, while building the indicator system of NIC, we should give full consideration to all and determine and arrange the evaluation indicators of the elements to form logical system complete structure and reasonable arrangement true of NIC.

(2) The factors inside NIC are an organic whole. The five aspects involved in NICsupplement one another and form an organic whole.

The innovation base is the carrier of national innovation in science and technology, the public platform supporting innovative activities of the entire country and the important basis NIC, is characterized by foundation, continuity and.ompetitiveness in innovation base is the most basic component of NIC as well as the evaluation basis for it, which reflects the foundation and level of a country in economic and social development and represents the input and contribution of a country in innovation development as well as the importance a country innovation ability.

The innovation environment is the important guarantee to enhance the competition level of a country in sci-tech innovation. Favorable innovation environment effectively gather innovation resources, facilitate positive factors to advance innovation development, quicken the innovation pace, and improve the innovation ability and level, but also foster the innovation carrier with strong competitiveness (enterprise, college or university, and research institute). Meanwhile, superior innovation environment also marketization of innovation results, improve innovation performance and accumulate the progressive capacity of innovation. The competitiveness in innovation environment is the primitive driving force for the formation of NIC and the necessity of NIC.

The innovation input is the crucial guarantee innovation activities and the innovation system. To enhance NIC, we should have substantial innovation input as the guarantee. ompetitiveness in innovation input is the and effective guarantee for the formation of NIC, which comprehensively reflects the contribution of a country. Without the input of innovation resource, innovation competitiveness will lose its material base.

The innovation output is the important standard the competitiveness level of a country in sci-tech innovation. The result and quality of innovation output directly determine the level of innovation competitiveness and represent the development and implementation dynamics of innovation activities. A high level of NIC certainly requires innovation output. ompetitiveness in innovation output, comprehensively capabilit.

Sustainable development of innovation is the important target for NIC. Only if we achieve sustainable development in innovation achieve sustainable enhancement of NIC. ompetitiveness in innovation sustainability is important embodiment for the formation of NIC. It involves both the influence of innovation on national production and life and the influence of the country on innovation and activities. It does not influence the innovation competitiveness of country, but also influence the innovation competitiveness of other countries.

The competitiveness in innovation basc, competitiveness in innovation environment, competitiveness in innovation input, competitiveness in innovation output and competitiveness in innovation sustainability are not mutually individuals but an interactive organic whole with element - structure - organization - function - optimization as the main line. Therefore, the indicator system, we should pay attention to the coordination and five and fully reflect interactive relation in the indicator system.

2. Principles of the Indicator System for NIC

Sci-tech innovation It is to make systematic overall evaluation and analysis on NIC. We should establish a scientific and evaluation indicator system. To do this, we should follow certain principles to ensure the indicators of the system scientific, representative and systematic, combination of some indicators. By and large, we should follow the important principles below to build the evaluation indicator system of NIC:

3. The Principle Combining Systematicness and Hierarchy.

The system of sci-tech innovation is a complex systemmany aspectsare connected mutually and combined. Accordingly, the indicator system of innovation competitiveness should also be an organic whole, which should describe and reflect the level and characteristics of the entire innovation system comprehensively, scientifically and accurately.

The innovation system, as a general system, can be further divided into several multi-layer sub-systems, which together influence the innovation competitiveness level and integrate the evaluation object and the indicators into an organic whole. we should multiple layers and sub-systems and go deepto adopt hierarchical method and follow the principle of hierarchy.

The principle combining systematicness and hierarchy is both to consider the complex and systematic characteristics and to classify the system into several levels for analysis so that the evaluation indicators represent the affiliation and interaction among the different levels of evaluation indicators. The indicators at the upper levels are the integration of those at the lower levels, which the establishment of lower levels indicators; the indicators at the lower levels are the decomposition of those at the upper levels. All of this forms an orderly and systematic hierarchical structure facilitating operation and application.

4. The Principle Combining Completeness and Independence.

The indicators and model for the indicator system of innovation competitiveness, as an organic whole, should try to reflect the whole characteristics and overall condition of the countries in the entire innovation system from different angles, as well as the principal information of the system so as to realize   The indicators at the same level should individually reflect one side of the system of this level without so as to reflect the overall development of the system with

5. The Principle Combining Universality and Comparability.

The indicators for the indicator system of innovation competitiveness should should be able to fully reflect the characteristics of the countries accurately reflect the conditions of the countries in innovation competitiveness. Besides the universality of the indicators, we should also take comparability into consideration and guarantee thThe indicators should be able to be compared with past and future ones, and with corresponding indicators of other countries so as to guarantee the overall and correct evaluation for innovation competitiveness. It is also easy, with the evaluation result, to make time and space comparison and analysis for innovation competitiveness and to find out the actual factors influencing innovation competitiveness.

6. The Principle Combining

In building the indicator system of innovation competitiveness, the specific indicators should be selected on scientific basis with full recognition and study of the innovative system, which should be logical, deliberation and verification, withstand the test of fact and history, and able to reflect the connotation, requirement,

On the basis of we should also pay attention to the operability of the indicator system. We should keep the indicators definite in concept, try to use universal names and concepts in the world and avoid mutual and repetition. The indicators should be identical in the statistical scope and the data should be easy to collect with authoritative and reliable resource. Even though some indicators may reflect some aspects of innovation competitiveness, if we find the data, we should abandon them adopt some others, the statistics, calculation, comparison and analysis for the indicators and mathematical model should be convenient and liable to comprehend so that the evaluation be conducted successfully with enough evaluation credibility.

7. The Principle Combining Dynamics and.

The innovation system is a historical, dynamic, continuous developing system, but at some time, it is static with dynamic and static. On one, improvement and modification for the indicator system with the development and variation of the innovation system; only On the other, once the indicator system established, we should not change the content effectively compare and analyze the development process of the system.

The above five principles are an organic whole relatively independent and also mutually related. We separate them but coordinate them and insist through the entire evaluation process of innovation competitiveness. Thus, they truly direct the building of the indicator system of innovation competitiveness and become the important guarantee to correctly and effectively evaluate, analyze and research innovation competitiveness.

II. Establishment of the Indicator System for NIC

In combination with and in accordance with the five principles for the establishment of the indicator model this report builds the evaluation and indicator system for NIC. In process of building, we have referred to many documents sci-tech competitiveness and innovation ability *World Knowledge Competitiveness Index* of Robert Huggins Associates, the *Global Competitiveness Report* of World Economic Forum (WEF), and the *World Competitiveness Yearbook* of International Institute for Management Development, Lausanne of Switzerland (IMD). On the basis of this, according to the definition and connotation of NIC made by this report, we   indicator system for NIC1 primary indicator, 5 secondary indicators and 35 tertiary indicators.

1. Basic to Build the Evaluation Indicator System of Innovation Competitiveness

According to the definition, connotation and mechanism of innovation competitiveness and following the five principles in building the indicator system, in the basic principles of system theory and cybernetics as well as the top-down and decomposition methods, this report divides the indicator system into three layers system layer, element layer and base layer (primary, secondary and tertiary indicators respectively) and builds the indicator system of innovation competitiveness classes and multiple elements and multiple layerspecific Fig. 3-1.

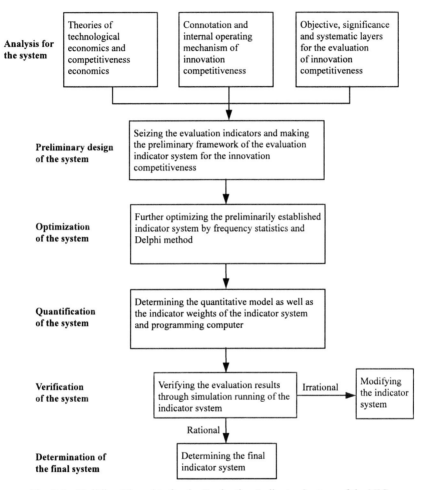

Fig. 3-1   Building Thoughts for the Evaluation Indicator System of the NIC

First, based on the theories in technological economics and competitiveness economics, according to the connotation and mechanism, confirm the objective, significance and system layer for the evaluation of innovation competitiveness, absorb existing essence on evaluation indicators of sci-tech competitiveness and innovation competitiveness, make careful analysis and comparison and take the availability of the indicators and data into consideration

Second, further optimize the evaluation indicator system in frequency statistics and Delphi method and ensure the and authority of the indicators, particularly, select frequently-used indicators, e. g. gross volume of R&D, total R&D personnel and protection of intellectual property right, to for reports and papers on innovation ability in science and technology as well as competitiveness in science and technology. Since th the connotation of NIC and most data of them are available, thecan be used to evaluate the environmental. On basis, we invited over 50 experts and scholars in the field of sci-tech innovation, including science and technology bureaus, academies of social sciences, development and research centers, colleges and universities etc. to form research group, further discuss, and improve the evaluation indicator system with consultation expert meeting law and Delphi method.

Third, based on the indicator system established above, determine the quantitative mathematical model as well as the weights of specific indicators, confirm the quantification methods of specific indicators and the algorithmic methods of quantity as well as the specific process related to the indicators, and then,

Fourth, the indicator data of some countries to and verify the result. If the resultrational, determine the evaluation indicator system of innovation competitiveness; if irrational, further modify the indicator system the research group and then

2. Selection the Indicators System Layer and Element Layer

In the evaluation indicator system of innovation competitiveness, there is only one indicator of the system layer (i.e. primary indicator), that is innovation competitiveness (A1). It is a comprehensive and systematic indicator to evaluate the innovation competitiveness of a country, covering all aspects of the innovation system, playing the role of general outline, and overall reflecting the innovation competitiveness level of a country. It is also the general objective for the whole indicator system.

Under the system layer is element layer. The indicators of this layer are mainly composed of the elements influence the innovation system, the supporting function of the elements to the whole innovation system. According to the connotation and mechanism of innovation competitiveness, the indicators of the element layer are mainly designed on five principal components of innovation competitiveness, that is: innovation base, innovation environment, innovation input, innovation output and innovation sustainability. Five secondary indicators are established and constitute the main part and principal framework of innovation competitiveness, as shown in Fig. 3-2.

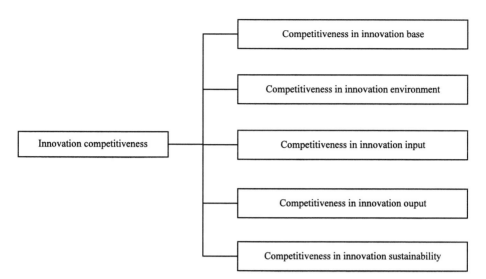

Fig. 3-2 Primary and Secondary Indicators of the Evaluation Indicator System for NIC

(1) Competitiveness in Innovation Base (B1). ompetitiveness in innovation base is the most basic element of NIC. Innovation base is the major factor reflecting the sci-tech input of the country, the creation of knowledge and the transformation and application of technology as well as the important factor   NIC. ompetitiveness in innovation base, on one, examines the impetus of national economic and social development and innovation ability, and on the other, examines the internal demand of national innovation ability. It represen the national economic and social development, the input and contribution of the country to innovation development, the degree of importance paid by the country to the enhancement of innovation abilitythe evaluation basis of NIC and the fundamental indicator the strength of innovation competitiveness.

(2) Competitiveness in Innovation Environment (B2). ompetitiveness in innovation environment is the primitive driving force for the formation of NIC and the necessity of NIC. Favorable innovation environment effectively gather the innovation resources but also foster the innovation carrier with strong competitiveness (enterprise, college or university, and research institute). Meanwhile, superior innovation environment   marketization of innovation achievements, thus to improve the innovation performance and accumulate progressive capacity of innovation, which is important   the strength of innovation competitiveness.

(3) Competitiveness in Innovation Input (B3). ompetitiveness in innovation input is the   and effective guarantee for the formation of NIC; without the input of innovation

resource, innovation competitiveness will lose its. The scale, quality and structural optimization of innovation resource input determine how much innovation output is and how innovation efficiency is. ompetitiveness in innovation input is the necessary guarantee for the formation of NIC, which comprehensively represents the contribution of the country to innovation input and is the key indicatorthe strength of innovation competitiveness.

(4) Competitiveness in Innovation Output (B4). ompetitiveness in innovation output is the carrier for the formation of NIC. The result and quality of innovation output directly determine the level of innovation ability and represent the development and implementation dynamics of innovation activities. ompetitiveness in innovation output, comprehensively reflect the executive capability the primary coverage to enhance NIC and important indicator the strength of innovation competitiveness.

(5) Competitiveness in Innovation Sustainability (B5). ompetitiveness in innovation sustainability is the important embodiment for the formation of NIC. It involves both the influence of innovation on national production and life and the influence of the country on innovation actions and activities, both the evaluation for the current situation of national innovation ability and the possible influence of innovation development. innovation activities, competitiveness in innovation sustainability does not influence the innovation competitiveness of this country, but also influence the innovation competitiveness of other countries by radiation, and thus It is also one of the important indicators the strength of innovation competitiveness.

3. Selection the Indicators Base layer

The indicators of element layer are the principal factor the innovation system, which is determined by the connotations and characteristics of the elements. These indicators are established through further division of the elements according to the connotations, components and characteristics of the five elements, innovation base, innovation environment, innovation input, innovation output and innovation sustainability.

The indicators of base layer are composed of the indicators and are the direct measurement of the element layer indicator and the most basic layer and operating layer for the entire indicator system of innovation competitiveness, on which, the evaluation of the entire indicator system lies. According to the definition of tertiary indicators, 35 tertiary indicators are established, seven base layer indicators for every element layer, as shown in Tab. 3-1.

Tab. 3-1 Secondary and Tertiary Indicators for the Indicator System
of Innovation Competitiveness

Secondary indicator	Tertiary indicator	Number
B1 Competitiveness in innovation base	GDP, per capita GDP, fiscal revenue, per capita fiscal revenue, direct foreign investment, gross attendance rate for higher education, overall labor productivity	7
B2 Competitiveness in innovation environment	Number of Internet users/1,000 persons, number of cell-phones/1,000 persons, number of new businesses, opening dates of businesses, macro tax burden, advanced technological products purchased by governments, protection of intellectual property right	7
B3 Competitiveness in innovation input	Gross R&D expenditure, proportion of gross R&D expenditure in GDP, per capita R&D expenditure, R&D personnel, proportion of R&D personnel to total employees, proportion of R&D personnel in businesses, proportion of R&D input in businesses	7
B4 Competitiveness in innovation output	Applications American patents, average patent authorizations of sci-tech personnel, publications of scientific papers, average paper publications of sci-tech personnel, royalty and license income, high-tech products export, proportion of high-tech products export in the manufacturing	7
B5 Competitiveness in innovation sustainability	Gross expenditure on public education, proportion of gross expenditure on public education to GDP, per capita expenditure on public education, proportion of persons of higher education, proportion of scientists and engineers, growth rate of sci-tech personnel, growth rate of sci-tech funds	7

4. Design Overview and Explanation for the Competitiveness Indicator System

The evaluation indicator system of NIC consists of three layers of indicators, that is, the system layer, the element layer and the base layer. The three layers correspond to one primary indicator, five secondary indicators and 35 tertiary indicators, among which, the primary and the secondary indicators are synthetic indirect indicators and the tertiary indicators are objective direct and measurable indicators. They are fundamental in the whole indicator system and, in the process of evaluation, released by authoritative international agencies World Bank and the UN. some data of the indicators are hard to access hence, some tertiary indicators have been ignored in this report. The building of the evaluation indicator system of innovation competitiveness will provide a reasonable and effective evaluation standard for evaluating G20 NIC.

III. Establishment of the Evaluation Model for NIC

ext step after building the evaluation indicator system of innovation competitiveness is to build the evaluation model of innovation competitiveness, which is also a vital link in the evaluation process of the entire innovation competitiveness. The establishment of the evaluation model of innovation competitiveness will simplify the evaluation of innovation competitiveness: only by putting the collected data into the evaluation model relative evaluation results will be obtained. This report builds the evaluation model of innovation competitiveness in three steps: first, conduct dimensionless treatment for the evaluation indicators; second, determine the weight of the evaluation indicators; establish mathematical model.

(I) Dimensionless Treatment for the Indicators

Due to different measuring units and dimensions of the base layer indicators (tertiary indicators) in the evaluation indicator system, and numeral values, the indicators not be used in calculation, but transformed into dimensionless index value or score value.

also known as standardization is a method to eliminate the influence of the dimension of original variables (indicators) through mathematical manipulation. There are many approaches, but usually there are four used: sum standardization, standardization of standard deviation, standardization of maximum and level difference standardization. The simple and practical standardization of maximum is in this report for the dimensionless treatment of the indicators.

When the indicator is positive (the bigger, the better), the dimensionless value (Xi) of the i indicator:

$$Xi = \frac{x_i - x_{min}}{x_{max} - x_{min}} \times 100$$

When the indicator is negative (the smaller, the better), the dimensionless value (Xi) of the i indicator:

$$Xi = \frac{x_{max} - x_i}{x_{max} - x_{min}} \times 100$$

In which, Xi refers to the value of the i indicator through dimensionless treatment, the dimensionless value of the i indicator for short; xi is the original value of this indicator; x_{max} and x_{min} respectively refers to the maximum and the minimum original values of the indicators of a kind in the comparison.

After polarity.

(II) Determin the Indicator Weights

Indicator weight refers to the dimension and degree of the indicators on the evaluation objective in the indicator system. The values of indicator weights directly influence the result of overall evaluation of innovation competitiveness and the fluctuation of the weights may cause variation in ranking of evaluated objects. Therefore, it is crucial for the success of an overall evaluation to determine the indicator weight in the indicator system of innovation competitiveness. Given the particularity for the evaluation of NIC, the international-common method of weighted average is in this report to determine the weight of the indicators, that is, at the element layer, the weight of each secondary indicator are the same, all 0.2; at the base layer, the weight of each tertiary indicator are the same, all 0.14.

(III) Establish the Model for Innovation Competitiveness

determin the weights is to build the model of innovation competitiveness for calculating the evaluation points of the innovation competitiveness of the countries. For a country, the higher the evaluation score, the stronger the overall innovation competitiveness is. The model for innovation competitiveness is as follows:

$$Y=\sum\sum x_{ij}w_{ij} \qquad \qquad \text{Formula (3.1)}$$

$$Y_i=\sum x_{ij}w_{ij} \qquad \qquad \text{Formula (3.2)}$$

In the above formula, Y is the overall evaluation point of innovation competitiveness, Y_i is the evaluation point of the i element indicator, x_{ij} is the dimensionless data value of the j base indicator for the i element, w_{ij} is the weight of the base indicator.

While evaluating the innovation competitiveness of a country after the evaluation model for innovation competitiveness, since the weights of the indicators are fixed, input the dimensionless data values of the indicators of the base layer for the country, we will get the evaluation point of the country in innovation competitiveness as well as the evaluation points of the indicators of the element and the base layers. According to the evaluation model of innovation competitiveness, we can make an overall evaluation for the innovation competitiveness of G20 nations and then make the ranking, comparison and analysis for the innovation competitiveness of all the G20 nations.

(IV) Establishthe Dynamic Prediction Model for Innovation Competitiveness

1. Innovation Competitiveness, a Dynamic Process of Change and Development

With economic and social development as well as the progress of science and technology, innovation competitiveness of countries is also advancing. It is a continuous and dynamic i, since innovation competitiveness is a relative concept, apart from the internal factors of the country itself, the external development factors of other countries should also be taken into.

On one, the development of a country itself, the progress of science and technology and the improvement of innovation ability will the scores and ranks of some indicators in the indicator system of innovation competitiveness for this country and thus the overall scores and ranks of innovation competitiveness; on the other, development of other countries, the progress of science and technology and the improvement of innovation ability will also scores and ranks of innovation competitiveness for this country., with the influence of them, innovation competitiveness of this country will also change in scores and ranks. Therefore, to understand the changes and situation of NIC in a more comprehensive, more specific and more profound way, we must make transverse dynamic analysis on innovation competitiveness.

2. Changes Innovation Competitiveness a

According to the practical research and development of innovation competitiveness, there are mainly six of change and development states for the indicators of the system.

(1) Continuously Rising, meaning the indicators These indicators are not only continuously rising in the development and change of the country itself but They are the key factor to enhance NIC. The more the continuously rising indicators, the stronger the NIC is.

(2) Rising Fluctuation, meaning the indicators That is, during the evaluation period, in despite of any variations to the ranks of these indicators, the ranks of them at the end of the evaluation period are always higher than at the beginning of the evaluation period. These indicators are also the important factor to enhance NIC.

(3) Continuously Unchanged, meaning the indicators remain unchanged in the rankings all along. It does not mean no change in the values or scores of these indicators. The values and scores may rise or drop, but due to external factors, in their ranks, a.

(4) Unchanged Fluctuation, meaning the indicators remain unchanged in overall trend but with some fluctuation during the evaluation period. That is, during the evaluation period, despite any variations to the ranks of these indicators, ranks of them at the end of the evaluation period must be the same withat the beginning of the evaluation period.

(5) Declining Fluctuation, meaning the indicators in overall trend but with some rising or unchanged That is, during the evaluation period, despite any variations to the ranks of these indicators, the ranks of them at the end of the evaluation period are always lower than that the beginning of the evaluation period. These indicators are the important factor drag down NIC.

(6) Continuously Declining, meaning the indicators continuousThese indicators are

not only continuously declining in the development and change of the country itself but also weak in comparison with other countries. They are the main factordown NIC.

3. Dynamic Model of Innovation Competitiveness

According to the indicator system and the changing types of innovation competitiveness, technological means of 3D 100% stacked area, variation curve chart and overall evaluation formbuild the dynamic model of innovation competitiveness. The computational formula of the evaluation points for the primary, secondary and tertiary indicators in specific indicator system of innovation competitiveness have been given before as follows:

$$Y=\sum\sum x_{ij}w_{ij}, \ Y_i=\sum x_{ij}w_{ij}$$

According to the measuring results of the above formula, the dynamic variation of NIC is showed with 100% stacked area as Fig. 3-3.

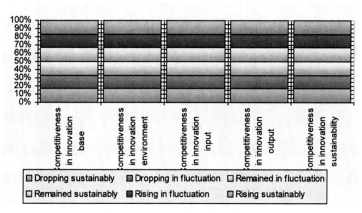

Fig. 3-3   Dynamic Model of NIC

Apart from the 100% stacked area for the dynamic variation of innovation competitiveness, in the process of the analysis, the variation curve chart and overall evaluation form are also used to describe the variations in rankings of the indicators in the evaluation periods.

IV. Approaches for NIC

1. Determination of the Evaluation Period and Coverage of Innovation Competitiveness

In evaluating innovation competitiveness, the innovation competitiveness of all countries in any periods not be involved, so we should determine the evaluation period and coverage.

(1) Evaluation Period. Based on the statistical data released by the authoritative international agencies of World Bank and the UN, it covers a time span of nine years from 2001 to the end of 2009.

(2) Countries Involv in the Evaluation. G20 nations are taken as the evaluation object. However, since the EU involves 27 member countries and some of them (e.g. the UK, France, and Germany) the evaluation for may cause repeated evaluation in this report, the EU is excluded from the evaluation system, instead of the evaluation object. Therefore, this report will mainly evaluat, analythe presentation and dynamic variation of the innovation competitiveness for the other 19 countries of G20.

(3) Regions Involv in the Evaluation. Based on the evaluation results of G20 nations, the 19 countries are divided according to their locations into six regions for simple evaluation, analysis and of innovation competitiveness. The six regions are North America, South America, Europe, Asia, Africa and Oceania. Furthermore, in view of the increasing international influence of BRICS (China, Russia, India, Brazil and South Africa), they are also involved in the analysis.

2. Determination of the Ranking Sections as well as Advantage and Weakness of the Indicators

According to the established indicator system, this report by years and in stages for the indicators of innovation competitiveness at all levels with technological tendency chartTo facilitate the evaluation on the analysis result, two evaluation standards are thus established.

(1) Standard to Determine the Ranking Sections. In order to judge the status of the innovation competitiveness of a country in G20, we determine No. 1-5 in the ranking as the first array, No. 6-10 as the second array, No. 11-15 as the third array, and No. 16-19 as the fourth array.

(2) Standard to Evaluate the Advantage and Weakness. We employ strength, advantage, medium and weakness to evaluate the quality of the indicators. The indicators ranking No. 1-5 are strength indicators; those ranking No. 6-10 are advantage indicators; those ranking No. 11-15 are medium indicators; and those ranking No. 16-19 are weakness indicators. The indicators of all levels are evaluated this standard.

3. Determination of the Dynamic Variation Tendency of the Indicators

According to the dynamic variation types of innovation competitiveness determined above, this report adopts the symbols of "continuously ↑" "↑ fluctuation" "continuously →" "→ fluctuation" "↓ fluctuation" and "continuously ↓" to represent the six variation states of the indicators continuously rising, rising continuously unchanged, unchanged fluctuation, declining fluctuation and continuously declining, which describes the specific variations of the indicators concisely and clearly.

Chapter 4

Evaluation and Analysis Approaches
anResult Verification

The study on NIC is a brand new research subject,mentioned by some scholars in analyzing the problems of national innovation ability or national competitiveness no special and systematic research on it yet. Of course, NIC, as a brand new research subject, in the theory and the method study of national innovation and national competitiveness. After all, theory and method study are always derived from the same origin. In view of this, this study the existing research and explor a brand new research perspective. This chapter in depth research thought, analytical approach and technical process for the analysis and evaluation of NIC and forms a rather complete evaluation frame for the research of NIC.

I. Overall Research

1. Guiding Ideology of the Research

Under the background of globalization, economic cooperation among countries is becoming more and more expansive; the circulation of various production factors and resources is becoming more and more frequent, but the imbalance of economic development intensifies the competition among countries and sci-tech competition turns to be the focus of the competition in comprehensive national strength. Enhancing the international competition capability through innovation has become the consensus of the whole world. Many countries around the world, especially developed countries, take sci-tech progress and innovation as the national strategy, substantially increasing sci-tech input, increasing the protection and utility of patents and intellectual property rights, developing high-tech industry, facilitating the application of high-tech industry, to take the initiative in international economy and sci-tech competition. Recently, China has witnessed remarkable achievement in economic growth: national power international status   But the competitive strength of developed countries, China still remains inslow in adjusting the economic restructure and transforming the economic development mode, requir adjustment in the growth mode of international trade, and in particular, inadequate in independent innovation ability with a greater gap between the overall sci-tech level of China and the sophisticated level of the. From the strategic and overall perspective, there is an urgent need of solid scientific foundation and powerful technological support to develop new industri, adjust the economic structure, transform the economic growth mode, accelerate the industrial optimization and maintain the national security and strategic interests. Hence, as early as during the period of the 11th Five-Year, China has proposed to improve the independent innovation ability with efforts and take it as one of the important objectives "to form a passel of advantageous enterprises with independent intellectual property rights, well-known brands and strong international competition capability." At the same time, China has worked out the national strategic plan for medium- and long-term sci-tech development and made the critical strategic decision "accelerat the construction of national innovation system" innovative countryindependent innovation China's scientific and technological development. Moreover, in a rather long period in the future, China will aim to promote scientific and technological progress and innovation, drive China's economic growth from resource-independent to innovation-driven and drive the economic and social development into a track of scientific development.

to research and evaluate the NIC is to analyze current situation of sci-tech innovation of countries summarize the characteristics and the inherent laws of the competitiveness in sci-tech innovation beginning with the relation between scientific   technical innovation and economic   social development, discuss the driving factors and the mechanisms of formation for NIC   NIC from multiple levels of theory, method and practice evaluate the innovation competitiveness of all countries in the world thus to make every effort to scientifically and objectively reflect the representation and variation trace of sci-tech innovation of countries in a long period, and interpret the characteristics and the differences of innovation competitiveness for countries, so as to provide helpful reference for China to enhance the independent innovation ability and improve innovation competitiveness.

2. Framework and Thoughts of the Research

The innovation system of a country is a systematic process, including both scientific and technological research and the relation between sci-tech and The research of NIC is relating to sci-tech innovation and many other content, with and meanwhile, it requires reasonable definition and objective evaluation for innovation competitiveness. nly by innovation and breakthrough approachesdiscuss NIC and Research and evaluation of innovation competitiveness also require comprehensive approaches. expand the researchenrich the theoretical connotation and bring forth new research approaches. In order to make the evaluation results of NIC as objective as possible and realize the research goal, we should select correct research method, design and execute the technical route for the research, so as to ensure research and improve the research quality. The technical route following in this research is shown in Fig.4-1.

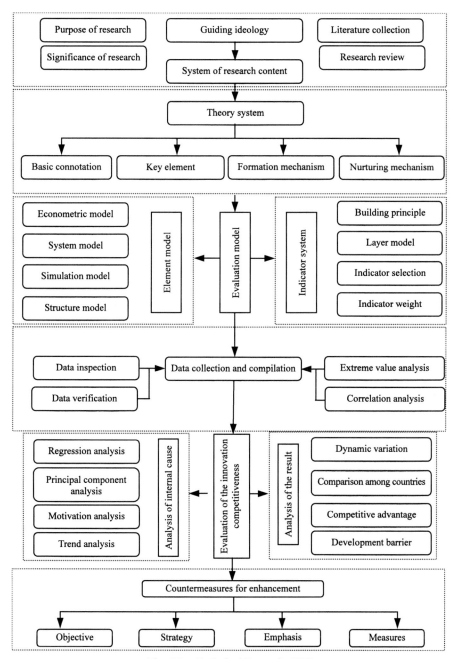

Fig. 4-1   Technical Route for NIC

In content and system, we should nail down the significance of research according to research objective determined by the guiding ideology, employ the theories of multiple disciplines like technical economics, quantitative economics, management and statistics through substantive literatures, clarify the importance and necessity to research and evaluate NIC under globalization in a and from various angles, draw on the relative research results of Chinese and foreign researchers, and based on research, build the theoretical system of NIC. ow to define the basic connotation of NIC and how to sum up the principal features, the and internal motive of NIC, esearch competitiveness cannot without evaluation, thus scientific and objective indicator system and evaluation model are required. evaluation model and method some limitation to restriction in cognition and knowledge, but the evaluation result on competitiveness as well as reflection development and formation of evaluation objects.

The indicator system and evaluation model of NIC should not only draw on Chinese and foreign mainstream research approaches, especially substantive research approaches and research results about the evaluation of national innovation ability which are the basis to research and evaluate NIC, but also combine with the characteristics of competitiveness and build the indicator system and evaluation model of NIC with unique characteristics. They should be able to objectively evaluate NIC, reflect the current situation and tendency of present international competition in science and technology, excavate the internal mechanism and the key points of NIC, and reflect the mechanisms of formation of NIC. The evaluation results should be able to reflect the guiding ideology for research and realize the research goal, facilitate the improvement of China's science and technology system, form extensive and multi-layer innovation cooperative mechanism, facilitate the cultivation and selection of skilled personnel in science and technology, develop scientific and technological talent team, increase the input in science and technology, improve resource allocation for science and technology, optimize the resource allocation of science and technology, improve output efficiency of scientific and technological input, and enhance the independent innovation capacity.

The evaluation model mainly includes two partsfactor model and indicator system. The factor model is which is the foundation for building the evaluation indicator system of NIC and provide basis to analyze the mechanisms of formation, the formation model and the internal motivation of innovation competitiveness. The indicator system is the basis for the evaluation of competitiveness. Building the indicator system to reflect the connotation of innovation competitiveness is important research and evaluate competitiveness. We should not choose the indicators at random but determine the weight of the indicator system through step-by-step decomposition, careful review each indicator In the evaluation method, we adopt the evaluation techniques frequently used at present to make overall evaluation on the innovation competitiveness of major G20 nations and interpret and analyze the evaluation results in anot only making comparison and and historical comparison but also making pointed analysis of comparative advantages and tendencies of countries, the reasons causing the competition results and the obstacles to the enhancement of competitiveness, analyzing the internal factors with influence on competitiveness, and judging and predicting the development trend of competitiveness.

Finally, we should sum up the value of the evaluation results, combining theory and practice tightly and expressing the relevant theories and evaluation results of NIC in different forms. Through the comparisons of innovation competitiveness, we see the and weakness of China in innovation competitiveness, summarize the fundamental distribution characteristics and the evolution trend of innovation competitiveness, find the primary indicators, the weak links and the roots restricting and affecting China's innovation competitiveness level and the potential development trend of innovation competitiveness in the future., we propose the goal and relevant strategies of China in innovation competitiveness as well as corresponding countermeasures to enhance innovation competitiveness, which be accelerat the development of China in science and technology and improv innovation ability of it.

II. Verification of the Indicator System

The indicator system is the basis evaluation of innovation competitiveness. On the whole, it has special function and significance, the indicator system is composed of many single indicatorshe correctness and integrity of each indicator very important n case that single indicator is may not meet the requirement of the and thus may the integrity of the whole indicator system and produce

1. Verification for Single Indicators

erification for single indicators mainly refers to verifying the indicators with available relevant data for integrity, consistency, fluctuation and extreme values so as to judge whether these indicators meet the demand and achieve the goal of the indicator system.

(1) Verification for Integrity and Consistency

The evaluation indicator system of NIC is composed of many indicators many fields of sci-tech, economy and society. Although countries have adopted the unified statistical and accounting system specified by the UN, because of different national situations and different development stages, the statistical systems of countries are not absolutely consistent, and the scopeand accounting processes of statistical inquiry are also different, thus some indicators are not consistent among different countries. Besides, some indicators have not been involved in the statistics of some countries, thus the indicator data of NIC is confronted with in integrity and consistency.

The verification for the integrity and consistency of the indicators is to check the connotation and data source of every indicator and ensure selected indicator recognized in the statistical system with clear accounting scope and definite meaning universal indicators. Furthermore, we should guarantee that identical indicators should have same data sources. As for indicators with different data sources, we should check them carefully and ensure th data and consistent. As to value indicators, since different monetary units, they are all converted into USD unified annual exchange rate.

(2) Verification for Fluctuation

Every indicator system has their specific function and unique effect and they are the of overall evaluation results, which reflect NIC from different aspects and should have some, fluctuation and coordination. The variation in the of the indicator should reflect the connotation variation in the measurement. Fluctuation requires that, under the situation that all the other indicators remain unchanged, the variation of this indicator could influence the measuring result, or the observed values of this indicator have certain fluctuation and distinctiveness. A coefficient of variation is usually used to judge the fluctuation of indicators as the following formula:

$$\delta = \sigma / \bar{x} \quad \sigma = \sqrt{\sum (x - \bar{x})^2 / (n-1)} \quad\quad (4\text{-}1)$$

(3) Verification for Extreme Values

It is very likely operation. In the statistics of substantive indicator data, some "noise" data (maximum value or minimum value) are inevitable, that is, individual dat deviates greatly from most other data, and thus, an indicator may vary with too large fluctuation different individuals. gap between the evaluation objects or errors occurred in the process of data collection and compilation. "Noise" data are unfavorable to the overall evaluation of competitiveness. In particular, the overall evaluation of competitiveness generally adopts compound weight method the score of overall competitiveness is obtained with the weighted scores of the lower-level indicators and the scores of the indicators with objective data are obtained through dimensionless treatment in the threshold method. That is to say, the total score of overall evaluation is obtained through multi-level for the scores of single indicator. If maximum value or minimum value emerges for an indicator, calculating with dimensionless formula in threshold method, the scores of the sample indicators may concentrate at one or zero. They are distributed and have influence on the overall evaluation of competitiveness. Seeing that the indicators may have extreme values, on one, we should analyze the characteristics of the indicators themselves and make the decision in combination with situation; on the other, we should select adequate quantitative method to find and dispose the extreme value that might exist for the indicators.

We mainly judge the extreme values of the indicator data according to the. The data have certain distribution characteristics at different samples. The distances between each datu and its mean value all meet certain rule, which is related to the standard deviation of the sample data. According to the law of number, 99.97% data are distributed within three mean square deviations to the mean value, i.e.:

$$P(|(x-\bar{x})/\sigma|<3)=0.9997 \quad \sigma=\sqrt{\sum(x-\bar{x})^2/(n-1)} \tag{4-2}$$

$\bar{x}$ is the mean value of the sample data and σ is the standard deviation of the sample data. In normal conditions, there is three tenthousandths probability that there is a greater gap between the indicator value and the mean value of a sample, exceeding three standard deviations, and it is less likely to go wrong; but if it is true for this case of small probability, Generally, this value can be regarded as the extreme and we should deal with it as required, to draw it back to a reasonable scope through re-check and modification.

2. Correlation Verification for the Indicators

During the evaluation of NIC, the indicator system is the core. In order to reflect all the factors influencing NIC, we design the system with coverage and many indicators to avoid inadequate information result from very few indicators and thus reflect NIC from different aspects, avoid the improper influence on the overall evaluation of abnormal fluctuation of individual indicator due to very few indicators and thus Howeverindicator system, indicators are selected analysis, selected   the formation model of NIC: obviously, they are selected subjectively and the relation among the indicators is not clear. correlation among the indicatorscomprehensive indicator system, i.e. different indicators identical information as well as information in the overall evaluation of NIC. If two indicators reflect content or have identical nature, they contain same information. If both are involved in the indicator system for the overall evaluation, it may cause indicator repetition and lead to information redundancy or even mutual contradiction. In the process of overall evaluation, the repeated calculation of this information affect the coordination for the evaluation of overall competitiveness.

The evaluation indicator system of NIC involves 5 secondary indicators and 35 tertiary indicators, which cover sci-tech, economics and education. Some indicators are in measuring content The repeated information among some indicators is adverse to the motive analysis for competitiveness. Therefore, we should analyze the correlation of each indicator. If significant correlation exist, certain approaches are required to eliminate the associative function among the indicators.

The analysis on the correlation of indicators is to research whether there is some dependence between research objects and then, as for the dependent objects, to discuss the correlation direction as well as the It is a statistical method correlation between random variables. According to the fluctuation direction of two variables, correlation involves positive correlation, negative correlation and non-correlation. 1) Positive Correlation: ne variable increases decreases and the other increases or decreases; both in the same direction: that is positive correlation. 2) Negative Correlation: ne variable increases or decreases and the other decreases or increases; both in opposite directions: that is negative correlation. 3) Non-correlation: the two variables, there is no correlation for the variation. Such a relation between the two variables is also called or zero correlation. Of course, this classification More precise statistical indicators are required to reflect the correlation between two variables, that is, to reflect the correlation between two variables with a statistic. According to different data categories of the variables, we should adopt different measuring approaches. The data of the indicator system for environmental competitiveness are all continuous variables at definite measurement and the correlative between variables can be measured by calculating the correlation coefficient in "short form" This method reflects the correlativity by the products of the variables and their own mean values, which is Pearson's formula:

$$r_{xy} = \frac{\sigma = \sum(x-\bar{x})(y-\bar{y})}{\sqrt{\sum(x-\bar{x})^2}\sqrt{\sum(y-\bar{y})^2}} \tag{4-3}$$

Here, x and y refer to the two variables to be measured for the correlation coefficient. r_{xy} is the correlation coefficient reflects the statistic of correlativity between x and y, also called simple correlation coefficient. Positive or negative r_{xy} determines the positive or negative relation between x and y. r_{xy} values between -1 and 1: the the absolute value to 1, the higher the correlativity of x and y; on the contrary, the the absolute value of ρ_{xy} to 0, the less obvious the linear relation of x and y. Certain reference standard is used to judge and verify the correlativity. The test statistic is:

$$t = \sqrt{\frac{r_{xy}^2(n-2)}{1-r_{xy}^2}} \sim t_{\partial/2}(n-2) \tag{4-4}$$

orrelation reflects the relationship degree between two indicators, but in a comprehensive indicator system, the relationship among multiple indicators is complicated correlation is to research the correlativity between a variable and another group of variables. It reflect the correlation of multiple indicators with the principle with one of simple correlation coefficient: the greater the value, the closer the relation of the variables. Generally, it is used for multiple regression, factorial analysis.

Multiple correlation also contains repeated information of multiple indicators. Partial correlation is to research the linear correlativity of two variables in the circumstance of multiple variables with the influence of other variables, i.e. net correlation between two variables the influence of other indicators. Therefore, compar with linear correlation coefficient, partial correlation coefficient reflect the relation between two variables. In conclusion, the calculation of partial correlation coefficient among indicators is to eliminate the influence of the other indicators on the basis of simple correlation coefficient, and the former formula should be modified as follows:

$$r_{12,3} = \frac{r_{12} - r_{13}r_{23}}{\sqrt{(1-r_{13}^2)(1-r_{23}^2)}} \tag{4-5}$$

In which, $r_{12,3}$ refers to the partial correlation of the first and the second indicators r_{12}, r_{13} and r_{23} respectively refer to the simple correlation between two indicators. We can use t to verify and the significance of partial correlation coefficient. Suppose the partial correlation coefficient deducting the influence of q variables is $r_{(-q)}$, and the test statistic is:

$$t = \frac{r_{(-q)}\sqrt{n-q-2}}{\sqrt{1-r_{(-q)}^2}} \sim t_{\partial/2}(n-q-2) \tag{4-6}$$

When multiple correlation or partial correlation among the indicators is rather obvious and pass the test of significance, we should principal component   evaluation indicators so as to eliminate redundant information of indicators.

3. Correlation Verification for the Indicators of the Competitiveness in Innovation Base

Calculate the correlation matrix among the seven tertiary indicators in the five secondary indicators respectively according to Formula (4-4) and Formula (4-6) and specify the corresponding two-tailed test values to every correlation coefficient. When the test value is less than 0.05 or 0.01, it means the correlation coefficient is larger than the critical value at the significance level of 0.05 and 0.01 respectively and the two indicators are correlatSince the evaluation of NIC from 2001-2009, long span ue to space limitations, we not list all the correlation coefficients and thus measure the correlation coefficients of secondary indicator in 2001, 2005 and 2009. Tab. 4-1, Tab. 4-2 and Tab. 4-3 are the analysis results of the indicators for the competitiveness in innovation base in 2001, 2005 and 2009 respectively.

Tab. 4-1 Correlation Verification for the Indicators of Competitiveness in Innovation Base in 2001

Indicator	Item	GDP	Per capita GDP	Fiscal revenue	Per capita fiscal revenue	FDI	Gross attendance rate for higher education	Labor productivity
GDP	Correlation coefficient	1	0.694**	0.991**	0.593**	0.873**	0.329	0.646**
	Test value		0.001	0	0.008	0	0.169	0.003
	Number of samples	19	19	19	19	19	19	19
Per capita GDP	Correlation coefficient	0.694**	1	0.740**	0.966**	0.576**	0.651**	0.986**
	Test value	0.001		0	0	0.01	0.003	0
	Number of samples	19	19	19	19	19	19	19
Fiscal revenue	Correlation coefficient	0.991**	0.740**	1	0.664**	0.882**	0.375	0.702**
	Test value	0	0		0.002	0	0.114	0.001
	Number of samples	19	19	19	19	19	19	19
Per capita fiscal revenue	Correlation coefficient	0.593**	0.966**	0.664**	1	0.546*	0.604**	0.976**
	Test value	0.008	0	0.002		0.016	0.006	0
	Number of samples	19	19	19	19	19	19	19
FDI	Correlation coefficient	0.873**	0.576**	0.882**	0.546*	1	0.269	0.546*
	Test value	0	0.01	0	0.016		0.265	0.016
	Number of samples	19	19	19	19	19	19	19
Gross attendance rate for higher education	Correlation coefficient	0.329	0.651**	0.375	0.604**	0.269	1	0.632**
	Test value	0.169	0.003	0.114	0.006	0.265		0.004
	Number of samples	19	19	19	19	19	19	19
Labor productivity	Correlation coefficient	0.646**	0.986**	0.702**	0.976**	0.546*	0.632**	1
	Test value	0.003	0	0.001	0	0.016	0.004	
	Number of samples	19	19	19	19	19	19	19

Note: ** means the significance level of correlation coefficient is 0.01 (two-sided test), * means the significance level of correlation coefficient is 0.05 (two-sided test).

Tab. 4-2 Correlation Verification for the Indicators of Competitiveness in Innovation Base in 2005

Indicator	Item	GDP	Per capita GDP	Fiscal revenue	Per capita fiscal revenue	FDI	Gross attendance rate for higher education	Labor productivity
GDP	Correlation coefficient	1	0.570*	0.985**	0.452	0.507*	0.375	0.531*
	Test value		0.011	0	0.052	0.027	0.114	0.019
	Number of samples	19	19	19	19	19	19	19
Per capita GDP	Correlation coefficient	0.570*	1	0.648**	0.961**	0.42	0.649**	0.986**
	Test value	0.011		0.003	0	0.073	0.003	0
	Number of samples	19	19	19	19	19	19	19
Fiscal revenue	Correlation coefficient	0.985**	0.648**	1	0.561*	0.532*	0.424	0.620**
	Test value	0	0.003		0.012	0.019	0.07	0.005
	Number of samples	19	19	19	19	19	19	19
Per capita fiscal revenue	Correlation coefficient	0.452	0.961**	0.561*	1	0.429	0.563*	0.974**
	Test value	0.052	0	0.012		0.067	0.012	0
	Number of samples	19	19	19	19	19	19	19
FDI	Correlation coefficient	0.507*	0.42	0.532*	0.429	1	0.136	0.412
	Test value	0.027	0.073	0.019	0.067		0.578	0.079
	Number of samples	19	19	19	19	19	19	19
Gross attendance rate for higher education	Correlation coefficient	0.375	0.649**	0.424	0.563*	0.136	1	0.616**
	Test value	0.114	0.003	0.07	0.012	0.578		0.005
	Number of samples	19	19	19	19	19	19	19
Labor productivity	Correlation coefficient	0.531*	0.986**	0.620**	0.974**	0.412	0.616**	1
	Test value	0.019	0	0.005	0	0.079	0.005	
	Number of samples	19	19	19	19	19	19	19

Note: ** means the significance level of correlation coefficient is 0.01 (two-sided test), * means the significance level of correlation coefficient is 0.05 (two-sided test).

Tab. 4-3 Correlation Verification for the Indicators of Competitiveness in Innovation Base in 2009

Indicator	Item	GDP	Per capita GDP	Fiscal revenue	Per capita fiscal revenue	FDI	Gross attendance rate for higher education	Labor productivity
GDP	Correlation coefficient	1	0.478*	0.974**	0.35	0.841**	0.276	0.441
	Test value		0.039	0	0.142	0	0.253	0.059
	Number of samples	19	19	19	19	19	19	19

Indicator	Item	GDP	Per capita GDP	Fiscal revenue	Per capita fiscal revenue	FDI	Gross attendance rate for higher education	Labor productivity
Per capita GDP	Correlation coefficient	0.478*	1	0.607**	0.959**	0.414	0.600**	0.984**
	Test value	0.039		0.006	0	0.078	0.007	0
	Number of samples	19	19	19	19	19	19	19
Fiscal revenue	Correlation coefficient	0.974**	0.607**	1	0.514*	0.832**	0.345	0.585**
	Test value	0	0.006		0.024	0	0.148	0.009
	Number of samples	19	19	19	19	19	19	19
Per capita fiscal revenue	Correlation coefficient	0.35	0.959**	0.514*	1	0.371	0.503*	0.972**
	Test value	0.142	0	0.024		0.118	0.028	0
	Number of samples	19	19	19	19	19	19	19
FDI	Correlation coefficient	0.841**	0.414	0.832**	0.371	1	0.18	0.388
	Test value	0	0.078	0	0.118		0.462	0.1
	Number of samples	19	19	19	19	19	19	19
Gross attendance rate for higher education	Correlation coefficient	0.276	0.600**	0.345	0.503*	0.18	1	0.561*
	Test value	0.253	0.007	0.148	0.028	0.462		0.012
	Number of samples	19	19	19	19	19	19	19
Labor productivity	Correlation coefficient	0.441	0.984**	0.585**	0.972**	0.388	0.561*	1
	Test value	0.059	0	0.009	0	0.1	0.012	
	Number of samples	19	19	19	19	19	19	19

Note: ** means the significance level of correlation coefficient is 0.01 (two-sided test), * means the significance level of correlation coefficient is 0.05 (two-sided test).

The analysis on the three correlation tables above indicates that there are three total amount indicators, GDP, fiscal revenue and FDI, two per capita indicators and two rate indicators. The three total amount indicators   related to economic scale and the correlation coefficients of them are very with significant correlation. The correlation coefficient between the two per capita indicators is relatively, but the correlation coefficients with the other indicators are relatively small. Of the two rate indicators, the correlation coefficients of gross attendance for higher education with the other indicators are all very small and test of significance, but the correlation coefficients of labor productivity with the other indicators are relatively big. Since the labor productivity is calculated on output and this group of indicators is mostly related to the scale of economic development, the correlation among some indicators is rather significant.

4. Correlation Verification for the Indicators of the Competitiveness in Innovation Environment

Tab. 4-4, Tab. 4-5 and Tab. 4-6 are the analysis results of the indicators for the competitiveness in innovation environment in 2001, 2005 and 2009 respectively.

Tab. 4-4   Correlation Verification for the Indicators of Competitiveness in Innovation Environment in 2001

Indicator	Item	Number of Internet users	Number of cell-phones	Number of new businesses	Average time required for enterprise development	Average tax burden of businesses	Purchase ability of governments for advanced technological products	Protection for intellectual property right
Number of Internet users	Correlation coefficient	1	0.744**	0.33	-0.685**	-0.187	0.617**	0.775**
	Test value		0	0.167	0.001	0.443	0.005	0
	Number of samples	19	19	19	19	19	19	19
Number of cell-phones	Correlation coefficient	0.744**	1	0.158	-0.610**	-0.044	0.27	0.684**
	Test value	0		0.519	0.006	0.859	0.264	0.001
	Number of samples	19	19	19	19	19	19	19
Number of new businesses	Correlation coefficient	0.33	0.158	1	-0.259	-0.157	0.348	0.186
	Test value	0.167	0.519		0.284	0.522	0.144	0.445
	Number of samples	19	19	19	19	19	19	19
Average time required for enterprise development	Correlation coefficient	-0.685**	-0.610**	-0.259	1	0.084	-0.414	-0.620**
	Test value	0.001	0.006	0.284		0.733	0.078	0.005
	Number of samples	19	19	19	19	19	19	19
Average tax burden of businesses	Correlation coefficient	-0.187	-0.044	-0.157	0.084	1	-0.526*	-0.352
	Test value	0.443	0.859	0.522	0.733		0.021	0.139
	Number of samples	19	19	19	19	19	19	19
Purchase ability of governments for advanced technological products	Correlation coefficient	0.617**	0.27	0.348	-0.414	-0.526*	1	0.668**
	Test value	0.005	0.264	0.144	0.078	0.021		0.002
	Number of samples	19	19	19	19	19	19	19
Protection for intellectual property right	Correlation coefficient	0.775**	0.684**	0.186	-0.620**	-0.352	0.668**	1
	Test value	0	0.001	0.445	0.005	0.139	0.002	
	Number of samples	19	19	19	19	19	19	19

Note: ** means the significance level of correlation coefficient is 0.01 (two-sided test), * means the significance level of correlation coefficient is 0.05 (two-sided test).

Tab. 4-5　Correlation Verification for the Indicators of Competitiveness in Innovation Environment in 2005

Indicator	Item	Number of Internet users	Number of cell-phones	Number of new businesses	Average time required for enterprise development	Average tax burden of businesses	Purchase ability of governments for advanced technological products	Protection for intellectual property right
Number of Internet users	Correlation coefficient	1	0.607**	0.331	-0.460*	-0.251	0.596**	0.778**
	Test value		0.006	0.167	0.048	0.3	0.007	0
	Number of samples	19	19	19	19	19	19	19
Number of cell-phones	Correlation coefficient	0.607**	1	0.271	-0.459*	-0.17	0.159	0.514*
	Test value	0.006		0.262	0.048	0.486	0.515	0.024
	Number of samples	19	19	19	19	19	19	19
Number of new businesses	Correlation coefficient	0.331	0.271	1	-0.056	-0.117	0.312	0.134
	Test value	0.167	0.262		0.821	0.633	0.193	0.584
	Number of samples	19	19	19	19	19	19	19
Average time required for enterprise development	Correlation coefficient	-0.460*	-0.459*	-0.056	1	0.065	-0.278	-0.481*
	Test value	0.048	0.048	0.821		0.791	0.25	0.037
	Number of samples	19	19	19	19	19	19	19
Average tax burden of businesses	Correlation coefficient	-0.251	-0.17	-0.117	0.065	1	-0.532*	-0.361
	Test value	0.3	0.486	0.633	0.791		0.019	0.128
	Number of samples	19	19	19	19	19	19	19
Purchase ability of governments for advanced technological products	Correlation coefficient	0.596**	0.159	0.312	-0.278	-0.532*	1	0.668**
	Test value	0.007	0.515	0.193	0.25	0.019		0.002
	Number of samples	19	19	19	19	19	19	19
Protection for intellectual property right	Correlation coefficient	0.778**	0.514*	0.134	-0.481*	-0.361	0.668**	1
	Test value	0	0.024	0.584	0.037	0.128	0.002	
	Number of samples	19	19	19	19	19	19	19

Note: ** means the significance level of correlation coefficient is 0.01 (two-sided test), * means the significance level of correlation coefficient is 0.05 (two-sided test).

Tab. 4-6 Correlation Verification for the Indicators of Competitiveness in Innovation Environment in 2009

Indicator	Item	Number of Internet users	Number of cell-phones	Number of new businesses	Average time required for enterprise development	Average tax burden of businesses	Purchase ability of governments for advanced technological products	Protection for intellectual property right
Number of Internet users	Correlation coefficient	1	0.255	0.451	-0.343	-0.192	0.427	0.634**
	Test value		0.292	0.053	0.151	0.43	0.068	0.004
	Number of samples	19	19	19	19	19	19	19
Number of cell-phones	Correlation coefficient	0.255	1	0.078	-0.223	-0.081	-0.15	0.013
	Test value	0.292		0.752	0.359	0.741	0.541	0.957
	Number of samples	19	19	19	19	19	19	19
Number of new businesses	Correlation coefficient	0.451	0.078	1	0.134	-0.047	0.313	0.189
	Test value	0.053	0.752		0.586	0.847	0.191	0.438
	Number of samples	19	19	19	19	19	19	19
Average time required for enterprise development	Correlation coefficient	-0.343	-0.223	0.134	1	0.297	-0.029	-0.39
	Test value	0.151	0.359	0.586		0.216	0.906	0.099
	Number of samples	19	19	19	19	19	19	19
Average tax burden of businesses	Correlation coefficient	-0.192	-0.081	-0.047	0.297	1	-0.543*	-0.424
	Test value	0.43	0.741	0.847	0.216		0.016	0.071
	Number of samples	19	19	19	19	19	19	19
Purchase ability of governments for advanced technological products	Correlation coefficient	0.427	-0.15	0.313	-0.029	-0.543*	1	0.550*
	Test value	0.068	0.541	0.191	0.906	0.016		0.015
	Number of samples	19	19	19	19	19	19	19
Protection for intellectual property right	Correlation coefficient	0.634**	0.013	0.189	-0.39	-0.424	0.550*	1
	Test value	0.004	0.957	0.438	0.099	0.071	0.015	
	Number of samples	19	19	19	19	19	19	19

Note: ** means the significance level of correlation coefficient is 0.01 (two-sided test), * means the significance level of correlation coefficient is 0.05 (two-sided test).

The analysis on the three correlation tables above indicates that, since there is only one total quantity indicator for the competitiveness in innovation environment, the number of new businesses, and the others all are average indicators or strength indicators, the correlation coefficients are very small and only a few pass the significance test for the 5% significance level. Some indicators even have reverse correlation.

5. Correlation Verification for the Indicators of the Competitiveness in Innovation Input

Tab. 4-7, Tab. 4-8 and Tab. 4-9 are the analysis results of the indicators for the competitiveness in innovation input in 2001, 2005 and 2009 respectively.

Tab. 4-7   Correlation Verification for the Indicators of Competitiveness in Innovation Input in 2001

Indicator	Item	Gross volume of R&D	Proportion of R&D to GDP	Per capita R&D	R&D personnel	Proportion of R&D personnel to total employees	Proportion of R&D personnel in the businesses	Proportion of R&D input in the businesses
Gross volume of R&D	Correlation coefficient	1	0.615**	0.728**	0.947**	0.565*	0.593**	0.512*
	Test value		0.005	0	0	0.012	0.007	0.025
	Number of samples	19	19	19	19	19	19	19
Proportion of R&D to GDP	Correlation coefficient	0.615**	1	0.935**	0.480*	0.913**	0.815**	0.788**
	Test value	0.005		0	0.038	0	0	0
	Number of samples	19	19	19	19	19	19	19
Per capita R&D	Correlation coefficient	0.728**	0.935**	1	0.564*	0.899**	0.748**	0.702**
	Test value	0	0		0.012	0	0	0.001
	Number of samples	19	19	19	19	19	19	19
R&D personnel	Correlation coefficient	0.947**	0.480*	0.564*	1	0.488*	0.566*	0.394
	Test value	0	0.038	0.012		0.034	0.012	0.095
	Number of samples	19	19	19	19	19	19	19
Proportion of R&D personnel to total employees	Correlation coefficient	0.565*	0.913**	0.899**	0.488*	1	0.754**	0.625**
	Test value	0.012	0	0	0.034		0	0.004
	Number of samples	19	19	19	19	19	19	19
Proportion of R&D personnel in the businesses	Correlation coefficient	0.593**	0.815**	0.748**	0.566*	0.754**	1	0.793**
	Test value	0.007	0	0	0.012	0		0
	Number of samples	19	19	19	19	19	19	19
Proportion of R&D input in the businesses	Correlation coefficient	0.512*	0.788**	0.702**	0.394	0.625**	0.793**	1
	Test value	0.025	0	0.001	0.095	0.004	0	
	Number of samples	19	19	19	19	19	19	19

Note: ** means the significance level of correlation coefficient is 0.01 (two-sided test), * means the significance level of correlation coefficient is 0.05 (two-sided test).

Tab. 4-8 Correlation Verification for the Indicators of Competitiveness in Innovation Input in 2005

Indicator	Item	Gross volume of R&D	Proportion of R&D to GDP	Per capita R&D	R&D personnel	Proportion of R&D personnel to total employees	Proportion of R&D personnel in the businesses	Proportion of R&D input in the businesses
Gross volume of R&D	Correlation coefficient	1	0.572*	0.675**	0.955**	0.508*	0.624**	0.516*
	Test value		0.01	0.002	0	0.026	0.004	0.024
	Number of samples	19	19	19	19	19	19	19
Proportion of R&D to GDP	Correlation coefficient	0.572*	1	0.927**	0.415	0.902**	0.755**	0.803**
	Test value	0.01		0	0.077	0	0	0
	Number of samples	19	19	19	19	19	19	19
Per capita R&D	Correlation coefficient	0.675**	0.927**	1	0.501*	0.924**	0.662**	0.691**
	Test value	0.002	0		0.029	0	0.002	0.001
	Number of samples	19	19	19	19	19	19	19
R&D personnel	Correlation coefficient	0.955**	0.415	0.501*	1	0.386	0.571*	0.371
	Test value	0	0.077	0.029		0.103	0.011	0.118
	Number of samples	19	19	19	19	19	19	19
Proportion of R&D personnel to total employees	Correlation coefficient	0.508*	0.902**	0.924**	0.386	1	0.609**	0.571*
	Test value	0.026	0	0	0.103		0.006	0.011
	Number of samples	19	19	19	19	19	19	19
Proportion of R&D personnel in the businesses	Correlation coefficient	0.624**	0.755**	0.662**	0.571*	0.609**	1	0.787**
	Test value	0.004	0	0.002	0.011	0.006		0
	Number of samples	19	19	19	19	19	19	19
Proportion of R&D input in the businesses	Correlation coefficient	0.516*	0.803**	0.691**	0.371	0.571*	0.787**	1
	Test value	0.024	0	0.001	0.118	0.011	0	
	Number of samples	19	19	19	19	19	19	19

Note: ** means the significance level of correlation coefficient is 0.01 (two-sided test), * means the significance level of correlation coefficient is 0.05 (two-sided test).

Tab. 4-9 Correlation Verification for the Indicators of Competitiveness in Innovation Input in 2009

Indicator	Item	Gross volume of R&D	Proportion of R&D to GDP	Per capita R&D	R&D personnel	Proportion of R&D personnel to total employees	Proportion of R&D personnel in the businesses	Proportion of R&D input in the businesses
Gross volume of R&D	Correlation coefficient	1	0.522*	0.626**	0.949**	0.453	0.617**	0.556*
	Test value		0.022	0.004	0	0.051	0.005	0.014
	Number of samples	19	19	19	19	19	19	19
Proportion of R&D to GDP	Correlation coefficient	0.522*	1	0.933**	0.359	0.929**	0.734**	0.762**
	Test value	0.022		0	0.131	0	0	0
	Number of samples	19	19	19	19	19	19	19
Per capita R&D	Correlation coefficient	0.626**	0.933**	1	0.425	0.935**	0.677**	0.697**
	Test value	0.004	0		0.07	0	0.001	0.001
	Number of samples	19	19	19	19	19	19	19
R&D personnel	Correlation coefficient	0.949**	0.359	0.425	1	0.292	0.534*	0.443
	Test value	0	0.131	0.07		0.225	0.018	0.058
	Number of samples	19	19	19	19	19	19	19
Proportion of R&D personnel to total employees	Correlation coefficient	0.453	0.929**	0.935**	0.292	1	0.667**	0.572*
	Test value	0.051	0	0	0.225		0.002	0.011
	Number of samples	19	19	19	19	19	19	19
Proportion of R&D personnel in the businesses	Correlation coefficient	0.617**	0.734**	0.677**	0.534*	0.667**	1	0.768**
	Test value	0.005	0	0.001	0.018	0.002		0
	Number of samples	19	19	19	19	19	19	19
Proportion of R&D input in the businesses	Correlation coefficient	0.556*	0.762**	0.697**	0.443	0.572*	0.768**	1
	Test value	0.014	0	0.001	0.058	0.011	0	
	Number of samples	19	19	19	19	19	19	19

Note: ** means the significance level of correlation coefficient is 0.01 (two-sided test), * means the significance level of correlation coefficient is 0.05 (two-sided test).

The indicators of competitiveness in innovation input mainly include three R&D expenditure, R&D personnel and scientific research input. The analysis on the three correlation tables above indicates that the correlation coefficient is relatively between the two total quantity indicators of R&D expenditure and R&D personnel; the correlation coefficient is also relatively between the two proportion indicators of the proportion of R&D to GDP and the proportion of R&D personnel to total employees. By and large, the correlation coefficients among this group of indicators are all relatively and most pass the significance test of 5% significance level. It indicates a manpower and material input in innovation.

6. Correlation Verification for the Indicators of the Competitiveness in Innovation Output

Tab. 4-10, Tab. 4-11 and Tab. 4-12 are the analysis results of the indicators for the competitiveness in innovation output in 2001, 2005 and 2009 respectively.

Tab. 4-10   Correlation Verification for the Indicators of Competitiveness in Innovation Output in 2001

Indicator	Item	Applications American patents	Average patent authorizations of sci-tech personnel	Publications of scientific papers	Average sci-tech paper publications of sci-tech personnel	Royalty and license income	High-tech products export	Proportion of high-tech products export to the manufacturing
Applications American patents	Correlation coefficient	1	0.715**	0.954**	-0.009	0.968**	0.874**	0.530*
	Test value		0.001	0	0.971	0	0	0.019
	Number of samples	19	19	19	19	19	19	19
Average patent authorizations of sci-tech personnel	Correlation coefficient	0.715**	1	0.653**	0.156	0.627**	0.744**	0.634**
	Test value	0.001		0.002	0.523	0.004	0	0.004
	Number of samples	19	19	19	19	19	19	19
Publications of scientific papers	Correlation coefficient	0.954**	0.653**	1	0.139	0.984**	0.913**	0.584**
	Test value	0	0.002		0.571	0	0	0.009
	Number of samples	19	19	19	19	19	19	19
Average sci-tech paper publications of sci-tech personnel	Correlation coefficient	-0.009	0.156	0.139	1	0.088	0.083	-0.042
	Test value	0.971	0.523	0.571		0.721	0.736	0.865
	Number of samples	19	19	19	19	19	19	19
Royalty and license income	Correlation coefficient	0.968**	0.627**	0.984**	0.088	1	0.872**	0.556*
	Test value	0	0.004	0	0.721		0	0.013
	Number of samples	19	19	19	19	19	19	19
High-tech products export	Correlation coefficient	0.874**	0.744**	0.913**	0.083	0.872**	1	0.747**
	Test value	0	0	0	0.736	0		0
	Number of samples	19	19	19	19	19	19	19
Proportion of high-tech products export to the manufacturing	Correlation coefficient	0.530*	0.634**	0.584**	-0.042	0.556*	0.747**	1
	Test value	0.019	0.004	0.009	0.865	0.013	0	
	Number of samples	19	19	19	19	19	19	19

Note: ** means the significance level of correlation coefficient is 0.01 (two-sided test), * means the significance level of correlation coefficient is 0.05 (two-sided test).

Tab. 4-11 Correlation Verification for the Indicators of Competitiveness in Innovation Output in 2005

Indicator	Item	Applications American patents	Average patent authorizations of sci-tech personnel	Publications of scientific papers	Average sci-tech paper publications of sci-tech personnel	Royalty and license income	High-tech products export	Proportion of high-tech products export to the manufacturing
Applications American patents	Correlation coefficient	1	0.832**	0.953**	0.055	0.976**	0.604**	0.445
	Test value		0	0	0.824	0	0.006	0.056
	Number of samples	19	19	19	19	19	19	19
Average patent authorizations of sci-tech personnel	Correlation coefficient	0.832**	1	0.785**	0.256	0.786**	0.634**	0.511*
	Test value	0		0	0.291	0	0.004	0.025
	Number of samples	19	19	19	19	19	19	19
Publications of scientific papers	Correlation coefficient	0.953**	0.785**	1	0.141	0.976**	0.709**	0.537*
	Test value	0	0		0.564	0	0.001	0.018
	Number of samples	19	19	19	19	19	19	19
Average sci-tech paper publications of sci-tech personnel	Correlation coefficient	0.055	0.256	0.141	1	0.116	-0.092	-0.185
	Test value	0.824	0.291	0.564		0.638	0.707	0.447
	Number of samples	19	19	19	19	19	19	19
Royalty and license income	Correlation coefficient	0.976**	0.786**	0.976**	0.116	1	0.601**	0.480*
	Test value	0	0	0	0.638		0.006	0.037
	Number of samples	19	19	19	19	19	19	19
High-tech products export	Correlation coefficient	0.604**	0.634**	0.709**	-0.092	0.601**	1	0.798**
	Test value	0.006	0.004	0.001	0.707	0.006		0
	Number of samples	19	19	19	19	19	19	19
Proportion of high-tech products export to the manufacturing	Correlation coefficient	0.445	0.511*	0.537*	-0.185	0.480*	0.798**	1
	Test value	0.056	0.025	0.018	0.447	0.037	0	
	Number of samples	19	19	19	19	19	19	19

Note: ** means the significance level of correlation coefficient is 0.01 (two-sided test), * means the significance level of correlation coefficient is 0.05 (two-sided test).

Tab. 4-12   Correlation Verification for the Indicators of Competitiveness in Innovation Output in 2009

Indicator	Item	Applications American patents	Average patent authorizations of sci-tech personnel	Publications of scientific papers	Average sci-tech paper publications of sci-tech personnel	Royalty and license income	High-tech products export	Proportion of high-tech products export to the manufacturing
Applications American patents	Correlation coefficient	1	0.843**	0.918**	0.07	0.984**	0.303	0.283
	Test value		0	0	0.776	0	0.207	0.241
	Number of samples	19	19	19	19	19	19	19
Average patent authorizations of sci-tech personnel	Correlation coefficient	0.843**	1	0.746**	0.261	0.808**	0.321	0.366
	Test value	0		0	0.28	0	0.18	0.123
	Number of samples	19	19	19	19	19	19	19
Publications of scientific papers	Correlation coefficient	0.918**	0.746**	1	0.118	0.942**	0.546*	0.444
	Test value	0	0		0.629	0	0.016	0.057
	Number of samples	19	19	19	19	19	19	19
Average sci-tech paper publications of sci-tech personnel	Correlation coefficient	0.07	0.261	0.118	1	0.116	-0.215	-0.155
	Test value	0.776	0.28	0.629		0.637	0.376	0.527
	Number of samples	19	19	19	19	19	19	19
Royalty and license income	Correlation coefficient	0.984**	0.808**	0.942**	0.116	1	0.308	0.307
	Test value	0	0	0	0.637		0.2	0.201
	Number of samples	19	19	19	19	19	19	19
High-tech products export	Correlation coefficient	0.303	0.321	0.546*	-0.215	0.308	1	0.715**
	Test value	0.207	0.18	0.016	0.376	0.2		0.001
	Number of samples	19	19	19	19	19	19	19
Proportion of high-tech products export to the manufacturing	Correlation coefficient	0.283	0.366	0.444	-0.155	0.307	0.715**	1
	Test value	0.241	0.123	0.057	0.527	0.201	0.001	
	Number of samples	19	19	19	19	19	19	19

Note: ** means the significance level of correlation coefficient is 0.01 (two-sided test), * means the significance level of correlation coefficient is 0.05 (two-sided test).

The indicators of competitiveness in innovation output mainly include three   patent, paper and technological products export. The analysis on the three correlation tables above indicates that the three total quantity indicators are all highly correlated, including applications American patents, the publications of scientific papers and the royalty and license income, but with less correlativity with another total quantity indicator of high-tech products export. The correlation coefficients of high-tech products export are all small with the other indicators, in total quantity in proportion, which indicates a between innovation results and application ability.

7. Correlation Verification for the Indicators of Competitiveness in Innovation Sustainability

Tab. 4-13, Tab. 4-14 and Tab. 4-15 are the analysis results of the indicators for competitiveness in innovation sustainability in 2001, 2005 and 2009 respectively.

Tab. 4-13   Correlation Verification for the Indicators of Competitiveness in Innovation Sustainability in 2001

Indicator	Item	Gross educational expenditure	Per capita educational expenditure	Proportion of educational expenditure to GDP	Proportion of persons of higher education	Proportion of scientists and engineers	Growth rate of sci-tech personnel	Growth rate of sci-tech funds
Gross educational expenditure	Correlation coefficient	1	0.728**	0.238	0.249	0.531*	0.005	-0.172
	Test value		0	0.327	0.305	0.019	0.984	0.481
	Number of samples	19	19	19	19	19	19	19
Per capita educational expenditure	Correlation coefficient	0.728**	1	0.527*	0.438	0.756**	0.143	-0.269
	Test value	0		0.02	0.061	0	0.561	0.266
	Number of samples	19	19	19	19	19	19	19
Proportion of educational expenditure to GDP	Correlation coefficient	0.238	0.527*	1	0.172	0.093	0.262	-0.315
	Test value	0.327	0.02		0.482	0.704	0.278	0.189
	Number of samples	19	19	19	19	19	19	19
Proportion of persons of higher education	Correlation coefficient	0.249	0.438	0.172	1	0.645**	0.062	-0.357
	Test value	0.305	0.061	0.482		0.003	0.802	0.133
	Number of samples	19	19	19	19	19	19	19
Proportion of scientists and engineers	Correlation coefficient	0.531*	0.756**	0.093	0.645**	1	-0.007	-0.035
	Test value	0.019	0	0.704	0.003		0.978	0.887
	Number of samples	19	19	19	19	19	19	19
Growth rate of sci-tech personnel	Correlation coefficient	0.005	0.143	0.262	0.062	-0.007	1	-0.195
	Test value	0.984	0.561	0.278	0.802	0.978		0.424
	Number of samples	19	19	19	19	19	19	19
Growth rate of sci-tech funds	Correlation coefficient	-0.172	-0.269	-0.315	-0.357	-0.035	-0.195	1
	Test value	0.481	0.266	0.189	0.133	0.887	0.424	
	Number of samples	19	19	19	19	19	19	19

Note: ** means the significance level of correlation coefficient is 0.01 (two-sided test), * means the significance level of correlation coefficient is 0.05 (two-sided test).

Tab. 4-14 Correlation Verification for the Indicators of Competitiveness in Innovation Sustainability in 2005

Indicator	Item	Gross educational expenditure	Per capita educational expenditure	Proportion of educational expenditure to GDP	Proportion of persons of higher education	Proportion of scientists and engineers	Growth rate of sci-tech personnel	Growth rate of sci-tech funds
Gross educational expenditure	Correlation coefficient	1	0.605**	0.288	0.311	0.502*	-0.329	-0.188
	Test value		0.006	0.232	0.194	0.029	0.169	0.441
	Number of samples	19	19	19	19	19	19	19
Per capita educational expenditure	Correlation coefficient	0.605**	1	0.623**	0.408	0.781**	-0.503*	-0.516*
	Test value	0.006		0.004	0.083	0	0.028	0.024
	Number of samples	19	19	19	19	19	19	19
Proportion of educational expenditure to GDP	Correlation coefficient	0.288	0.623**	1	0.23	0.268	-0.628**	-0.675**
	Test value	0.232	0.004		0.344	0.267	0.004	0.002
	Number of samples	19	19	19	19	19	19	19
Proportion of persons of higher education	Correlation coefficient	0.311	0.408	0.23	1	0.654**	-0.472*	-0.219
	Test value	0.194	0.083	0.344		0.002	0.041	0.367
	Number of samples	19	19	19	19	19	19	19
Proportion of scientists and engineers	Correlation coefficient	0.502*	0.781**	0.268	0.654**	1	-0.525*	-0.297
	Test value	0.029	0	0.267	0.002		0.021	0.217
	Number of samples	19	19	19	19	19	19	19
Growth rate of sci-tech personnel	Correlation coefficient	-0.329	-0.503*	-0.628**	-0.472*	-0.525*	1	0.406
	Test value	0.169	0.028	0.004	0.041	0.021		0.085
	Number of samples	19	19	19	19	19	19	19
Growth rate of sci-tech funds	Correlation coefficient	-0.188	-0.516*	-0.675**	-0.219	-0.297	0.406	1
	Test value	0.441	0.024	0.002	0.367	0.217	0.085	
	Number of samples	19	19	19	19	19	19	19

Note: ** means the significance level of correlation coefficient is 0.01 (two-sided test), * means the significance level of correlation coefficient is 0.05 (two-sided test).

Tab. 4-15 Correlation Verification for the Indicators of Competitiveness in Innovation Sustainability in 2009

Indicator	Item	Gross educational expenditure	Per capita educational expenditure	Proportion of educational expenditure to GDP	Proportion of persons of higher education	Proportion of scientists and engineers	Growth rate of sci-tech personnel	Growth rate of sci-tech funds
Gross educational expenditure	Correlation coefficient	1	0.561*	0.209	0.266	0.418	-0.264	-0.225
	Test value		0.013	0.39	0.271	0.075	0.274	0.355
	Number of samples	19	19	19	19	19	19	19
Per capita educational expenditure	Correlation coefficient	0.561*	1	0.455	0.366	0.750**	-0.575*	-0.348
	Test value	0.013		0.05	0.123	0	0.01	0.144
	Number of samples	19	19	19	19	19	19	19
Proportion of educational expenditure to GDP	Correlation coefficient	0.209	0.455	1	0.314	0.17	-0.362	0.157
	Test value	0.39	0.05		0.19	0.488	0.128	0.52
	Number of samples	19	19	19	19	19	19	19
Proportion of persons of higher education	Correlation coefficient	0.266	0.366	0.314	1	0.642**	-0.25	-0.121
	Test value	0.271	0.123	0.19		0.003	0.303	0.622
	Number of samples	19	19	19	19	19	19	19
Proportion of scientists and engineers	Correlation coefficient	0.418	0.750**	0.17	0.642**	1	-0.507*	-0.428
	Test value	0.075	0	0.488	0.003		0.027	0.067
	Number of samples	19	19	19	19	19	19	19
Growth rate of sci-tech personnel	Correlation coefficient	-0.264	-0.575*	-0.362	-0.25	-0.507*	1	0.261
	Test value	0.274	0.01	0.128	0.303	0.027		0.28
	Number of samples	19	19	19	19	19	19	19
Growth rate of sci-tech funds	Correlation coefficient	-0.225	-0.348	0.157	-0.121	-0.428	0.261	1
	Test value	0.355	0.144	0.52	0.622	0.067	0.28	
	Number of samples	19	19	19	19	19	19	19

Note: ** means the significance level of correlation coefficient is 0.01 (two-sided test), * means the significance level of correlation coefficient is 0.05 (two-sided test).

The indicators of competitiveness in innovation sustainability mainly includes two growth trend of educational input and sci-tech input, most of which are mean indicators and proportion indicators. The analysis on the three correlation tables above indicates that the correlation coefficient is universally small among the indicators, except for the higher correlativity of two proportion indicators (the proportion of scientists and engineers and the per capita educational expenditure) with other indicators. it still indicate a significant relation among them.

Part 2 General Report

Overall Evaluation and Comparative Analysis of G20 NIC

In the world today, as an important platform of international dialogue and cooperation between developed countries and countries of newly emerging markets, G20 plays a more and more important roles especially in the fields of international economic cooperation as well as sci-tech innovation. 65% population of the globe, 90% GDP 80% trade volume of the globe, and 65% equity shares in International Monetary Fund and World Bank. It is that G20 holds a vital position in the global economy. At present, the world is on the eve of a new revolution in science and technology and major countries are all striving for new economic development modes to commence a new round competition commanding height in science and technology and development. In the global competition, innovation undoubtedly becomes the principal driving force for the development of economic society and innovation competitiveness is the core element of national competitiveness. G20, as the important "locomotive" of global economic development, will decide the future and direction of world sci-tech innovation with competitiveness and vitality of it reflected in global sci-tech innovation. Through analysis of G20 NIC during 2001-2009 as well as analysis of the variations in rankings of the elements in the innovation competitiveness, this part.

I. Overall Evaluation of G20 NIC

(I) Evaluation Results of G20 NIC

According to the indicator model and mathematical model of NIC, the evaluation is made for G20 NIC during 2001-2009. Tab. 1 lists the rankings and variations in rankings of G20 NIC during the evaluation period as well as the evaluation results of the subordinate five secondary indicators. Fig. 1, Fig. 2 and Fig. 3 show the rankings and variations in rankings of G20 NIC during 2001-2009.

Tab. 1 Evaluation and Comparison of G20 NIC during 2001-2009

Countries Items	Argentina	Australia	Brazil	Canada	China	France	Germany	India	Indonesia	Italy	Japan	Korea	Mexico	Russia	Saudi Arabia	South Africa	Turkey	UK	USA	Highest scores	Lowest scores	Average scores
Overall variations in NIC during 2001-2009	4.1	2.7	5.7	0.1	10.8	1.8	2.9	1.6	6.2	0.9	-5.5	0.4	-0.3	1.8	6.9	-1.2	4.1	-4.1	-5.0	-5.0	6.2	1.8
	0	0	2	0	2	1	1	0	0	0	0	1	-2	-2	0	-2	2	-3	0	-	-	-
2001 Innovation competitiveness	16.3	44.2	18.6	47.4	23.3	48.5	49.8	13.2	7.7	36.9	58.5	48.3	20.7	27.0	24.2	21.9	17.0	52.1	88.8	88.8	7.7	35.0
	17	8	15	7	12	5	4	18	19	9	2	6	14	10	11	13	16	3	1	-	-	-
Competitiveness in innovation base	17.9	36.5	8.3	43.4	6.9	49.2	45.8	1.4	1.3	40.8	55.9	26.9	12.7	13.2	16.3	4.6	6.7	49.5	97.1	97.1	1.3	28.1
	10	8	14	6	15	4	5	18	19	7	2	9	13	12	11	17	16	3	1	-	-	-
Competitiveness in innovation environment	14.2	70.2	23.0	64.8	31.5	60.7	62.2	22.6	16.9	48.4	62.5	73.0	28.7	36.2	42.8	44.5	29.9	74.1	84.0	84.0	14.2	46.9
	19	4	16	5	13	8	7	17	18	9	6	3	15	12	11	10	14	2	1	-	-	-
Competitiveness in innovation input	8.1	38.2	22.2	50.3	30.4	49.9	58.2	7.7	0.7	26.0	75.2	55.6	11.3	35.7	15.1	19.0	14.4	43.4	95.3	95.3	0.7	34.6
	17	8	12	5	10	6	3	18	19	11	2	4	16	9	14	13	15	7	1	-	-	-
Competitiveness in innovation output	9.1	20.7	13.0	27.6	16.1	29.1	34.9	9.8	6.2	26.1	48.5	36.1	15.6	8.0	5.6	10.9	9.9	41.4	91.0	91.0	5.6	24.2
	16	9	12	7	10	6	5	15	18	8	2	4	11	17	19	13	14	3	1	-	-	-
Competitiveness in innovation sustainability	32.2	55.3	26.5	50.8	31.7	53.7	47.6	24.5	13.3	43.3	50.2	49.9	35.5	41.9	41.4	30.3	24.3	51.9	76.3	76.3	13.3	41.1
	13	2	16	5	14	3	8	17	19	9	6	7	12	10	11	15	18	4	1	-	-	-
2002 Innovation competitiveness	14.4	46.0	18.8	48.1	25.7	50.1	52.7	13.1	8.0	37.7	58.4	49.0	21.6	28.9	24.3	21.8	17.5	54.4	89.6	89.6	8.0	35.8
	17	8	15	7	11	5	4	18	19	9	2	6	14	10	12	13	16	3	1	-	-	-
Competitiveness in innovation base	12.5	40.5	8.9	44.5	12.1	55.5	54.8	1.9	1.7	44.7	53.7	28.4	14.3	14.3	15.2	3.8	7.3	52.1	98.5	98.5	1.7	29.7
	13	8	15	7	14	2	3	18	19	6	4	9	12	11	10	17	16	5	1	-	-	-
Competitiveness in innovation environment	13.7	69.8	24.1	67.3	32.4	60.3	65.0	22.6	17.1	47.4	63.1	73.3	29.5	37.2	44.5	44.9	31.5	78.3	84.6	84.6	13.7	47.7
	19	4	16	5	13	8	6	17	18	9	7	3	15	12	11	10	14	2	1	-	-	-
Competitiveness in innovation input	8.6	40.9	21.9	50.4	32.6	51.0	58.7	7.5	0.7	27.0	76.4	55.9	12.7	35.9	15.1	19.6	13.5	44.0	94.5	94.5	0.7	35.1
	17	8	12	6	10	5	3	18	19	11	2	4	16	9	14	13	15	7	1	-	-	-
Competitiveness in innovation output	8.9	21.8	13.0	27.1	19.6	29.3	36.9	9.7	7.6	26.7	50.1	37.2	16.2	11.8	6.2	11.2	11.1	40.6	92.0	92.0	6.2	25.1
	17	9	12	7	10	6	5	16	18	8	2	4	11	13	19	14	15	3	1	-	-	-
Competitiveness in innovation sustainability	28.3	57.1	26.1	51.6	32.0	54.5	48.3	23.9	12.8	42.5	48.8	50.4	35.6	45.2	40.8	29.6	24.2	57.0	78.6	78.6	12.8	41.4
	15	2	16	5	13	4	8	18	19	10	7	6	12	9	11	14	17	3	1	-	-	-
2003 Innovation competitiveness	16.8	44.6	17.3	47.3	26.4	49.8	52.6	12.0	8.3	36.9	58.0	48.7	19.6	29.0	24.0	21.2	17.0	52.9	88.8	88.8	8.3	35.3
	17	8	15	7	11	5	4	18	19	9	2	6	14	10	12	13	16	3	1	-	-	-
Competitiveness in innovation base	13.4	40.6	8.5	44.2	14.9	61.2	56.9	2.0	1.7	50.6	53.5	29.3	13.9	15.6	16.4	5.0	9.1	55.6	96.3	96.3	1.7	31.0
	14	8	16	7	12	2	3	18	19	6	5	9	13	11	10	17	15	4	1	-	-	-
Competitiveness in innovation environment	16.8	70.2	24.2	67.2	32.7	64.2	65.6	21.8	17.4	47.9	62.7	73.5	30.1	39.8	45.2	45.2	34.8	79.1	84.9	84.9	16.8	48.6
	19	4	16	5	14	7	6	17	18	9	8	3	15	12	10	11	13	2	1	-	-	-

Countries / Items		Argentina	Australia	Brazil	Canada	China	France	Germany	India	Indonesia	Italy	Japan	Korea	Mexico	Russia	Saudi Arabia	South Africa	Turkey	UK	USA	Highest scores	Lowest scores	Average scores
2003	Competitiveness in innovation input	8.4	41.2	20.5	49.2	33.7	48.8	58.5	7.4	0.6	25.8	76.5	56.7	12.3	34.2	14.6	19.8	11.7	42.5	94.0	94.0	0.6	34.6
		17	8	12	5	10	6	3	18	19	11	2	4	15	9	14	13	16	7	1	-	-	-
	Competitiveness in innovation output	8.5	19.8	10.0	26.0	25.1	27.9	37.2	8.8	6.4	26.1	50.5	36.1	16.8	11.0	5.4	9.9	8.7	36.5	90.9	90.9	5.4	24.3
		17	10	13	8	9	6	3	15	18	7	2	5	11	12	19	14	16	4	1	-	-	-
	Competitiveness in innovation sustainability	36.9	51.3	23.5	49.9	25.4	46.7	44.7	20.2	15.2	34.1	46.6	47.7	25.2	44.6	38.3	25.9	21.0	50.5	78.0	78.0	15.2	38.2
		11	2	16	4	14	6	8	18	19	12	7	5	15	9	10	13	17	3	1	-	-	-
2004	Innovation competitiveness	18.1	46.9	18.0	47.9	27.6	50.6	52.6	12.8	7.9	38.0	58.7	50.4	21.8	27.7	23.4	23.5	20.2	53.6	87.9	87.9	7.9	36.2
		16	8	17	7	11	5	4	18	19	9	2	6	14	10	13	12	15	3	1	-	-	-
	Competitiveness in innovation base	14.4	47.9	9.3	44.6	10.9	57.5	51.0	2.5	2.7	51.1	53.9	30.5	13.2	17.7	18.9	6.6	10.9	58.5	95.1	95.1	2.5	31.4
		12	7	16	8	14	3	6	19	18	5	4	9	13	11	10	17	15	2	1	-	-	-
	Competitiveness in innovation environment	19.0	70.1	26.1	66.7	33.0	64.0	68.3	23.5	17.7	48.1	64.6	73.4	30.7	44.1	46.8	46.2	35.3	78.7	85.0	85.0	17.7	49.5
		18	4	16	6	14	8	5	17	19	9	7	3	15	12	10	11	13	2	1	-	-	-
	Competitiveness in innovation input	9.3	42.3	19.8	49.9	36.4	49.0	58.4	7.4	0.6	25.6	76.7	59.2	15.6	32.5	14.6	18.5	12.0	41.8	92.8	92.8	0.6	34.9
		17	7	12	5	9	6	4	18	19	11	2	3	14	10	15	13	16	8	1	-	-	-
	Competitiveness in innovation output	7.6	18.9	10.0	23.3	29.7	27.3	38.3	8.4	7.4	26.2	49.6	34.7	15.8	7.8	4.9	9.0	10.3	33.7	90.1	90.1	4.9	23.8
		17	10	13	9	6	7	3	15	18	8	2	4	11	16	19	14	12	5	1	-	-	-
	Competitiveness in innovation sustainability	40.3	55.1	25.0	54.8	27.8	55.4	47.3	22.5	11.2	39.1	49.0	54.0	33.9	36.2	31.9	37.3	32.4	55.3	76.8	76.8	11.2	41.3
		9	4	17	5	16	2	8	18	19	10	7	6	13	12	15	11	14	3	1	-	-	-
2005	Innovation competitiveness	17.8	46.1	20.1	48.4	29.1	49.9	52.8	15.7	11.4	38.0	57.3	49.9	22.6	27.9	24.8	22.2	21.1	55.3	86.1	86.1	11.4	36.7
		17	8	16	7	10	6	4	18	19	9	2	5	13	11	12	14	15	3	1	-	-	-
	Competitiveness in innovation base	16.1	45.3	11.7	50.6	13.3	60.7	54.5	4.0	4.6	51.2	52.4	33.2	14.5	20.3	24.5	9.0	14.3	65.5	91.2	91.2	4.0	33.5
		12	8	16	7	15	3	4	19	18	6	5	9	13	11	10	17	14	2	1	-	-	-
	Competitiveness in innovation environment	21.1	69.8	26.6	67.2	34.1	63.9	69.5	25.8	23.4	48.9	65.1	72.6	34.4	49.6	51.2	48.5	36.3	77.6	85.1	85.1	21.1	51.1
		19	4	16	6	15	8	5	17	18	11	7	3	14	10	9	12	13	2	1	-	-	-
	Competitiveness in innovation input	8.0	42.7	20.7	48.1	38.9	46.7	57.1	13.6	0.7	24.2	77.5	60.6	16.3	28.9	14.5	17.1	14.5	39.7	91.3	91.3	0.7	34.8
		18	7	12	5	9	6	4	17	19	11	2	3	14	10	16	13	15	8	1	-	-	-
	Competitiveness in innovation output	7.4	18.8	10.8	24.6	32.2	27.9	39.4	7.9	7.6	25.6	46.5	32.4	15.4	5.5	5.5	10.7	10.5	36.5	90.0	90.0	5.5	24.0
		17	10	12	9	6	7	3	15	16	8	2	5	11	18	19	13	14	4	1	-	-	-
	Competitiveness in innovation sustainability	36.2	53.7	30.7	51.4	27.1	50.0	43.6	27.0	20.6	40.1	44.8	50.9	32.4	35.2	28.4	25.9	29.9	57.5	73.1	73.1	20.6	39.9
		10	3	13	4	16	6	8	17	19	9	7	5	12	11	15	18	14	2	1	-	-	-

Countries / Items		Argentina	Australia	Brazil	Canada	China	France	Germany	India	Indonesia	Italy	Japan	Korea	Mexico	Russia	Saudi Arabia	South Africa	Turkey	UK	USA	Highest scores	Lowest scores	Average scores
2006	Innovation competitiveness	19.5	46.5	20.2	48.0	29.2	49.4	52.7	12.5	11.6	38.6	55.3	50.8	18.8	30.8	26.7	22.7	20.6	54.9	87.3	87.3	11.6	36.6
		16	8	15	7	11	6	4	18	19	9	2	5	17	10	12	13	14	3	1	-	-	-
	Competitiveness in innovation base	14.8	47.2	10.9	52.6	11.3	56.7	52.3	2.7	2.4	50.3	46.5	32.2	12.6	20.6	23.9	6.4	13.6	60.9	95.6	95.6	2.4	32.3
		12	7	16	4	15	3	5	18	19	6	8	9	14	11	10	17	13	2	1	-	-	-
	Competitiveness in innovation environment	23.3	68.9	27.3	67.2	33.8	63.7	69.5	25.8	22.8	49.1	64.6	72.4	34.2	49.8	56.1	48.7	38.2	76.8	84.8	84.8	22.8	51.4
		18	5	16	6	15	8	4	17	19	11	7	3	14	10	9	12	13	2	1	-	-	-
	Competitiveness in innovation input	7.4	43.9	20.3	46.7	40.5	46.7	57.2	7.5	0.7	24.6	77.4	63.0	15.5	28.1	14.0	16.9	15.4	40.1	91.3	91.3	0.7	34.6
		18	7	12	5	8	6	4	17	19	11	2	3	14	10	16	13	15	9	1	-	-	-
	Competitiveness in innovation output	7.2	18.4	10.2	24.8	31.7	27.6	38.3	8.0	5.5	24.7	45.3	29.8	15.4	5.1	5.4	10.3	10.3	39.0	88.1	88.1	5.1	23.4
		16	10	14	8	5	7	4	15	17	9	2	6	11	19	18	12	13	3	1	-	-	-
	Competitiveness in innovation sustainability	44.5	53.9	32.2	48.3	28.9	52.5	46.2	18.4	26.8	44.1	42.8	56.3	16.1	50.4	34.3	31.3	25.6	57.5	76.7	76.7	16.1	41.4
		9	4	13	7	15	5	8	18	16	10	11	3	19	6	12	14	17	2	1	-	-	-
2007	Innovation competitiveness	18.5	45.1	20.5	47.2	30.6	49.4	51.4	13.3	11.0	37.2	52.2	50.0	19.2	28.9	27.8	20.2	23.8	51.9	84.4	84.4	11.0	35.9
		17	8	14	7	10	6	4	18	19	9	2	5	16	11	12	15	13	3	1	-	-	-
	Competitiveness in innovation base	14.5	48.9	12.4	55.8	14.9	59.3	55.3	2.8	1.8	52.0	45.1	32.4	12.2	23.2	22.1	6.0	14.0	64.9	94.1	94.1	1.8	33.3
		13	7	15	4	12	3	5	18	19	6	8	9	16	10	11	17	14	2	1	-	-	-
	Competitiveness in innovation environment	24.9	68.3	28.5	66.6	34.1	66.7	69.2	27.1	26.2	49.9	63.3	71.5	34.4	50.8	59.8	49.1	40.0	78.3	83.9	83.9	24.9	52.3
		19	5	16	7	15	6	4	17	18	11	8	3	14	10	9	12	13	2	1	-	-	-
	Competitiveness in innovation input	7.0	44.8	19.5	44.8	42.6	46.9	56.9	7.5	0.6	25.4	77.4	64.7	15.4	28.1	13.7	15.5	17.8	39.4	91.2	91.2	0.6	34.7
		18	6	12	7	8	5	4	17	19	11	2	3	15	10	16	14	13	9	1	-	-	-
	Competitiveness in innovation output	7.4	18.3	10.8	25.2	32.7	26.3	35.1	8.0	4.9	24.8	41.9	28.9	14.6	5.0	5.5	10.9	9.8	30.1	86.5	86.5	4.9	22.5
		16	10	13	8	4	7	3	15	19	9	2	6	11	18	17	12	14	5	1	-	-	-
	Competitiveness in innovation sustainability	38.6	45.2	31.0	43.6	28.6	47.6	40.4	21.1	21.3	33.9	33.3	52.7	19.4	37.2	38.1	19.7	37.1	46.6	66.2	66.2	19.4	36.9
		8	5	14	6	15	3	7	17	16	12	13	2	19	10	9	18	11	4	1	-	-	-
2008	Innovation competitiveness	21.7	49.2	23.9	48.7	35.8	51.7	54.8	15.8	15.6	39.6	52.7	50.6	22.0	31.8	31.2	21.9	22.4	51.0	83.4	83.4	15.6	38.1
		17	7	13	8	10	4	2	18	19	9	3	6	15	11	12	16	14	5	1	-	-	-
	Competitiveness in innovation base	15.8	52.5	14.6	50.5	16.1	57.9	53.8	3.1	2.6	50.6	47.1	29.1	11.8	25.9	27.3	5.6	14.1	52.2	91.3	91.3	2.6	32.7
		13	4	14	7	12	2	3	18	19	6	8	9	16	11	10	17	15	5	1	-	-	-
	Competitiveness in innovation environment	26.3	71.5	34.9	71.3	44.4	68.2	72.6	31.2	39.1	48.8	64.3	69.2	38.2	55.6	68.4	49.5	42.4	80.2	70.5	80.2	26.3	55.1
		19	3	17	4	13	8	2	18	15	12	9	6	16	10	7	11	14	1	5	-	-	-
	Competitiveness in innovation input	7.4	46.7	20.1	44.9	45.4	47.7	58.7	9.3	2.3	28.1	77.2	67.1	16.7	28.3	14.4	16.0	18.8	39.5	92.7	92.7	2.3	35.9
		18	6	12	8	7	5	4	17	19	11	2	3	14	10	16	15	13	9	1	-	-	-

Continued

Year	Items	Argentina	Australia	Brazil	Canada	China	France	Germany	India	Indonesia	Italy	Japan	Korea	Mexico	Russia	Saudi Arabia	South Africa	Turkey	UK	USA	Highest scores	Lowest scores	Average scores
2008	Competitiveness in innovation output	8.3	18.4	11.1	26.2	33.8	27.7	34.6	8.7	5.1	24.8	41.9	28.5	16.6	5.3	4.9	11.1	10.2	30.0	85.6	85.6	4.9	22.8
		16	10	13	8	4	7	3	15	18	9	2	6	11	17	19	12	14	5	1	-	-	-
	Competitiveness in innovation sustainability	50.6	56.8	38.9	50.3	39.3	57.3	54.4	26.8	28.7	45.7	33.1	59.3	26.6	43.7	41.2	27.5	26.6	53.2	76.9	76.9	26.6	44.0
		7	4	13	8	12	3	5	17	15	9	14	2	19	10	11	16	18	6	1	-	-	-
2009	Innovation competitiveness	20.4	46.9	24.3	47.5	34.1	50.3	52.6	14.8	13.9	37.8	53.0	48.7	20.5	28.9	31.2	20.7	21.1	48.0	83.8	83.8	13.9	36.8
		17	8	13	7	10	4	3	18	19	9	2	5	16	12	11	15	14	6	1	-	-	-
	Competitiveness in innovation base	15.7	50.8	15.8	47.4	19.5	60.7	56.3	5.3	2.7	52.7	50.6	28.2	10.4	22.8	19.6	5.9	13.1	50.2	92.8	92.8	2.7	32.7
		14	5	13	8	12	2	3	18	19	4	6	9	16	10	11	17	15	7	1	-	-	-
	Competitiveness in innovation environment	25.3	67.7	35.0	69.9	41.5	64.0	70.0	29.1	39.6	47.7	62.9	62.2	37.4	51.5	71.8	43.8	41.7	74.9	81.6	81.6	25.3	53.6
		19	6	17	5	14	7	4	18	15	11	8	9	16	10	3	12	13	2	1	-	-	-
	Competitiveness in innovation input	7.8	47.0	20.3	44.3	48.0	47.2	58.0	9.8	2.8	28.3	78.1	67.7	16.7	27.8	14.4	15.8	18.0	38.2	91.6	91.6	2.8	35.9
		18	7	12	8	5	6	4	17	19	10	2	3	14	11	16	15	13	9	1	-	-	-
	Competitiveness in innovation output	8.1	20.3	12.2	27.8	34.8	28.5	35.3	10.1	5.9	24.9	41.3	28.0	18.0	6.3	4.9	12.1	10.0	32.4	80.7	80.7	4.9	23.2
		16	10	12	8	4	6	3	14	18	9	2	7	11	17	19	13	15	5	1	-	-	-
	Competitiveness in innovation sustainability	45.2	48.7	38.2	47.8	26.9	51.1	43.6	19.7	18.7	35.4	32.0	57.4	19.9	35.8	45.1	25.8	22.8	44.4	72.1	72.1	18.7	38.4
		6	4	10	5	14	3	9	18	19	12	13	2	17	11	7	15	16	8	1	-	-	-

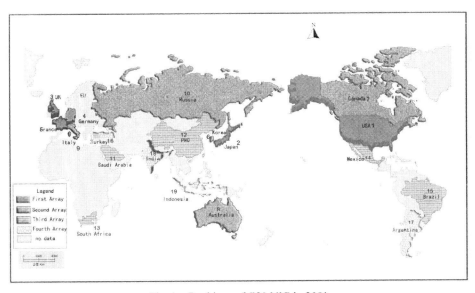

Fig. 1 Rankings of G20 NIC in 2001

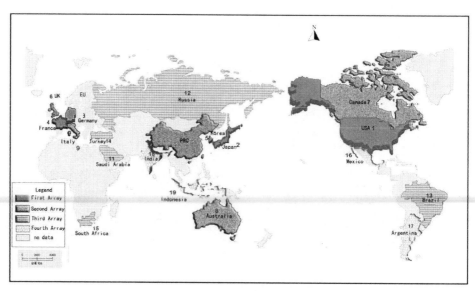

Fig. 2   Rankings of G20 NIC in 2009

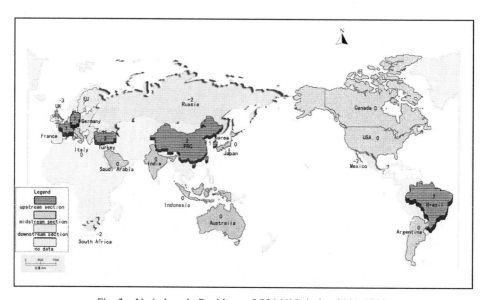

Fig. 3   Variations in Rankings of G20 NIC during 2001-2009

1. Overall Rankings of G20 NIC

Fig. 4 shows the scores of G20 NIC in 2009 and the rankings of the countries during 2001-2009.

As for G20 NIC in 2009, the following countries were in the first (No. 1-5): the US,

Japan, Germany, France, Korea; the following in the second (No. 6-10): the UK, Canada, Australia, Italy, China; the following in the third (No. 11-15): Saudi Arabia, Russia, Brazil, Turkey, South Africa; and the following in the fourth (No. 16-19): Mexico, Argentina, India, Indonesia.

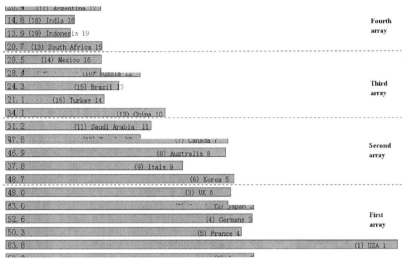

Fig. 4   Scores and Rankings of G20 NIC during 2001-2009

Note: In the figure, the left of the column, the are the rankings of the countries in innovation competitiveness in 2009, and the figures in the parenthesis are the rankings of the countries in innovation competitiveness in 2001.

As for the G20 NIC in 2001, the following countries were in the first (No. 1-5): the US, Japan, the UK, Germany, France; the following in the second (No. 6-10): Korea, Canada, Australia, Italy, Russia; the following in the third (No. 11-15): Saudi Arabia, China, South Africa, Mexico, Brazil; and the following in the fourth (No. 16-19): Turkey, Argentina, India, Indonesia.

2. Overall Scores of G20 NIC

According to Fig. 4, NIC was distributed in a pattern among G20 nations. In 2009, only the US scored above 80 points in innovation competitiveness and the rest all below 60. Among them, three countries scored between 50-60 points; four countries between 40-50 points; three countries between 30-40 points; six countries between 20-30 points; two countries between 10-20 points; and none scored below 10 points.

The countries with higher NIC were mainly developed countries, and in the first and second, there were eight developed countriesthese countries science and technology input, scientific and technological resources of human talents and sci-tech innovation system, and therefore, they are endowed with stronger NIC. The countries with lower NIC were mainly developing countries in the third and fourth. That because, in these countries, the economic and social development level relatively low, and there still a clear gap in innovation environment, innovation input and innovation efficiency between them and developed countries. Great efforts needed to change this situation and enhance the NIC of them.

See Fig. 5 and Tab. 2 for the variations in scores of G20 NIC.

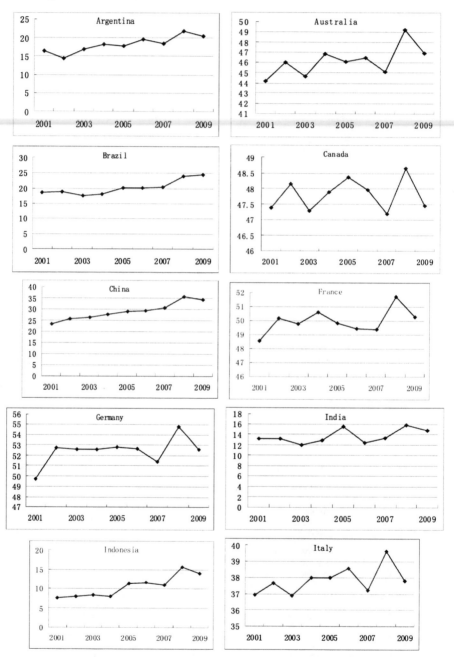

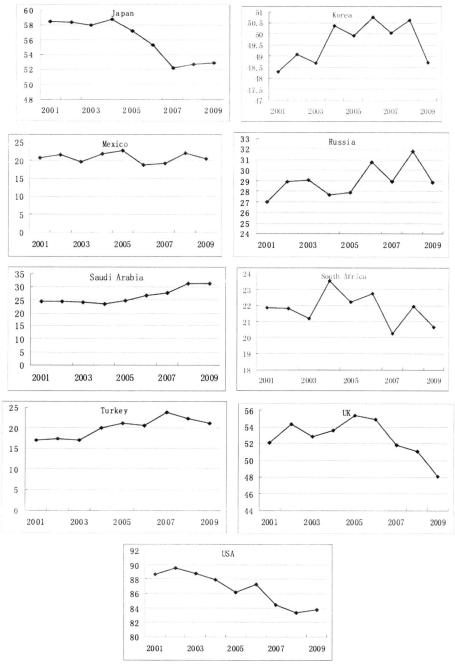

Fig. 5   Variations in Scores of G20 NIC during 2001-2009

According to Fig. 5, during 2001-2009, most countries showed a rising trend in the scores of innovation competitiveness except for some fluctuation in specific years. ix countries Argentina, Brazil, China, Indonesia, Saudi Arabia and Turkey showed an obvious rising trend with minor fluctuation. ight countries Australia, Canada, France, Germany, India, Italy, Korea and Russia greater fluctuation. ive countries Japan, Mexico, South Africa, the UK and the US showed a dropping trend, especially Japan, the US and the UK with major fluctuations.

According to Tab. 2, during 2001-2009, the NIC of China grew fastest in scores, by 10.8 points in recent 10 years, far beyond the average level of scores (1.8) for G20 NIC. It indicated that the NIC of China rose quickest. The scores of Saudi Arabia and Indonesia also grew faster with growth rate above 6 points. The scores of the US and Japan declined very, by 5.0 and 5.5 points respectively. Even though they still ranked No. 1 and 2 in G20, the gaps among them and the other countries were narrowing. Additionally, the score of the UK also declined very, by 4.1 points.

Overall, during 2001-2009, the scores of G20 NIC rose slowly, by 1.8 points on average. Among them, 14 countries witnessed rise in the scores of NIC, by 3.6 points on average; only five countries witnessed decline, by 3.2 points on average. On the whole, the rising countries than declining countries, indicating that the integral level of G20 NIC was rising during the evaluation period.

Tab. 2 Rankings of the Variations in Scores of G20 NIC during 2001-2009

Rankings in 2009	Countries	Scores in 2001	Scores in 2009	Variations in scores (2001-2009)	Rankings of fluctuation pace in scores
1	USA	88.8	83.8	-5.0	19
2	Japan	58.5	53.0	-5.5	20
3	Germany	49.8	52.6	2.9	7
4	France	48.5	50.3	1.8	11
5	Korea	48.3	48.7	0.4	14
6	UK	52.1	48.0	-4.1	18
7	Canada	47.4	47.5	0.1	15
8	Australia	44.2	46.9	2.7	8
9	Italy	36.9	37.8	0.9	13
10	China	23.3	34.1	10.8	1
11	Saudi Arabia	24.2	31.2	6.9	2
12	Russia	27.0	28.9	1.8	9
13	Brazil	18.6	24.3	5.7	4
14	Turkey	17.0	21.1	4.1	5
15	South Africa	21.9	20.7	-1.2	17
16	Mexico	20.7	20.5	-0.3	16
17	Argentina	16.3	20.4	4.1	6
18	India	13.2	14.8	1.6	12
19	Indonesia	7.7	13.9	6.2	3
Average scores		35.0	36.8	1.8	-

3. Scores of the Elements of G20 NIC

Tab. 1 lists the evaluation results of secondary indicators of G20 NIC during 2001-2009 and shows the scores and rankings as well as the fluctuation of the five secondary indicators of NIC.

According to the variations in scores, the highest score of NIC in 2009 was 83.8, down by 5.0 points over that in 2001; the lowest score was 13.9, up by 6.2 points over that in 2001; the average score was 36.8, up by 1.8 points over that in 2001. It indicated a slight rise in the integral level of G20 NIC. While in the secondary indicators, the scores of competitiveness in innovation environment rose fastest the average score from 46.9 in 2001 to 53.6 in 2009, by 6.7 points, the lowest score from 14.2 in 2001 to 25.3 in 2009, but the highest score from 84.0 in 2001 to 81.6 in 2009. The scores of competitiveness in innovation base also rose the average score up by 4.5 points, the lowest score up by 1.4 points, but the highest score down by 4.3 points. The scores of competitiveness in innovation input rose slowly the average score up by 1.3 points, the lowest score up by 2.1 points, but the highest score down by 3.7 points. The average scores of the other two secondary indicators declined. The competitiveness in innovation sustainability dropped most the average score down by 2.6 points, the highest score down by 4.2 points, but the lowest score up by 5.4 points. The highest score, the lowest score and the average score of competitiveness in innovation output all declined, down by 10.3, 0.7 and 1.0 points respectively.

By comparing the variations in scores of G20 NIC during 2001-2009, we conclude that the integral level of innovation competitiveness showed a rising trend mainly to the drive enhancement of competitiveness in innovation base, competitiveness in innovation environment, and competitiveness in innovation input. should go on strengthening the efforts in the three aspects. Meanwhile, special attention should be paid to competitiveness in innovation output and competitiveness in innovation sustainability, especially in the process of sci-tech innovation.

(II) Comparative Analysis on the Evaluation of G20 NIC

1. Comparative Analysis on the Variations in Rankings of G20 NIC

According to Fig. 6, a comparison between 2009 and 2001, six countries rose in the rankings of NIC, including Brazil, China, France, Germany, Korea and Turkey, among which, Brazil, China and Turkey by 2 places and France, Germany and Korea up by 1 place;

unchanged, Argentina, Australia, Canada, India, Indonesia, Italy, Japan, Saudi Arabia and the US; four countries Mexico, Russia, South Africa and the UK, among which, the UK dropped at the greatest rate by 3 places and the other three countries all by 2 places.

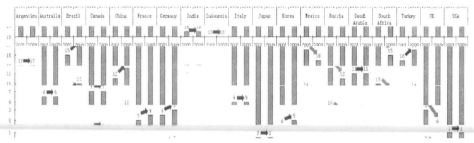

Fig. 6   Variations in Rankings of G20 NIC during 2001-2009

2. Analysis on the Arrays of G20 NIC

Tab. 3 lists the average scores of the arrays of G20 in NIC during 2001-2009. According to this table, we see that the average scores of the first array in NIC declined fluctuation, from 59.5 points in 2001 to 57.7 points in 2009; the average scores of the second array rose fluctuation, 2009 up by 1.2 points over 2001, point in 2003, then 42.6 points in 2006, and down 0.7 point in 2007, then up to the peak value of 44.8 points in 2008, and then, down to 42.9 in 2009; the average scores of the third array except for slight declines in 2003 and 2009; the average scores of the fourth array rose fluctuation, 3.8 points on the whole. By and large, except for the first array, the scores in innovation competitiveness of the second, third and fourth arrays all rose to some degree; in particular, the scores of the fourth array rose to the degree.

Tab. 3   Average Scores of the Arrays in NIC during 2001-2009

Average scores Items		Innovation competitiveness	Competitiveness in innovation base	Competitiveness in innovation environment	Competitiveness in innovation input	Competitiveness in innovation output	Competitiveness in innovation sustainability
First array	2001	59.5	59.5	73.2	66.9	50.4	57.6
	2002	61.1	62.9	74.7	67.3	51.3	59.8
	2003	60.4	64.7	75.0	67.0	50.2	55.5
	2004	60.7	63.2	75.1	67.4	49.3	59.5
	2005	60.3	64.9	74.9	66.9	49.0	57.3
	2006	60.2	63.6	74.5	67.1	48.5	59.4
	2007	58.0	65.9	74.2	67.4	45.3	51.7
	2008	58.7	61.5	73.2	68.7	45.2	61.0
	2009	57.7	62.7	73.7	68.7	44.9	55.4
	Variations in scores	-1.8	3.2	0.4	1.8	-5.5	-2.2

Average scores Items		Innovation competitiveness	Competitiveness in innovation base	Competitiveness in innovation environment	Competitiveness in innovation input	Competitiveness in innovation output	Competitiveness in innovation sustainability
Second array	2001	40.8	33.1	55.7	39.6	23.9	46.6
	2002	42.0	34.7	56.1	40.7	24.9	47.0
	2003	41.3	36.2	57.1	40.1	25.0	44.2
	2004	42.2	38.6	58.0	40.4	25.1	45.9
	2005	42.3	41.0	59.4	39.4	25.8	42.9
	2006	42.6	40.0	60.3	39.9	25.1	46.7
	2007	41.9	40.3	61.5	39.9	24.7	39.6
	2008	44.8	40.9	65.1	41.0	25.1	48.7
	2009	42.9	39.9	61.7	41.0	25.9	43.3
	Variations in scores	2.1	6.8	6.0	1.4	2.0	-3.3
Third array	2001	21.8	11.5	33.8	19.3	11.9	34.2
	2002	22.5	12.4	35.0	19.4	12.7	33.3
	2003	21.7	13.4	36.5	18.6	11.3	29.5
	2004	23.3	13.4	37.9	18.8	10.7	34.4
	2005	23.7	15.7	40.4	18.6	11.1	31.3
	2006	23.9	14.6	40.8	18.5	10.8	33.9
	2007	24.2	15.6	41.5	18.7	10.8	32.8
	2008	26.3	17.3	44.8	19.9	11.5	36.2
	2009	25.2	16.7	42.9	19.7	12.5	31.2
	Variations in scores	3.5	5.3	9.1	0.4	0.6	-3.0
Fourth array	2001	13.6	3.5	19.2	6.9	7.2	22.1
	2002	13.2	3.7	19.4	7.3	8.1	21.8
	2003	13.5	4.3	20.0	7.0	7.2	20.0
	2004	14.2	5.3	21.6	7.3	6.9	21.6
	2005	16.2	7.3	24.2	9.2	6.5	25.2
	2006	15.6	5.6	24.8	7.4	5.8	21.7
	2007	15.5	5.7	26.7	7.2	5.7	20.4
	2008	18.7	5.8	32.7	8.3	5.9	26.8
	2009	17.4	6.1	31.7	8.7	6.3	20.3
	Variations in scores	3.8	2.6	12.5	1.8	-0.9	-1.9

secondary indicators, variations in scores in Fig. 7, Fig. 8, Fig. 9 and Fig. 10. The scores of the four arrays in competitiveness in innovation base all rose fluctuation, among which, the scores of the second array rose the most, indicatingcompetitiveness in innovation base, especially The scores of the four arrays in the competitiveness in innovation environment also rose major fluctuation, among which, the scores of the fourth array rose the most, indicating an obvious rise the level of the competitiveness in innovation environment, especially fourth array Similarly, the scores of the four arrays in the competitiveness in innovation input all rose but minor fluctuation. The scores of the first and the fourth arrays in the competitiveness in innovation output declined major fluctuation whereas the second and the third arrays rose minor fluctuation, thus the level of competitiveness in innovation output declined slightly. The scores of the four arrays in competitiveness in innovation sustainability declined fluctuation, among which, the scores of the second array declined the most, indicating decline level of competitiveness in innovation sustainability, especially the second array.

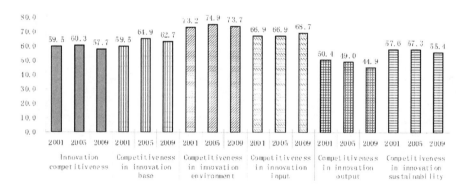

Fig. 7   Scores Comparisons of the First Array in NIC and the Secondary Indicators

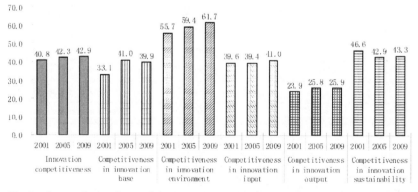

Fig. 8   Scores Comparisons of the Second Array in NIC and the Secondary Indicators

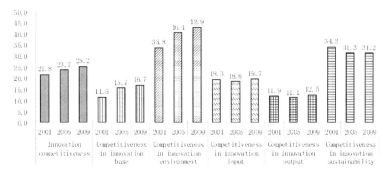

Fig. 9   Scores Comparisons of the Third Array in NIC and the Secondary Indicators

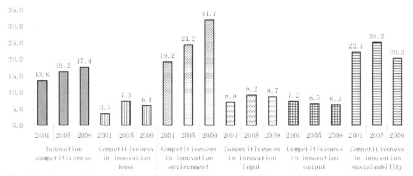

Fig. 10   Scores Comparisons of the Fourth Array in NIC and the Secondary Indicators

Fig. 11 shows the variations in rankings of the arrays for G20 NIC. According to this figure, during 2001-2009, six countries witnessed great changes in the rankings of innovation competitiveness: the UK fell into the second array, Russia fell into the third array, and Mexico into the fourth array; while Korea rose into the first array from the second array, China rose into the second array from the third array, and Turkey rose into the third array from the fourth array.

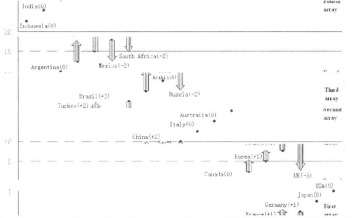

Fig. 11   Across-Array Variations in Rankings of G20 NIC during 2001-2009

II. Regional Distribution of G20 NIC

(I) Analysis on the Equilibrium of G20 NIC

The scores and rankings of G20 NIC through dimensionless and weighted average with threshold method reflect the innovation competitiveness of countries. To represent the actual variations and overall situation of G20 NIC more accurately, we should also analyze the score distribution of NIC and study and the actual variations and equilibrium of the scores in competitiveness. Fig. 12, Fig. 13 and Fig. 14 respectively show the distribution of evaluation points of G20 NIC in 2001, 2005 and 2009.

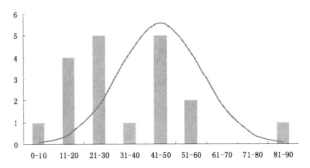

Fig. 12   Distribution of the Evaluation Points of G20 NIC in 2001

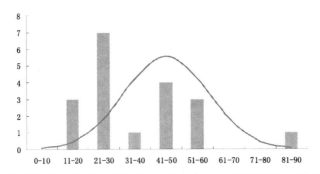

Fig. 13   Distribution of the Evaluation Points of G20 NIC in 2005

According to Fig. 12, Fig. 13 and Fig. 14, it innovation competitiveness was distributed in an unbalanced way among different countries and most countries scored 21-30 points 41-50 points. On the whole, it was neither symmetrical distribution nor normal distribution. According to the comparison of changes during the nine years, the scores in 2009 tended to be more concentrated and the number of the countries scoring 21-60 points increased to 13 from 11, whereas the number of countries scoring 11-20 points decreased by two and countries scoring below 10 points decreased by one.

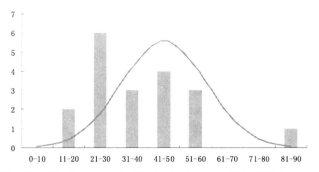

Fig. 14　Distribution of the Evaluation Points of G20 NIC in 2009

According to the overall scores of innovation competitiveness by different countries, the gap was big and equilibrium of distribution was also very poor, as shown in Tab. 1. In 2009, Indonesiathe lowest score only scored 13.9 points, merely 1/6 of the USgap of 69.9 points. In addition, the countries the first array witnessed the biggest gap: the US No. 1 score of innovation competitiveness 1.72 times of Korea No. 5, 35.1 points. The countries the second, third and fourth arrays also witnessed rather obvious gap of scores. The countries ranking first in each array were about 1.41, 1.51 and 1.47 times the last one respectively.

According to the average scores of the four arrays, the gap was also very big. The average value for innovation competitiveness of the five countries in the first array was 57.7 points; the average score of the five countries in the second array was 42.9 points; the average score of the five countries in the third array was 25.2 points; and the average score of the five countries in the fourth array was 17.4 points. The ratio was 3.3: 2.5: 1.5: 1.

(II) Evaluation and Analysis of G20 NIC by Regions

As per the distribution of G20 in the six continents, Tab. 4 lists the average scores and variations of G20 NIC during 2001-2009.

According to the scores, the evaluation points of G20 for NIC in the six continents were: 50.6 points for North America, 22.4 for South America, 39.8 for Europe, 32.5 for Asia, 20.7 for Africa and 46.9 for Oceania. The ratio was 2.4: 1.1: 1.9: 1.6: 1: 2.3, big gap. The case was similar Generally speaking, 2001-2009 rather big gaps among the six regions.

According to the variations in point values, during 2001-2009, the six continents of the globe witnessed rather small variations in scores of G20 NIC. The point values of North America and Africa fell slightly by 1.7 and 1.2 points respectively while the other four continents all rose somewhat, especially South America4.9 points and Asia by 4.2 points.

Tab. 4   Average Scores and the Variations of NIC by Regions during 2001-2009

	Scores Items	2001	2002	2003	2004	2005	2006	2007	2008	2009	Variations in scores during 2001-2009
North America	USA	88.8	89.6	88.8	87.9	86.1	87.3	84.4	83.4	83.8	-5.0
	Canada	47.4	48.1	47.3	47.9	48.4	48.0	47.2	48.7	47.5	0.1
	Mexico	20.7	21.6	19.6	21.8	22.6	18.8	19.2	22.0	20.5	-0.3
	Average scores	52.3	53.1	51.9	52.5	52.4	51.3	50.3	51.3	50.6	-1.7
South America	Argentina	16.3	14.4	16.8	18.1	17.8	19.5	18.5	21.7	20.4	4.1
	Brazil	18.6	18.8	17.3	18.0	20.1	20.2	20.5	23.9	24.3	5.7
	Average scores	17.5	16.6	17.1	18.1	18.9	19.8	19.5	22.8	22.4	4.9
Europe	France	48.5	50.1	49.8	50.6	49.9	49.4	49.4	51.7	50.3	1.8
	Germany	49.8	52.7	52.6	52.6	52.8	52.7	51.4	54.8	52.6	2.9
	Italy	36.9	37.7	36.9	38.0	38.0	38.6	37.2	39.6	37.8	0.9
	Russia	27.0	28.9	29.0	27.7	27.9	30.8	28.9	31.8	28.9	1.8
	Turkey	17.0	17.5	17.0	20.2	21.1	20.6	23.8	22.4	21.1	4.1
	UK	52.1	54.4	52.9	53.6	55.3	54.9	51.9	51.0	48.0	-4.1
	Average scores	38.6	40.2	39.7	40.5	40.8	41.2	40.4	41.9	39.8	1.2
Asia	China	23.3	25.7	26.4	27.6	29.1	29.2	30.6	35.8	34.1	10.8
	India	7.7	8.0	8.3	7.9	11.4	11.6	11.0	15.6	13.9	6.2
	Indonesia	7.7	8.0	8.3	7.9	11.4	11.6	11.0	15.6	13.9	6.2
	Japan	58.5	58.4	58.0	58.7	57.3	55.3	52.2	52.7	53.0	-5.5
	Korea	48.3	49.0	48.7	50.4	49.9	50.8	50.0	50.6	48.7	0.4
	Saudi Arabia	24.2	24.3	24.0	23.4	24.8	26.7	27.8	31.2	31.2	6.9
	Average scores	28.3	28.9	28.9	29.3	30.7	30.9	30.4	33.6	32.5	4.2
Africa	South Africa	21.9	21.8	21.2	23.5	22.2	22.7	20.2	21.9	20.7	-1.2
Oceania	Australia	44.2	46.0	44.6	46.9	46.1	46.5	45.1	49.2	46.9	2.7

Tab. 5 lists the average scores and overall fluctuations in scores of BRICS in NIC and Fig. 15 shows the variation tendency in scores of BRICS more intuitively.

According to the comparison the scores of BRICS in innovation competitiveness, during 2001-2009 the scores of China and Russia in NIC were all higher than the three countries and China and Russia competed with each other. However, since 2007, the score of China has been higher than that of Russia with the gap year by year. Before 2007, the score of Brazil in NIC was lower than that of South Africa, but thereafter, it was higher than South Africa with the gap year by year. India scored the lowest score in NIC, only 15.6 points and 7.7 points, the other countries.

Tab. 5 Variations in Scores of the BRICS in NIC during 2001-2009

	2001	2002	2003	2004	2005	2006	2007	2008	2009	Variations in scores during 2001-2009
China	23.3	25.7	26.4	27.6	29.1	29.2	30.6	35.8	34.1	10.8
Russia	27.0	28.9	29.0	27.7	27.9	30.8	28.9	31.8	28.9	1.8
India	7.7	8.0	8.3	7.9	11.4	11.6	11.0	15.6	13.9	6.2
Brazil	18.6	18.8	17.3	18.0	20.1	20.2	20.5	23.9	24.3	5.7
South Africa	21.9	21.8	21.2	23.5	22.2	22.7	20.2	21.9	20.7	-1.2

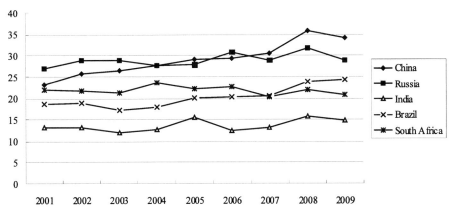

Fig. 15   Variation Tendency in the Evaluation Points of BRICS in NIC during 2001-2009

According to the fluctuations in scores of BRICS in NIC, China witnessed the greatest growth rate, rising by 10.8 points; India, the next, rising by 6.2 points; Brazil rising by 5.7 points; Russia rising by 1.8 points South Africa by 1.2 points.

(III) Evaluation and Analysis of G20 NIC within the Regions

G20 covers six continents of the globe To analyze the variations of G20 NIC within the regions further, Tab. 6, Tab. 7, Tab. 8 and Tab. 9 respectively list the rankings of North America, South America, Europe and Asia in G20 NIC during 2001-2009. the rankings and comparison of the countries for variations analysis, we clearly see of the countries within the corresponding regions as well as the within G20, and analyze the variations from two dimensions of G20 and the regions, thus the results more comprehensive and objective. We also find the variations of the arrays where the countries are located as well as In combination with Tab. 4, we regions.

Tab. 6　Rankings and Comparisons of North American Countries in G20 in NIC

Countries Items		USA	Canada	Mexico
Rankings in North America	2001	1	2	3
	2002	1	2	3
	2003	1	2	3
	2004	1	2	3
	2005	1	2	3
	2006	1	2	3
	2007	1	2	3
	2008	1	2	3
	2009	1	2	3
	Variations in rankings	0	0	0
Ranking in G20	2001	1	7	14
	2002	1	7	14
	2003	1	7	14
	2004	1	7	14
	2005	1	7	13
	2006	1	7	17
	2007	1	7	16
	2008	1	8	15
	2009	1	7	16
	Variations in rankings	0	0	-2

According to Tab. 6, it there were very gaps in rankings among the three North American countries of G20: the US ranked No. 1, always in the first array; Canada ranked No. 7 or 8, always in the second array; and Mexico ranking, down to the fourth array.

According to the scores in NIC, there were also obvious gaps within the three North American countries of G20. As shown in Tab. 4, in 2009, the score of the US was 83.8 points, Canada was 47.5, and Mexico was 20.5. The ratio was 4.1: 2.3: 1, reflecting very gaps.

On the whole, the overall rankings of the three North American countries of G20 in innovation competitiveness steady with little variations and the average score was 50.6

points. The level of competitiveness was This was mainly attributed to the US, which pulled forward the level of North America in innovation competitiveness.

Tab. 7   Rankings and Comparisons of South American Countries in G20 in NIC

Countries Items		Argentina	Brazil
Rankings in South America	2001	2	1
	2002	2	1
	2003	2	1
	2004	1	2
	2005	2	1
	2006	2	1
	2007	2	1
	2008	2	1
	2009	2	1
	Variations in rankings	0	0
Rankings in G20	2001	17	15
	2002	17	15
	2003	17	15
	2004	16	17
	2005	17	16
	2006	16	15
	2007	17	14
	2008	17	13
	2009	17	13
	Variations in rankings	0	2

According to Tab. 7, there was a smaller gap in rankings between the two South American countries of G20, Argentina and Brazil. Argentina ranked No. 17 or 16, always in the fourth array; Brazil, ranking, fell into the fourth array in 2004, but   the third array and ranked No. 13 in 2006.

According to the scores of NIC, the gap between the two countries was also small. As shown in Tab. 4, in 2009, the score of Argentina was 20.4 points and Brazil was 24.3, a gap of 3.9 points and ratio of 1.2: 1.

On the whole, the overall rankings of the two South American countries of G20 in innovation competitiveness steady with few change average score of 22.4 points. The level of competitiveness for them was.

Tab. 8   Rankings and Comparisons of European Countries in G20 in NIC

Countries Items		France	Germany	Italy	Russia	Turkey	UK
Rankings in Europe	2001	3	2	4	5	6	1
	2002	3	2	4	5	6	1
	2003	3	2	4	5	6	1
	2004	3	2	4	5	6	1
	2005	3	2	4	5	6	1
	2006	3	2	4	5	6	1
	2007	3	2	4	5	6	1
	2008	2	1	4	5	6	3
	2009	2	1	4	5	6	3
	Variations in rankings	1	1	0	0	0	-2
Rankings in G20	2001	5	4	9	10	16	3
	2002	5	4	9	10	16	3
	2003	5	4	9	10	16	3
	2004	5	4	9	10	15	3
	2005	6	4	9	11	15	3
	2006	6	4	9	10	14	3
	2007	6	4	9	11	13	3
	2008	4	2	9	11	14	5
	2009	4	3	9	12	14	6
	Variations in rankings	1	1	0	-2	2	-3

According to Tab. 8, it that there were greater gaps in rankings among the five European countries of G20 across three arrays. For instance, in 2001, UK, France and Germany first array, Turkey fourth array; in 2009, first, second and third arrays and there were 11 places between Turkey No. 14 and Germany No. 3.

luctuations of the countries were also very great. During 2001-2009, the UK dropped 3 places, from the first array to the second array; Russia dropped 2 places, from the second array to the third array; while Turkey rose 2 places, from the fourth array to the third array.

According to the scores of NIC, the gaps among the five European countries in innovation competitiveness were also great. As shown in Tab. 4, in 2009, the highest score Germany was 52.6 points, the lowest score by Turkey was 21.1 pointsthe former was 2.5 times of the latter.

Tab. 9　Rankings and Comparisons of Asian Countries in G20 in NIC

Countries Items		China	India	Indonesia	Japan	Korea	Saudi Arabia
Rankings in Asia	2001	4	5	6	1	2	3
	2002	3	5	6	1	2	4
	2003	3	5	6	1	2	4
	2004	3	5	6	1	2	4
	2005	3	5	6	1	2	4
	2006	3	5	6	1	2	4
	2007	3	5	6	1	2	4
	2008	3	5	6	1	2	4
	2009	3	5	6	1	2	4
	Variations in rankings	1	0	0	0	0	-1
Rankings in G20	2001	12	18	19	2	6	11
	2002	11	18	19	2	6	12
	2003	11	18	19	2	6	12
	2004	11	18	19	2	6	13
	2005	10	18	19	2	5	12
	2006	11	18	19	2	5	12
	2007	10	18	19	2	5	12
	2008	10	18	19	3	6	12
	2009	10	18	19	2	5	11
	Variations in rankings	2	0	0	0	1	0

On the whole, the five European countries of G20 witnessed greater gaps in the overall rankings of innovation competitiveness average score of 39.8 points. The level of competitiveness for them was.

According to Tab. 9, it that there are greater gaps in rankings among the six Asian countries of G20four arrays. For instance, in 2009, Japan and Korea were in the first array, China in the second array, Saudi Arabia in the third array, and India and Indonesia in the fourth array; there were 17 places between Indonesia No. 19 and Japan No. 2.

According to the scores of NIC, the gaps among the six Asian countries in innovation competitiveness were also great. As shown in Tab. 4, in 2009, the highest score Japan was 53.0 points, the lowest score by Turkey was 21.1 pointsthe former was 2.5 times of the latter.

On the whole, the six Asian countries of G20 witnessed greater gaps in the rankings of overall NIC average score of 39.8 points. The level of competitiveness for them was.

III. Overall Evaluation and Comparative Analysis of G20 National Competitiveness in Innovation Base

(I) Evaluation Results of G20 National Competitiveness in Innovation Base

According to the indicator model and mathematical model of national competitiveness in innovation base, the evaluation is made for the G20 national competitiveness in innovation base during 2001-2009. Tab. 10 lists the rankings and the variations in rankings of G20 national competitiveness in innovation base during the evaluation period as well as the evaluation results of the seven tertiary indicators. Fig. 16, Fig. 17 and Fig. 18 show the rankings and variations in rankings of G20 national competitiveness in innovation base during 2001-2009.

According to Tab. 10, in 2009, the highest score of competitiveness in innovation base was 92.8 points, by 4.3 points over that in 2001; the lowest score was 2.7 points, by 1.4 points over that in 2001; the average score was 32.6 points, by 4.5 points over that in 2001. It indicated a rise in the level of G20 in national competitiveness in innovation base. While in the tertiary indicators, the average scores of per capita GDP the most, by 9.9 points; then overall labor productivity and FDI, by 7.4 and 6.8 points respectively; none of the indicators declined.

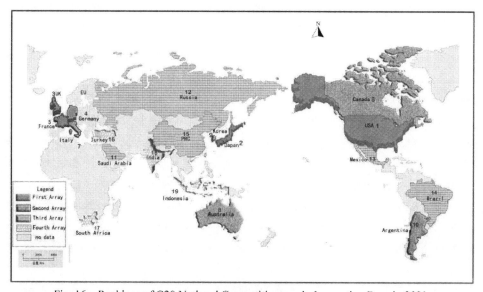

Fig. 16   Rankings of G20 National Competitiveness in Innovation Base in 2001

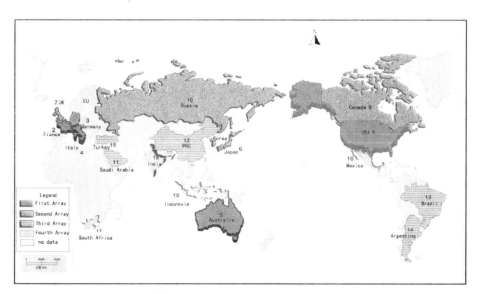

Fig. 17   Rankings of G20 National Competitiveness in Innovation Base in 2009

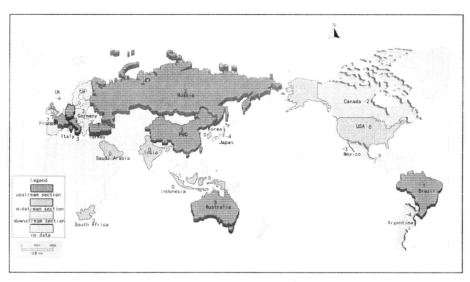

Fig. 18   Variations in Rankings of G20 National Competitiveness in Innovation Base During
2001-2009

By comparing the variations in scores of G20 national competitiveness in innovation base during 2001-2009, we conclude that the integral level of competitiveness in innovation base and the principal factors for per capita GDP, overall labor productivity and direct foreign investment.

Tab. 10 Evaluation and Comparison of G20 National Competitiveness in Innovation Base during 2001-2009

Countries / Items		Argentina	Australia	Brazil	Canada	China	France	Germany	India	Indonesia	Italy	Japan	Korea	Mexico	Russia	Saudi Arabia	South Africa	Turkey	UK	USA	Highest score	Lowest score	Average score
Overall variations in national competitiveness in innovation base during 2001-2009		-2.2	14.3	7.5	4.1	12.6	11.5	10.5	3.9	1.4	11.8	-5.3	1.3	-2.2	9.6	3.3	1.3	6.4	0.7	-4.3	-4.3	1.4	4.5
		-4	3	1	-2	3	2	2	0	0	3	-4	0	-3	2	0	0	1	-4	0	-	-	-
2001	Competitiveness in innovation base	17.9	36.5	8.3	43.4	6.9	49.2	45.8	1.4	1.3	40.8	55.9	26.9	12.7	13.2	16.3	4.6	6.7	49.5	97.1	97.1	1.3	28.1
		10	8	14	6	15	4	5	18	19	7	2	9	13	12	11	17	16	3	1	-	-	-
	GDP	1.5	2.6	4.3	5.9	11.9	12.1	17.5	3.6	0.4	9.9	39.3	3.8	5.0	1.9	0.6	0.0	0.8	13.4	100.0	100.0	0.0	12.3
		15	13	10	8	6	5	3	12	18	7	2	11	9	14	17	19	16	4	1	-	-	-
	Per capita GDP	19.0	54.0	7.5	63.6	1.6	60.4	63.5	0.0	0.9	54.0	89.6	28.8	16.4	4.6	23.2	6.1	6.9	68.9	100.0	100.0	0.0	35.2
		11	8	13	4	17	6	5	19	18	7	2	9	12	16	10	15	14	3	1	-	-	-
	Fiscal revenue	1.0	3.1	4.6	7.9	4.9	18.4	23.5	1.5	0.1	13.6	35.1	2.4	2.7	2.4	1.4	0.0	0.7	15.2	100.0	100.0	0.0	12.5
		16	10	9	7	8	4	3	14	18	6	2	13	11	12	15	19	17	5	1	-	-	-
	Per capita fiscal revenue	13.3	56.1	8.0	78.7	0.7	88.8	83.4	0.0	0.6	71.4	79.8	18.6	9.4	5.7	29.7	4.5	5.7	76.3	100.0	100.0	0.0	38.5
		11	8	13	5	17	2	3	19	18	7	4	10	12	14	9	16	15	6	1	-	-	-
	Direct foreign investment	3.0	6.6	15.0	18.1	27.8	31.4	17.1	5.0	0.0	10.5	5.4	3.8	19.3	3.4	1.8	6.0	3.7	33.4	100.0	100.0	0.0	16.4
		17	10	8	6	4	3	7	13	19	9	12	14	5	16	18	11	15	2	1	-	-	-
	Gross attendance rate for higher education	65.5	77.5	10.8	67.0	0.3	60.1	48.3	0.0	6.9	57.3	54.0	100.0	14.6	70.0	17.0	6.0	18.5	67.0	79.8	100.0	0.0	43.2
		7	3	15	5	18	8	11	19	16	9	10	1	14	4	13	17	12	6	2	-	-	-
	Overall labor productivity	22.1	55.7	7.9	62.3	0.9	73.2	67.3	0.0	0.6	69.0	88.0	30.7	21.3	4.4	40.4	9.3	10.5	72.5	100.0	100.0	0.0	38.7
		11	8	15	7	17	3	6	19	18	5	2	10	12	16	9	14	13	4	1	-	-	-
2009	Competitiveness in innovation base	15.7	50.8	15.8	47.4	19.5	60.7	56.3	5.3	2.7	52.7	50.6	28.2	10.4	22.8	19.6	5.9	13.1	50.2	92.8	92.8	2.7	32.7
		14	5	13	8	12	2	3	18	19	4	6	9	16	10	11	17	15	7	1	-	-	-
	GDP	0.2	4.7	9.5	7.7	34.2	17.0	22.1	8.0	1.9	13.3	34.5	4.0	4.4	6.8	0.7	0.0	2.4	13.7	100.0	100.0	0.0	15.0
		18	12	8	10	3	5	4	9	16	7	2	14	13	11	17	19	15	6	1	-	-	-
	Per capita GDP	14.4	92.2	15.8	86.2	5.7	88.6	88.6	0.0	2.6	76.0	85.9	35.7	15.8	16.7	30.5	10.2	15.8	76.2	100.0	100.0	0.0	45.1
		15	2	12	5	17	4	3	19	18	8	6	9	13	11	10	16	14	7	1	-	-	-
	Fiscal revenue	0.7	5.5	11.9	10.4	22.0	28.5	33.5	4.4	0.2	21.7	33.6	3.0	2.9	8.2	2.0	0.0	2.8	17.3	100.0	100.0	0.0	16.2
		17	11	8	9	5	4	3	12	18	6	2	13	14	10	16	19	15	7	1	-	-	-
	Per capita fiscal revenue	12.1	71.2	14.1	76.7	2.7	100.0	91.7	0.0	0.7	82.8	58.7	19.9	8.2	14.0	30.9	6.8	12.2	65.5	70.2	100.0	0.0	38.9
		14	5	11	4	17	1	2	19	18	3	8	10	15	12	9	16	13	7	6	-	-	-
	Direct foreign investment	1.8	15.8	18.3	13.8	57.6	43.9	28.3	24.8	2.5	20.6	7.8	0.0	9.7	26.5	6.8	2.9	5.2	53.6	100.0	100.0	0.0	23.2
		18	10	9	11	2	4	5	7	17	8	13	19	12	6	14	16	15	3	1	-	-	-
	Gross attendance rate for higher education	66.3	79.0	26.4	61.6	10.4	46.9	44.5	0.0	9.1	63.6	50.8	100.0	14.3	72.9	20.2	7.6	29.7	51.3	83.3	100.0	0.0	44.1
		5	3	13	7	16	10	11	19	17	6	9	1	15	4	14	18	12	8	2	-	-	-
	Overall labor productivity	14.3	87.0	14.3	75.6	3.8	100.0	85.4	0.0	1.9	90.5	83.0	34.7	17.7	14.8	46.1	13.5	23.7	73.9	96.4	100.0	0.0	46.1
		15	4	14	7	17	1	5	19	18	3	6	10	12	13	9	16	11	8	2	-	-	-

According to Fig. 19, national competitiveness in innovation base was distributed in a pattern among G20 nations. In 2009, only the US scored above 90 points in competitiveness in innovation base, France 60 points, and below 60. Among them, five countries scored between 50-60 points; one between 40-50 points; none between 30-40 points; two between 20-30 points; six between 10-20 points; and three scored below 10 points.

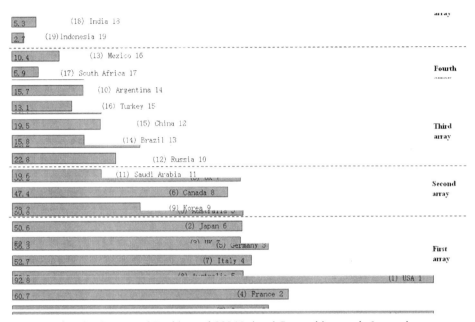

Fig. 19   Scores and Rankings of G20 National Competitiveness in Innovation
Base during 2001-2009

Note: In the figure, the left of the column, the are the rankings of the countries in competitiveness in innovation base in 2009, and the figures in the parenthesis are the rankings of the countries in competitiveness in innovation base in 2001.

ountries with higher national competitiveness in innovation base were developed countries in the first and second arrays, there were eight developed countries. It that the strong economic strength in the developed countries lays a solid foundation for them in sci-tech innovation. The developing countries are generally lower in national competitiveness in innovation base. None of them scores above 30 points, with developed countries. Indonesia No. 19 only score2.7 points,

(II) Analysis on the Variations in Rankings of G20 National Competitiveness in Innovation Base

According to Fig. 20, a comparison between 2009 and 2001, eight countries rose in the rankings of national competitiveness in innovation base. Three countries Australia, China and Italy all by 3 places; three countries France, Germany and Russia all by 2 places, and two countries Brazil and Turkey by 1 place. Six countries unchanged in the rankings, India, Korea, Saudi Arabia, South Africa and the US. Five countries declined in the rankings: Argentina, Japan and the UK all by 4 places; then Mexico, by 3 places; and Canada by 2 places.

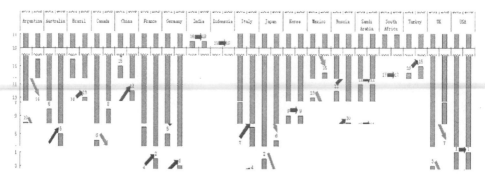

Fig. 20   Variations in Rankings of G20 National Competitiveness in Innovation
Base During 2001-2009

(III) Analysis on Across-Array Variations and Motivation of G20 National Competitiveness in Innovation Base

As for the G20 national competitiveness in innovation base in 2009, the following countries were in the first array (No. 1-5): the US, France, Germany, Italy, Australia; the following in the second array (No. 6-10): Japan, the UK, Canada, Korea, Russia; the following in the third array (No. 11-15): Saudi Arabia, China, Brazil, Argentina, Turkey; and the following in the fourth array (No. 16-19): Mexico, South Africa, India, Indonesia.

As for the G20 national competitiveness in innovation base in 2001, the following countries were in the first array (No. 1-5): the US, Australia, France, the UK, Canada; the following in the second array (No. 6-10): Japan, Korea, Germany, Italy, Russia; the following in the third array (No. 11-15): Saudi Arabia, Mexico, Argentina, China, South Africa; and the following in the fourth array (No. 16-19): Brazil, India, Turkey, Indonesia.

During the evaluation period, some countries acrossarray in the competitiveness in innovation base. Japan and the UK fell from the first array to the second array, Argentina from the second array to the third array and Mexico from the third array to the fourth array; whereas Australia and Italy rose from the second array to the first array, Russia from the third array to the second array and Turkey from the fourth array to the third array.

As for NIC the secondary indicator, its variation is synthetically caused by variations tertiary indicators. Tab. 10 also lists the variations of seven tertiary indicators.

According to the above countries in rankings of he competitiveness in innovation base, Japan declined by 4 places in the ranking of competitiveness in innovation base mainly per capita GDP, per capita fiscal revenue and overall labor productivity; the UK declined by 4 places mainly   per capita GDP and overall labor productivity; Mexico declined by 4 places mainly direct foreign investment and GDP.

Whereas, Australia rose by 4 places in the ranking of competitiveness in innovation base mainly from per capita GDP and overall labor productivity; Italy rose by 3 places mainly from per capita fiscal revenue and gross attendance rate for higher education; Russia rose by 2 places mainly from direct foreign investment and per capita GDP; Turkey rose by 1 place mainly from fiscal revenue, per capita fiscal revenue and over labor productivity.

It from the above analysis that per capita GDP, per capita fiscal revenue and overall labor productivity have the greatest influence on the competitiveness in innovation base and just these three indicators mainly embody the gaps of the countries in competitiveness in innovation base.

IV. Overall Evaluation and Comparative Analysis of G20 National Competitiveness in Innovation Environment

(I) Evaluation Results of G20 National Competitiveness in Innovation Environment

According to the indicator model and mathematical model of national competitiveness in innovation environment, G20 national competitiveness in innovation environment during 2001-2009. Tab. 11 lists the rankings and variations in rankings of G20 national competitiveness in innovation environment during the evaluation period as well as the evaluation results of the seven tertiary indicators. Fig. 21, Fig. 22 and Fig. 23 show the rankings and variations in rankings of G20 national competitiveness in innovation environment during 2001-2009.

According to Tab. 11, in 2009, the highest score of competitiveness in innovation environment was 81.6 points, 2.4 points over that in 2001; the lowest score was 25.2 points, 11 points over that in 2001; the average score was 53.6 points, 6.7 points over that in 2001. It indicated a rise in the level of G20 in national competitiveness in innovation environment. While in the tertiary indicators, the average score of number of Internet users/1,000 persons increased the most, by 16.8 points; then the advanced technological products purchased by governments and the opening dates of businesses, by 12.3 and 11.8 points respectively; the macro taxation burden and the number of cell-phones/1,000 persons, by 5.0 and 3.7 points respectively. The average scores of number of new businesses and protection of intellectual property right both declined by 1.5 and 1.1 points respectively.

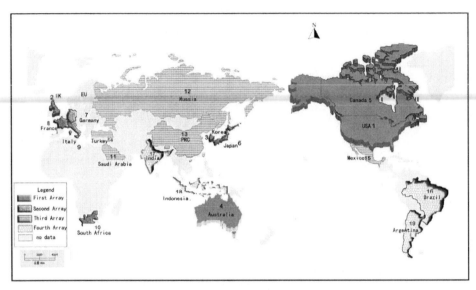

Fig. 21   Rankings of G20 National Competitiveness in Innovation Environment in 2001

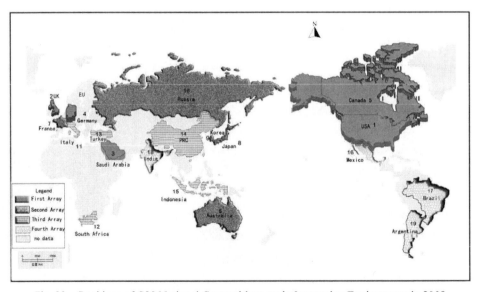

Fig. 22   Rankings of G20 National Competitiveness in Innovation Environment in 2009

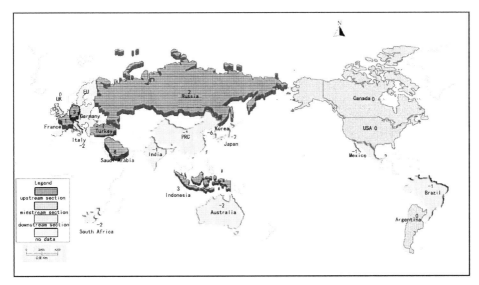

Fig. 23　Variations in Rankings of G20 National Competitiveness in Innovation Environment during 2001-2009

Tab. 11　Evaluation and Comparison of G20 National Competitiveness in Innovation Environment during 2001-2009

Countries Items		Argentina	Australia	Brazil	Canada	China	France	Germany	India	Indonesia	Italy	Japan	Korea	Mexico	Russia	Saudi Arabia	South Africa	Turkey	UK	USA	Highest scores	Lowest scores	Average scores
Overall variations in national competitiveness in innovation environment during 2001-2009		11.0	-2.5	12.0	5.1	10.0	3.3	7.8	6.6	22.7	-0.7	0.4	-10.8	8.7	15.4	29.0	-0.7	11.8	0.8	-2.4	-2.4	11.0	6.7
		0	-2	-1	0	-1	1	3	-1	3	-2	-2	-6	-1	2	8	-2	1	0	0	-	-	-
2001	Competitiveness in innovation environment	14.2	70.2	23.0	64.8	31.5	60.7	62.2	22.6	16.9	48.4	62.5	73.0	28.7	36.2	42.8	44.5	29.9	74.1	84.0	84.0	14.2	46.9
		19	4	16	5	13	8	7	17	18	9	6	3	15	12	11	10	14	2	1	-	-	-
	Number of Internet users/1,000 persons	17.5	100.0	7.3	85.2	3.7	49.4	59.4	0.0	2.5	51.3	72.7	97.7	12.5	4.2	7.7	11.0	8.7	63.1	95.0	100.0	0.0	39.4
		10	1	15	4	17	9	7	19	18	8	5	2	11	16	14	12	13	6	3	-	-	-
	Number of cell-phones/1,000 persons	19.1	62.9	16.9	37.1	11.2	69.7	75.3	0.0	2.2	100.0	65.2	67.4	23.6	4.5	12.4	25.8	31.5	86.5	49.4	100.0	0.0	40.0
		13	7	14	9	16	4	3	19	18	1	6	5	12	17	15	11	10	2	8	-	-	-
	Number of new businesses	1.6	13.9	38.0	22.8	4.7	17.8	9.4	5.4	2.7	10.8	17.4	8.7	6.4	65.4	0.0	5.5	6.0	62.9	100.0	100.0	0.0	21.0
		18	8	4	5	16	6	10	15	17	9	7	11	12	2	19	14	13	3	1	-	-	-
	Opening dates of businesses	61.4	100.0	9.6	99.4	72.3	76.5	74.1	47.6	0.0	87.3	82.5	91.0	66.3	74.7	58.4	78.3	78.3	93.4	97.6	100.0	0.0	71.0
		15	1	18	2	13	10	12	17	19	6	7	5	14	11	16	8	8	4	3	-	-	-
	Macro tax burden	0.0	59.1	42.0	63.0	30.0	45.0	62.9	45.5	75.6	32.7	58.8	76.6	56.0	60.8	100.0	74.8	58.9	77.2	66.3	100.0	0.0	57.1
		19	10	16	7	18	15	8	14	4	17	12	3	13	9	1	5	11	2	6	-	-	-
	Advanced technological products purchased by governments	0.0	58.3	29.2	58.3	62.5	66.7	54.2	29.2	29.2	8.3	50.0	100.0	20.8	37.5	66.7	37.5	16.7	54.2	91.7	100.0	0.0	45.8
		19	6	13	6	5	3	8	13	13	18	10	1	16	11	3	11	17	8	2	-	-	-
	Protection of intellectual property right	0.0	97.0	18.2	87.9	36.4	100.0	100.0	30.3	6.1	48.5	90.9	69.7	15.2	6.1	54.5	78.8	9.1	81.8	87.9	100.0	0.0	53.6
		19	3	14	5	12	1	1	13	17	11	4	9	15	17	10	8	16	7	5	-	-	-

Countries / Items		Argentina	Australia	Brazil	Canada	China	France	Germany	India	Indonesia	Italy	Japan	Korea	Mexico	Russia	Saudi Arabia	South Africa	Turkey	UK	USA	Highest scores	Lowest scores	Average scores
2009	Competitiveness in innovation environment	25.3	67.7	35.0	69.9	41.5	64.0	70.0	29.1	39.6	47.7	62.9	62.2	37.4	51.5	71.8	43.8	41.7	74.9	81.6	81.6	25.3	53.6
		19	6	17	5	14	7	4	18	15	11	8	9	16	10	3	12	13	2	1	-	-	-
	Number of Internet users/1,000 persons	32.2	85.6	43.5	92.9	30.2	84.7	95.3	0.0	4.4	55.5	92.9	97.0	27.2	47.2	42.7	4.7	38.5	100.0	93.5	100.0	0.0	56.2
		14	7	11	5	15	8	3	19	18	9	5	2	16	10	12	17	13	1	4	-	-	-
	Number of cell-phones/1,000 persons	63.6	50.0	34.1	17.4	8.3	37.9	62.9	0.0	18.2	79.5	34.1	40.2	25.0	88.6	100.0	37.1	29.5	64.4	39.4	100.0	0.0	43.7
		5	7	12	17	18	10	6	19	16	3	12	8	15	2	1	11	14	4	9	-	-	-
	Number of new businesses	1.2	12.9	48.2	26.3	1.0	19.3	9.4	6.6	3.9	10.0	17.9	7.7	6.2	39.8	0.0	3.2	6.3	50.4	100.0	100.0	0.0	19.5
		17	8	3	5	18	6	10	12	15	9	7	11	14	4	19	16	13	2	1	-	-	-
	Opening dates of businesses	79.7	100.0	0.0	97.5	69.5	95.8	89.0	77.1	61.9	96.6	82.2	89.8	94.1	76.3	97.5	83.1	96.6	90.7	96.6	100.0	0.0	82.8
		14	1	19	2	17	7	11	15	18	4	13	10	8	16	2	12	4	9	4	-	-	-
	Macro tax burden	0.0	64.4	41.8	84.3	47.7	45.3	64.0	47.9	75.7	42.3	63.6	83.7	61.6	65.8	100.0	82.9	68.0	75.7	65.5	100.0	0.0	62.1
		19	10	18	2	15	16	11	14	5	17	12	3	13	8	1	4	7	5	9	-	-	-
	Advanced technological products purchased by governments	0.0	70.0	60.0	80.0	90.0	65.0	75.0	40.0	75.0	15.0	70.0	70.0	30.0	40.0	95.0	25.0	50.0	55.0	100.0	100.0	0.0	58.2
		19	7	11	4	3	10	5	14	5	18	7	7	16	14	2	17	13	12	1	-	-	-
	Protection of intellectual property right	0.0	91.2	17.6	91.2	44.1	100.0	94.1	32.4	38.2	35.3	79.4	47.1	17.6	2.9	67.6	70.6	2.9	88.2	76.5	100.0	0.0	52.5
		19	3	15	3	11	1	2	14	12	13	6	10	15	17	9	8	17	5	7	-	-	-

By comparing the variations in scores of G20 national competitiveness in innovation environment during 2001-2009, we conclude that the level of competitiveness in innovation environment somewhat and the principal factors for the number of Internet users/1,000 persons, advanced technological products purchased by governments, and the opening dates of businesses.

According to Fig. 24, national competitiveness in innovation environment was distributed in a pattern among G20 nations. In 2009, only the US scored above 80 points in competitiveness in innovation environment; three countries between 70-80 points; five between 60-70; one between 50-60; four between 40-50; three between 30-40; two between 20-30; and none scored below 20 points.

The countries with higher competitiveness in innovation environment were mainly developed countries. Out of the countries ranked first 11 places, only three were developing countries and the others all were developed countries. It indicate that the developed countries favorable environment sci-tech innovation. The developing countries generally lower in national competitiveness in innovation environment. Except for Saudi Arabia, the developing countries all scored below 65 points, gap with developed countries. Argentina No. 19 only scored 25.3 points, less than 1/3 of th

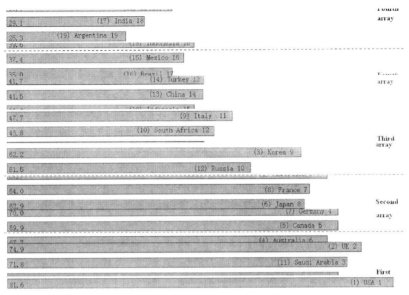

Fig. 24   Scores and Rankings of G20 National Competitiveness in Innovation Environment
during 2001-2009

Note: In the figure, in competitiveness in innovation environment in 2009, and the figures in the parenthesis
are the rankings of the countries in competitiveness in innovation environment in 2001.

(II) Analysis on the Variations in Rankings of G20 National Competitiveness in Innovation Environment

According to Fig. 25, a comparison between 2009 and 2001, six countries rose in the rankings of national competitiveness in innovation environment. Saudi Arabia two countries Germany and Indonesia both by 3 places; Russia by 2 places, and two countries France and Turkey both by 1 place. Four countries unchanged in the rankings, Argentina, Canada, the UK and the US. Nine countries declined in the rankings: Korea witnessed the greatest decline by 6 places; then Australia, Italy, Japan and South Africa, all 2 places; and Brazil, China, India and Mexico all by 1 place.

Fig. 25   Variations in Rankings of G20 National Competitiveness in Innovation Environment
during 2001-2009

(III) Analysis on Across-Array Variations and Motivation of G20 National Competitiveness in Innovation Environment

As for G20 national competitiveness in innovation environment in 2009, the following countries were in the first array (No. 1-5): the US, the UK, Saudi Arabia, Germany, Canada; the following in the second array (No. 6-10): Australia, France, Japan, Korea, Russia; the following in the third array (No. 11-15): Italy, South Africa, Turkey, China, Indonesia; and the following in the fourth array (No. 16-19): Mexico, Brazil, India, Argentina.

As for G20 national competitiveness in innovation environment in 2001, the following countries were in the first array (No. 1-5): the US, the UK, Korea, Australia, Canada; the following in the second array (No. 6-10): Japan, Germany, France, Italy, South Africa; the following in the third array (No. 11-15): Saudi Arabia, Russia, China, Turkey, Mexico; and the following in the fourth array (No. 16-19): Brazil, India, Indonesia, Argentina.

During the evaluation period, some countries in the competitiveness in innovation environment. Australia and Korea fell from the first array to the second array, Italy and South Africa from the second array to the third array and Mexico from the third array to the fourth array; whereas Germany rose from the second array to the first array, Saudi Arabia from the third array to the first array, Russia from the third array to the second array and Indonesia from the fourth array to the third array.

As for NIC the secondary indicator, its variation is synthetically caused by the variations of tertiary indicators. Tab. 11 also lists the variations of seven tertiary indicators.

According to the above countries in rankings of competitiveness in innovation environment, Australia declined by 2 places in the ranking of competitiveness in innovation environment mainly number of Internet users/1,000 persons; Korea declined by 6 places mainly the advanced technological products purchased by governments and the opening dates of businesses respectively; Italy declined by 2 places mainly the number of cell-phones/1,000 persons and protection of intellectual property right; South Africa declined by 2 places mainly advanced technological products purchased by governments, the number of Internet users/1,000 persons and the opening dates of businesses respectively; Mexico declined by 1 place mainly the number of Internet users/1,000 persons.

Whereas, Australia rose by 4 places in the ranking of competitiveness in innovation environment mainly from thethe number of Internet users/1,000 persons and the advanced technological products purchased by governments respectively; Saudi Arabia rose by 8 places mainly both the number of cell-phones/1,000 persons and the opening dates of businesses; Russia rose by 2 places mainly from number of cell-phones/1,000 persons and the number of Internet users/1,000 persons; Indonesia rose by 3 places mainly from the advanced technological products purchased by governments and the protection of intellectual property right respectively.

It is observed from the above analysis that the number of Internet users/1,000 persons, the number of cell-phones/1,000 persons and the advanced technological products purchased by governments have the greatest influence on the competitiveness in innovation environment and just these three indicators mainly embody the gaps of the countries in competitiveness in innovation environment.

V. Overall Evaluation and Comparative Analysis of G20 National Competitiveness in Innovation Input(I) Evaluation Results of G20 National Competitiveness in Innovation Input

According to the indicator model and mathematical model of national competitiveness in innovation input, evaluation is made for the G20 national competitiveness in innovation input during 2001-2009. Tab. 12 lists the rankings and variations in rankings of G20 national competitiveness in innovation input during the evaluation period as well as the evaluation results of the seven tertiary indicators. Fig. 26, Fig. 27 and Fig. 28 show the rankings and variations in rankings of G20 national competitiveness in innovation input during 2001-2009.

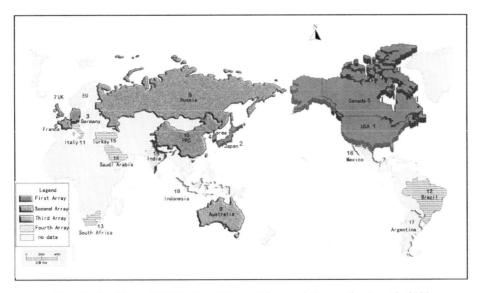

Fig. 26   Rankings of G20 National Competitiveness in Innovation Input in 2001

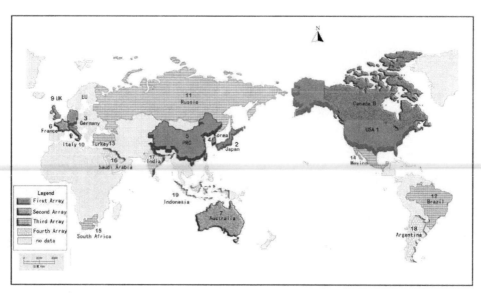

Fig. 27   Rankings of G20 National Competitiveness in Innovation Input in 2009

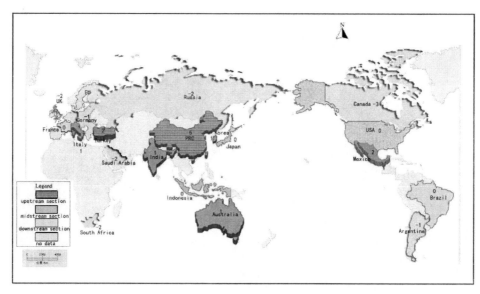

Fig. 28   Variations in Rankings of G20 National Competitiveness in Innovation Input During
2001-2009

Tab. 12　Evaluation and Comparison of G20 National Competitiveness in Innovation Input during 2001-2009

	Countries Items	Argentina	Australia	Brazil	Canada	China	France	Germany	India	Indonesia	Italy	Japan	Korea	Mexico	Russia	Saudi Arabia	South Africa	Turkey	UK	USA	Highest scores	Lowest scores	Average scores
	Overall variations in national competitiveness in innovation input during 2001-2009	-0.3	8.8	-1.9	-6.0	17.6	-2.7	-0.2	2.1	2.1	2.3	2.9	12.2	5.4	-7.9	-0.7	-3.2	3.6	-5.3	-3.7	-3.7	2.1	1.3
2001	Competitiveness in innovation input	8.1	38.2	22.2	50.3	30.4	49.9	58.2	7.7	0.7	26.0	75.2	55.6	11.3	35.7	15.1	19.0	14.4	43.4	95.3	95.3	0.7	34.6
		17	8	12	5	10	6	3	18	19	11	2	4	16	9	14	13	15	7	1	-	-	-
	Gross R&D expenditure	0.4	3.1	4.7	6.8	11.2	12.8	19.5	4.5	0.0	6.0	37.3	7.6	1.2	4.5	0.0	0.7	1.0	10.4	100.0	100.0	0.0	12.2
		17	13	10	8	5	4	3	11	18	9	2	7	14	12	19	16	15	6	1	-	-	-
	Proportion of gross R&D expenditure in GDP	12.3	52.7	32.4	66.3	29.4	69.9	78.5	22.8	0.0	33.8	100.0	78.9	11.3	36.7	0.9	22.3	15.9	56.6	86.9	100.0	0.0	42.5
		16	8	11	6	12	5	4	13	19	10	1	3	17	9	18	14	15	7	2	-	-	-
	Per capita R&D expenditure	3.7	46.2	7.5	62.6	2.4	59.9	67.7	1.2	0.0	30.1	83.8	45.9	3.6	8.8	1.0	5.1	4.5	50.5	100.0	100.0	0.0	30.8
		14	7	11	4	16	5	3	17	19	9	2	8	15	10	18	12	13	6	1	-	-	-
	R&D personnel	0.7	2.5	3.4	4.6	25.6	8.7	12.7	7.1	1.1	3.9	23.2	4.2	0.9	27.0	0.0	0.3	0.5	7.8	100.0	100.0	0.0	12.3
		16	13	12	9	3	6	5	8	14	11	4	10	15	2	19	18	17	7	1	-	-	-
	Proportion of R&D personnel in total employees	15.2	72.8	8.7	71.6	9.7	68.7	67.3	2.9	3.7	28.7	100.0	61.9	8.2	71.2	0.0	8.4	9.2	63.8	89.7	100.0	0.0	40.1
		11	3	14	4	12	6	7	18	17	10	1	9	16	5	19	15	13	8	2	-	-	-
	Proportion of R&D personnel in businesses	14.1	31.5	48.8	79.3	64.9	61.8	74.2	7.3	0.0	49.2	82.0	91.4	27.6	69.6	50.4	25.4	18.0	62.0	100.0	100.0	0.0	50.4
		17	13	12	4	7	9	5	18	19	11	3	2	14	6	10	15	16	8	1	-	-	-
	Proportion of R&D input in businesses	10.5	58.8	49.9	61.0	69.8	67.7	87.3	7.9	0.0	30.2	100.0	99.0	26.0	32.4	53.7	70.5	51.7	52.9	90.9	100.0	0.0	53.7
		17	9	13	8	6	7	4	18	19	15	1	2	16	14	10	5	12	11	3	-	-	-
2009	Competitiveness in innovation input	7.8	47.0	20.3	44.3	48.0	47.2	58.0	9.8	2.8	28.3	78.1	67.7	16.7	27.8	14.4	15.8	18.0	38.2	91.6	91.6	2.8	35.9
		18	7	12	8	5	6	4	17	19	10	2	3	14	11	16	15	13	9	1	-	-	-
	Gross R&D expenditure	0.7	4.8	6.2	5.8	32.8	11.3	19.9	7.0	0.1	5.8	37.7	11.7	1.4	7.8	0.0	1.1	1.9	9.5	100.0	100.0	0.0	14.0
		17	13	10	11	3	6	4	9	18	12	2	5	15	8	19	16	14	7	1	-	-	-
	Proportion of gross R&D expenditure in GDP	14.0	68.3	30.5	53.8	41.3	61.1	78.8	18.6	0.0	34.1	98.0	100.0	8.3	33.3	0.0	24.9	22.0	51.3	77.3	100.0	0.0	42.9
		16	5	12	7	9	6	3	15	19	10	2	1	17	11	18	13	14	8	4	-	-	-
	Per capita R&D expenditure	6.0	68.3	9.8	53.8	7.3	54.1	74.8	1.6	0.0	29.8	90.8	74.1	4.0	17.0	1.2	7.5	8.2	47.8	100.0	100.0	0.0	34.5
		15	5	11	7	14	6	3	17	19	9	2	4	16	10	18	13	12	8	1	-	-	-
	R&D personnel	1.2	3.2	6.0	5.6	54.3	9.4	12.7	15.4	2.7	5.6	20.9	7.9	1.4	20.5	0.0	0.6	1.5	7.8	100.0	100.0	0.0	14.6
		17	13	10	12	2	7	6	5	14	11	3	8	16	4	19	18	15	9	1	-	-	-
	Proportion of R&D personnel in total employees	22.7	80.4	13.0	76.9	21.7	78.7	70.8	2.8	1.1	38.7	100.0	97.8	7.7	56.5	0.0	9.9	21.3	74.3	86.1	100.0	0.0	45.3
		11	4	14	6	12	5	8	17	18	10	1	2	16	9	19	15	13	7	3	-	-	-
2009	Proportion of R&D personnel in businesses	9.0	34.6	44.1	74.2	87.7	70.4	71.1	0.0	1.2	45.0	99.1	94.1	50.7	59.6	53.5	38.9	43.3	40.5	100.0	100.0	0.0	53.5
		17	16	12	5	4	7	6	19	18	11	2	3	10	8	9	15	13	14	1	-	-	-
	Proportion of R&D input in businesses	1.2	69.4	32.6	40.0	90.8	45.7	78.0	23.1	14.2	39.1	100.0	88.7	43.4	0.0	46.4	27.5	27.5	36.0	77.9	100.0	0.0	46.4
		18	6	13	10	2	8	4	16	17	11	1	3	9	19	7	15	14	12	5	-	-	-

According to Tab. 12, in 2009, the highest score of competitiveness in innovation input was 91.6 points, 3.7 points over that of 2001; the lowest score was 2.8, by 2.1 points over that of 2001; the average score was 35.9 points, by 1.3 points over that of 2001. It indicated a slight rise in the level of G20 national competitiveness innovation input. While in the tertiary indicators, the average scores of the proportion of R&D personnel of total employees rose the most, by 5.2 points; then per capita R&D expenditure and proportion of R&D personnel in businesses, by 3.8 and 3.1 points respectively; the R&D personnel, the gross R&D expenditure and the proportion of gross R&D expenditure to GDP rose by 2.2 points, 1.8 points and 0.4 point respectively; while the average score of the proportion of R&D input in businesses by 7.3 points.

By comparing the variation in scores of G20 national competitiveness in innovation input during 2001-2009, we conclude that the level of innovation competitiveness slightly and the principal factors for include the proportion of R&D personnel of total employees, per capita R&D expenditure and the proportion of R&D personnel in businesses.

According to Fig. 29, national competitiveness in innovation input was distributed in a pattern among G20 nations. In 2009, only the US scored above 90 points in competitiveness in innovation input; one country between 70-80 points; one between 60-70; one between 50-60; four between 40-50; one between 30-40; three between 20-30; four between 10-20; and three scored below 10 points.

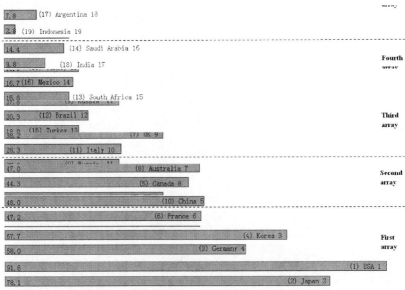

Fig. 29 Scores and Rankings of G20 National Competitiveness in Innovation Input during 2001-2009
Note: In the figure, the left of the column are the scores, the are the rankings of the countries in competitiveness in innovation input in 2009, and the figures in the parenthesis are the rankings of the countries in competitiveness in innovation input in 2001.

The countries with higher national competitiveness in innovation base were mainly developed countries, and in the first and second arrays except for China and Korea. that strong economic foundation and strength in the developed countries provided favorable conditions for them in sci-tech innovation input. The developing countries in competitiveness in innovation input, great gap with developed countries. Indonesia No. 19 only scored 2.8 points, merely 3% of the USNo. 1; Korea scored the highest point of 67.7 points, yet with the US.

(II) Analysis on the Variations in Rankings of G20 National Competitiveness in Innovation Input

According to Fig. 30, a comparison between 2009 and 2001, seven countries rose in the rankings of national competitiveness in innovation input. China by 5 places; two countries Mexico and Turkey by 2 place, and four countries Australia, India, Italy and Korea all by 1 place. Five countries unchanged in the rankings, Brazil, France, Indonesia, Japan and the US. Seven countries in the rankings: Canada witnessed the greatest by 3 places; then Russia, Saudi Arabia, South Africa and the UK, all by 2 places; and Argentina and Germany by 1 place.

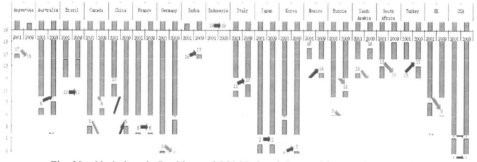

Fig. 30   Variations in Rankings of G20 National Competitiveness in Innovation
Input During 2001-2009

(III) Analysis on the Across-Array Variations and Motivation of G20 National Competitiveness in Innovation Input

As for G20 national competitiveness in innovation input in 2009, the following countries were in the first array (No. 1-5): the US, Japan, Korea, Germany, China; the following in the second array (No. 6-10): France, Australia, Canada, the UK, Italy; the following in the third array (No. 11-15): Russia, Brazil, Turkey, Mexico, South Africa; and the following in the fourth array (No. 16-19): Saudi Arabia, India, Argentina, Indonesia.

As for G20 national competitiveness in innovation input in 2001, the following countries were in the first array (No. 1-5): the US, Japan, Germany, Korea, Canada; the following in the second array (No. 6-10): France, the UK, Australia, Russia, China; the following in the third array (No. 11-15): Italy, Brazil, South Africa, Saudi Arabia, Turkey; and the following in the fourth array (No. 16-19): Mexico, Argentina, India, Indonesia.

During the evaluation period, some countries acrossarray in the competitiveness in innovation input. Canada fell from the first array to the second array, Russia from the second array to the third array and Saudi Arabia from the third array to the fourth array; whereas China rose from the second array to the first array, Italy from the third array to the second array and Mexico from the fourth array to the third array.

As for national competitiveness in innovation input as the secondary indicator, its variation is synthetically caused by the variations of tertiary indicators. Tab. 12 also lists the variations of seven tertiary indicators.

According to the above countries in the rankings of competitiveness in innovation input, Canada declined by 3 places in the ranking of competitiveness in innovation input mainly the rankings of gross R&D expenditure, per capita R&D expenditure and R&D personnel; Russia declined the rankings of the proportion of R&D input in businesses and the proportion of R&D personnel to total employees.

China rose by 5 places mainly from therankings of the proportion of R&D input in businesses, the proportion of gross R&D expenditure to GDP, and R&D personnel in businesses; Italy rose by 1 place mainly from rankings of the proportion of R&D input in businesses; Mexico rose by 2 places mainly from rankings of the proportion of R&D input in businesses and the proportion of R&D personnel in businesses.

It is from the above analysis that the proportion of R&D input in businesses and the proportion of R&D personnel in businesses have the greatest influence on the competitiveness in innovation input and just these two indicators mainly embody the gaps of the countries in competitiveness in innovation input.

VI. Overall Evaluation and Comparative Analysis of G20 National Competitiveness in Innovation Output

(I) Evaluation Results of G20 National Competitiveness in Innovation Output

According to the indicator model and mathematical model of national competitiveness in innovation output, evaluation is made for G20 national competitiveness in innovation output during 2001-2009. Tab. 13 lists the rankings and variations in rankings of G20 national competitiveness in innovation output during the evaluation period as well as the evaluation results of the seven tertiary indicators. Fig. 31, Fig. 32 and Fig. 33 show the rankings and variations in rankings of G20 national competitiveness in innovation output during 2001-2009.

Tab. 13 Evaluation and Comparison of G20 National Competitiveness in Innovation Output during 2001-2009

Countries / Items	Argentina	Australia	Brazil	Canada	China	France	Germany	India	Indonesia	Italy	Japan	Korea	Mexico	Russia	Saudi Arabia	South Africa	Turkey	UK	USA	Highest scores	Lowest scores	Average scores
Overall variations in national competitiveness in innovation output during 2001-2009	-1.0	-0.4	-0.8	0.2	18.7	-0.6	0.3	0.2	-0.3	-1.1	-7.2	-8.1	2.4	-1.8	-0.7	1.2	0.2	-9.0	-10.3	-10.3	-0.7	-1.0
2001 Competitiveness in innovation output	9.1	20.7	13.0	27.6	16.1	29.1	34.9	9.8	6.2	26.1	48.5	36.1	15.6	8.0	5.6	10.9	9.9	41.4	91.0	91.0	5.6	24.2
(rank)	16	9	12	7	10	6	5	15	18	8	2	4	11	17	19	13	14	3	1	-	-	-
Applications of American patents	0.1	1.5	0.1	4.4	2.0	3.8	10.9	0.8	0.0	1.6	43.1	10.6	0.1	0.2	0.0	0.1	0.0	3.9	100.0	100.0	0.0	9.6
(rank)	16	10	13	5	8	7	3	11	19	9	2	4	15	12	17	14	18	6	1	-	-	-
Average patent authorizations of sci-tech personnel	2.6	27.4	1.9	49.6	3.4	27.5	52.9	11.1	0.0	31.3	84.6	100.0	2.3	0.5	6.6	10.1	1.2	27.0	97.1	100.0	0.0	28.3
(rank)	14	8	16	5	13	7	4	10	19	6	3	1	15	18	12	11	17	9	2	-	-	-
Publications of scientific papers	1.4	7.5	3.6	11.4	11.0	16.0	22.3	5.6	0.0	11.5	29.4	5.7	1.6	8.1	0.2	1.1	2.1	23.8	100.0	100.0	0.0	13.8
(rank)	16	10	13	7	8	5	4	12	19	6	2	11	15	9	18	17	14	3	1	-	-	-
Average paper publications of sci-tech personnel	33.6	62.7	26.3	57.3	7.4	51.4	48.0	33.7	0.0	100.0	24.9	23.4	24.3	8.1	32.5	48.1	54.6	75.2	42.8	100.0	0.0	39.7
(rank)	11	3	13	4	18	6	8	10	19	1	14	16	15	17	12	7	5	2	9	-	-	-
Royalty and license income s	0.1	0.8	0.3	5.9	0.3	6.4	8.2	0.1	0.5	1.1	25.7	2.3	0.1	0.1	0.0	0.0	0.1	20.1	100.0	100.0	0.0	9.0
(rank)	14	9	11	6	12	5	4	17	10	8	2	7	16	13	19	18	15	3	1	-	-	-
High-tech products export	0.4	1.5	3.4	15.2	27.5	31.1	49.9	1.0	2.5	11.4	55.7	22.7	16.8	1.8	0.0	0.5	0.6	40.0	100.0	100.0	0.0	20.1
(rank)	18	14	11	9	6	5	3	15	12	10	2	7	8	13	19	17	16	4	1	-	-	-
Proportion of high-tech products export in manufacturing	25.5	43.4	55.3	49.3	61.3	67.2	52.3	16.5	40.4	25.5	76.2	88.1	64.2	37.4	0.0	16.5	10.6	100.0	97.0	100.0	0.0	48.8
(rank)	14	11	8	10	7	5	9	16	12	14	4	3	6	13	19	16	18	1	2	-	-	-
2009 Competitiveness in innovation output	8.1	20.3	12.2	27.8	34.8	28.5	35.3	10.1	5.9	24.9	41.3	28.0	18.0	6.3	4.9	12.1	10.0	32.4	80.7	80.7	4.9	23.2
(rank)	16	10	12	8	4	6	3	14	18	9	2	7	11	17	19	13	15	5	1	-	-	-
Applications of American patents	0.1	1.0	0.1	4.1	0.2	4.6	12.9	0.2	0.0	2.0	37.9	4.0	0.1	0.3	0.0	0.1	0.0	4.5	100.0	100.0	0.0	9.1
(rank)	16	9	14	6	11	4	3	12	18	8	2	7	15	10	18	13	17	5	1	-	-	-
Average patent authorizations of sci-tech personnel	1.8	15.2	1.3	38.9	0.2	28.1	58.9	1.2	0.0	27.3	86.2	22.1	3.4	0.9	0.0	9.5	0.3	26.5	100.0	100.0	0.0	22.2
(rank)	12	9	13	4	17	5	3	14	18	6	2	8	11	15	18	10	16	7	1	-	-	-
Publications of scientific papers	1.6	9.1	6.2	14.0	34.5	14.5	20.4	10.1	0.0	12.9	23.6	9.7	2.0	6.3	0.2	1.4	4.5	22.5	100.0	100.0	0.0	15.4
(rank)	16	11	13	7	2	6	5	9	19	8	3	10	15	12	18	17	14	4	1	-	-	-
Average paper publications of sci-tech personnel	25.9	75.3	32.1	71.6	11.7	46.5	49.4	29.1	0.0	100.0	26.8	26.8	40.8	7.9	34.3	56.3	60.5	71.4	53.0	100.0	0.0	43.1
(rank)	16	2	12	3	17	9	8	13	19	1	14	15	10	18	11	6	5	4	7	-	-	-
Royalty and license income s	0.1	0.9	0.5	3.6	0.5	10.5	15.3	0.2	0.0	1.2	24.2	3.5	0.7	0.5	0.0	0.0	0.2	14.4	100.0	100.0	0.0	9.3
(rank)	16	9	12	6	13	5	3	14	18	8	2	7	10	11	19	17	15	4	1	-	-	-
High-tech products export	0.4	1.0	2.4	7.2	100.0	24.1	40.9	2.9	1.7	7.5	28.5	29.7	10.7	1.3	0.0	0.4	0.4	16.4	40.6	100.0	0.0	16.6
(rank)	16	15	12	10	1	6	2	11	13	9	5	4	8	14	19	18	17	7	3	-	-	-
Proportion of high-tech products export in manufacturing	26.7	39.5	42.7	55.4	96.8	71.3	49.0	26.7	39.5	23.5	61.8	100.0	68.1	26.7	0.0	17.2	4.4	71.3	71.3	100.0	0.0	47.0
(rank)	13	11	10	8	2	3	9	13	11	16	7	1	6	13	19	17	18	3	3	-	-	-

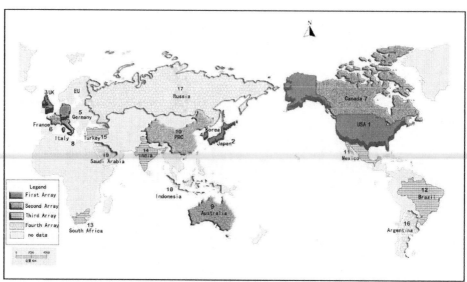

Fig. 31   Rankings of G20 National Competitiveness in Innovation Output in 2001

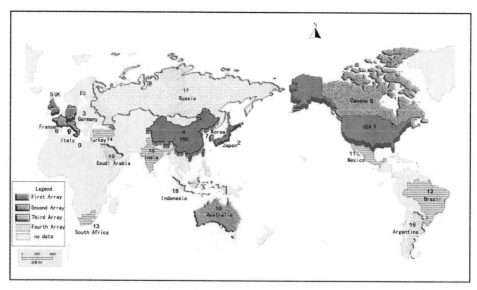

Fig. 32   Rankings of G20 National Competitiveness in Innovation Output in 2009

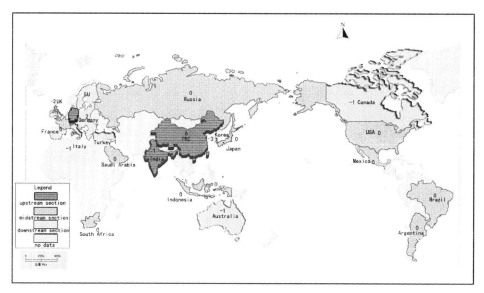

Fig. 33   Variations in Rankings of G20 National Competitiveness in Innovation Output During 2001-2009

According to Tab. 13, in 2009, the highest score of competitiveness in innovation output was 80.7 points, by 10.3 points over that in 2001; the lowest score was 4.9 points, by 0.7 point over that in 2001; the average score was 23.2 points, by 1.0 point over that in 2001. It a slight rise in the level of G20 in the national competitiveness in innovation output. While in the tertiary indicators, the average patent authorizations of sci-tech personnel the most, by 6.1 points; then high-tech products export, the proportion of high-tech products export in the manufacturing and the applications of American patents, by 3.5 points, 1.8 points and 0.6 point respectively; whereas the average scores of average paper publications of sci-tech personnel, publications of scientific papers, and the royalty and license income rose by 3.4 points, 1.6 points and 0.2 point respectively.

By comparing the variations in scores of G20 national competitiveness in innovation output during 2001-2009, we conclude that the level of competitiveness in innovation output and the principal factors for the decline of it include the average patent authorizations of sci-tech personnel, high-tech products export, and the proportion of high-tech products export in manufacturing.

According to Fig. 34, national competitiveness in innovation output was distributed in a pattern among G20 nations. In 2009, only the US scored a bit than 80 points in competitiveness in innovation output, Japan a bit than 40 points, and the rest all below 40. Among them, three countries scored between 30-40 points, five between 20-30 points, five between 10-20 points, and four below 10 points.

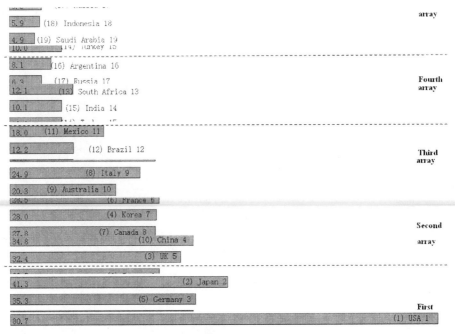

Fig. 34   Scores and Rankings of G20 National Competitiveness in Innovation Output
during 2001-2009

Note: In the figure, the left of the column are the scores, theare the rankings of the countries in competitiveness in
innovation output in 2009, and the figures in the parenthesis are the rankings of the countries in competitiveness in
innovation output in 2001.

ountries with higher national competitiveness in innovation output were mainly
developed countries, and in the first and second arrays except for China and Korea
developing countries.   that the developed countries higher sci-tech innovation output. The
developing countries very low in competitiveness in innovation output and developed
countries. Saudi Arabia No. 19 only scored 4.9 points, 6% of US No. 1; China scored the
highest point of 34.8 points, yet

(II) Analysis on the Variations in Rankings of G20 National Competitiveness in Innovation Output

According to Fig. 35, a comparison between 2009 and 2001, three countries in the
rankings of national competitiveness in innovation output. China by 6 places, Germany by
2 places, and India by 1 place. Ten countries unchanged in the rankings, Argentina, Brazil,
France, Indonesia, Japan, Mexico, Russia, Saudi Arabia, South Africa and the US. Six
countries in the rankings: Korea by 3 places; then the UK, by 2 places; and Australia,
Canada, Italy, and Turkey all by 2 places.

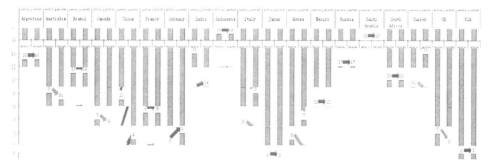

Fig. 35   Variations in Rankings of G20 National Competitiveness in Innovation Output
During 2001-2009

(III) Analysis on the Across-Array Variations and Motivation of G20 National Competitiveness in Innovation Output

As for the G20 national competitiveness in innovation output in 2009, the following countries were in the first array (No. 1-5): the US, Japan, Germany, China, the UK; the following in the second array (No. 6-10): France, Korea, Canada, Italy, Australia; the following in the third array (No. 11-15): Mexico, Brazil, South Africa, India, Turkey; and the following in the fourth array (No. 16-19): Argentina, Russia, Indonesia, Saudi Arabia.

As for the G20 national competitiveness in innovation output in 2001, the following countries were in the first array (No. 1-5): the US, Japan, the UK, Korea, Germany; the following in the second array (No. 6-10): France, Canada, Italy, Australia, China; the following in the third array (No. 11-15): Mexico, Brazil, South Africa, Turkey, India; and the following in the fourth array (No. 16-19): Argentina, Russia, Indonesia, Saudi Arabia.

During the evaluation period, some countries in competitiveness in innovation output. Korea fell from the first array to the second array, whereas China rose from the second array to the first array.

As for national competitiveness in innovation output as the secondary indicator, its variation is synthetically caused by the variations of tertiary indicators. Tab. 13 also lists the variations of seven tertiary indicators.

According to the above countries in the rankings of competitiveness in innovation output, Korea declined by 3 places in the ranking of competitiveness in innovation output mainly rankings of average patent authorizations of sci-tech personnel and the applications of American patents.

Whereas, China rose by 6 places mainly rankings of publications of scientific papers, high-tech products export, and proportion of high-tech products export in manufacturing.

It is from the above analysis and in combination with the fluctuations of the other countries in the rankings that the average patent authorizations of sci-tech personnel, the average paper publications of sci-tech personnel, and the high-tech products export have the greatest influence on competitiveness in innovation output and just these three indicators mainly embody the gaps of the countries in competitiveness in innovation output.

VII. Overall Evaluation and Comparative Analysis of G20 National Competitiveness in Innovation Sustainability

(I) Evaluation Results of G20 National Competitiveness in Innovation Sustainability

According to the indicator model and mathematical model of national competitiveness in innovation sustainability, evaluation is made for G20 national competitiveness in innovation sustainability during 2001-2009. Tab. 14 lists the rankings and variations in rankings of G20 national competitiveness in innovation sustainability during the evaluation period as well as the evaluation results of the seven tertiary indicators. Fig. 36, Fig. 37 and Fig. 38 show the rankings and variations in rankings of G20 national competitiveness in innovation sustainability during 2001-2009.

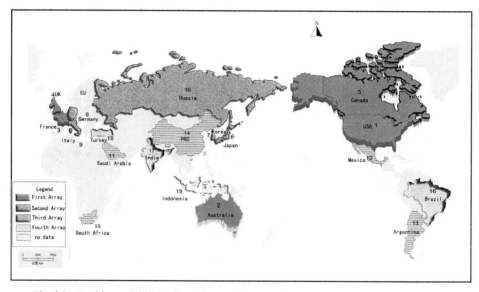

Fig. 36   Rankings of G20 National Competitiveness in Innovation Sustainability in 2001

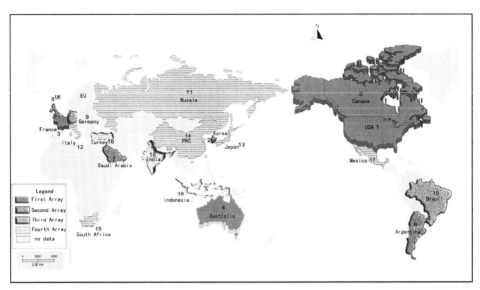

Fig. 37   Rankings of G20 National Competitiveness in Innovation Sustainability in 2009

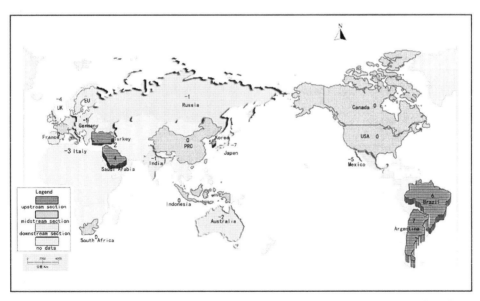

Fig. 38   Variations in Rankings of G20 National Competitiveness in Innovation Sustainability
during 2001-2009

Tab. 14 Evaluation and Comparison of G20 National Competitiveness in Innovation Sustainability during 2001-2009

Countries / Items	Argentina	Australia	Brazil	Canada	China	France	Germany	India	Indonesia	Italy	Japan	Korea	Mexico	Russia	Saudi Arabia	South Africa	Turkey	UK	USA	Highest scores	Lowest scores	Average scores
Overall variations in national competitiveness in innovation output during 2001-2009	13.0	-6.6	11.7	-3.0	-4.8	-2.6	-4.1	-4.8	5.4	-7.9	-18.3	7.5	-15.6	-6.1	3.7	-4.5	-1.4	-7.5	-4.2	-4.2	5.4	-2.6
	7	-2	6	0	0	0	-1	-1	0	-3	-7	5	-5	-1	4	0	2	-4	0	-	-	-
2001 Competitiveness in innovation sustainability	32.2	55.3	26.5	50.8	31.7	53.7	47.6	24.5	13.3	43.3	50.2	49.9	35.5	41.9	41.4	30.3	24.3	51.9	76.3	76.3	13.3	41.1
	13	2	16	5	14	3	8	17	19	9	6	7	12	10	11	15	18	4	1	-	-	-
Gross expenditure on public education	1.5	2.5	3.0	5.6	5.7	12.2	13.9	2.1	0.0	8.8	24.8	2.9	4.9	0.9	1.8	0.4	0.2	11.0	100.0	100.0	0.0	10.6
	15	12	10	8	7	4	3	13	19	6	2	11	9	16	14	17	18	5	1	-	-	-
Proportion of gross expenditure on public education in GDP	16.3	46.5	5.3	57.0	0.7	59.5	49.8	0.0	0.2	46.6	56.3	20.8	15.3	2.4	32.6	6.1	3.1	55.6	100.0	100.0	0.0	30.2
	11	8	14	3	17	2	6	19	18	7	4	10	12	16	9	13	15	5	1	-	-	-
Per capita expenditure on public education	43.4	45.3	26.4	49.1	5.4	58.5	37.1	15.6	0.0	45.3	20.8	30.2	50.9	11.3	100.0	52.8	3.8	39.6	60.4	100.0	0.0	36.6
	9	7	13	6	17	3	11	15	19	7	14	12	5	16	1	4	18	10	2	-	-	-
Proportion of persons of higher education	74.6	62.9	17.6	53.6	0.0	45.1	45.7	3.4	12.2	40.6	40.1	100.0	22.0	70.0	22.1	11.7	28.0	46.3	66.3	66.3	0.0	40.1
	2	5	15	6	19	9	8	18	16	10	11	1	14	3	13	17	12	7	4	-	-	-
Proportion of scientists and engineers	11.8	68.8	6.9	71.3	9.8	55.6	61.8	0.0	2.3	21.4	100.0	55.3	5.9	66.9	3.0	4.5	4.9	59.3	90.0	100.0	0.0	36.8
	11	4	13	3	12	8	6	19	18	10	1	9	14	5	17	16	15	7	2	-	-	-
Growth rate of sci-tech personnel	77.9	90.0	89.3	76.7	100.0	88.1	74.6	100.0	0.0	93.1	59.4	85.1	73.0	64.9	85.1	72.4	89.8	99.0	77.9	100.0	0.0	78.8
	12	5	7	13	1	8	14	1	19	4	18	10	15	17	9	16	6	3	11	-	-	-
Growth rate of sci-tech funds	0.0	71.2	37.2	42.7	100.0	56.5	50.6	50.2	78.3	47.4	50.4	54.8	76.3	76.9	45.1	64.2	40.1	52.8	39.8	100.0	0.0	54.4
	19	5	18	15	1	7	10	12	2	13	11	8	4	3	14	6	16	9	17	-	-	-
2009 Competitiveness in innovation sustainability	45.2	48.7	38.2	47.8	26.9	51.1	43.6	19.7	18.7	35.4	32.0	57.4	19.9	35.8	45.1	25.8	22.8	44.4	72.1	72.1	18.7	38.4
	6	4	10	5	14	3	9	18	19	12	13	2	17	11	7	15	16	8	1	-	-	-
Gross expenditure on public education	0.2	3.3	9.5	6.4	18.2	17.5	17.7	4.1	0.2	10.2	20.7	3.2	3.5	4.6	0.8	0.0	0.3	13.8	100.0	100.0	0.0	12.3
	17	13	8	9	3	5	4	11	18	7	2	14	12	10	15	19	16	6	1	-	-	-
Proportion of gross expenditure on public education in GDP	15.5	72.9	16.6	75.1	3.0	91.0	72.0	0.0	1.3	60.6	52.8	31.3	14.1	12.7	32.1	10.9	8.0	76.5	100.0	100.0	0.0	39.3
	12	5	11	4	17	2	6	19	18	7	8	10	13	14	9	15	16	3	1	-	-	-
Per capita expenditure on public education	96.7	53.2	93.0	69.1	6.1	100.0	57.5	15.6	5.2	54.3	18.4	68.0	67.0	44.6	100.0	91.7	0.0	94.9	94.8	100.0	0.0	59.5
	3	13	6	8	17	1	11	16	18	12	15	9	10	14	2	7	19	4	5	-	-	-
Proportion of persons of higher education	79.1	77.1	33.7	56.5	14.5	38.1	42.1	0.0	13.5	36.5	29.9	95.3	20.0	100.0	28.9	12.8	40.1	46.1	85.1	100.0	0.0	44.7
	4	5	12	6	16	10	8	19	17	11	13	2	15	1	14	18	9	7	3	-	-	-
Proportion of scientists and engineers	19.8	80.1	12.3	83.4	24.0	67.5	70.7	2.4	0.0	30.5	92.0	100.0	5.0	57.7	2.7	6.2	12.9	73.2	86.8	100.0	0.0	43.5
	12	5	14	4	11	8	7	18	19	10	2	1	16	9	17	15	13	6	3	-	-	-
Growth rate of sci-tech personnel	81.8	40.0	66.1	38.2	100.0	38.6	42.2	100.0	85.1	55.5	0.0	83.4	25.2	14.0	51.2	42.2	78.5	5.8	29.9	100.0	0.0	51.5
	5	12	7	14	1	13	11	1	3	8	19	4	16	17	9	10	6	18	15	-	-	-
Growth rate of sci-tech funds	23.2	14.4	36.6	5.9	22.3	4.6	2.8	15.8	25.4	0.0	9.9	20.4	4.5	17.3	100.0	16.7	19.9	0.5	8.0	100.0	0.0	18.3
	4	11	2	14	5	15	17	10	3	19	12	6	16	8	1	9	7	18	13	-	-	-

According to Tab. 14, in 2009, the highest score of competitiveness in innovation sustainability was 72.1 points, by 4.2 points over that in 2001; the lowest score was 18.7 points, by 5.4 points over that in 2001; the average score was 38.4 points, by 2.6 points over that in 2001. It indicate a rise in the level of G20 in national competitiveness in innovation sustainability. While in the tertiary indicators, the average scores of the growth rate of sci-tech funds dropped the most, by 36.1 points; then the growth rate of sci-tech personnel, by 27.3 points; the average scores of the other five indicators rose but minor fluctuations.

By comparing the variations in scores of G20 national competitiveness in innovation sustainability during 2001-2009, we conclude that the level of competitiveness in innovation sustainability and the principal factors for decline include the growth rate of sci-tech funds and the growth rate of sci-tech personnel.

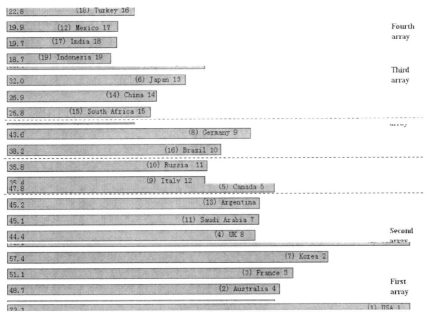

Fig. 39   Scores and Rankings of G20 National Competitiveness in Innovation Sustainability during 2001-2009

Note: In the figure, the left of the column are the scores, the are the rankings of the countries in competitiveness in innovation sustainability in 2009, and the figures in the parenthesis are the rankings of the countries in competitiveness in innovation sustainability in 2001.

According to Fig. 39, national competitiveness in innovation sustainability was distributed in a pattern among G20 nations. In 2009, only the US scored   than 70 points in competitiveness in innovation sustainability and the rest all below 60. Among them, two countries scored between 50-60 points, six between 40-50 points, four between 30-40 points, three between 20-30 points, three between 10-20 points, and none below 10 points.

ountries with higher competitiveness in innovation environment were mainly developed countries. Out of the countries in the first and second arrays, only three were developing countries and the rest were developed countries. that the developed countries did well in sustainable development of sci-tech innovation. eveloping countries generally lower in national competitiveness in innovation sustainability,   in which, Korea ranked No. 2 and Argentina ranked No. 6.

(II) Analysis on the Variations in Rankings of G20 National Competitiveness in Innovation Sustainability

According to Fig. 40, a comparison between 2009 and 2001, five countries in the rankings of national competitiveness in innovation sustainability. Argentina by 7 places, then Brazil by 6 places, and Korea, Saudi Arabia and Turkey by 5, 4 and 2 places respectively. Six countries unchanged in the rankings, Canada, China, France, Indonesia, South Africa and the US. Eight countries in the rankings: Japan the greatest by 7 places; then Mexico by 5 places, the UK, Italy and Australia by 4, 3 and 2 places respectively, and Germany, India and Russia all by 1 place.

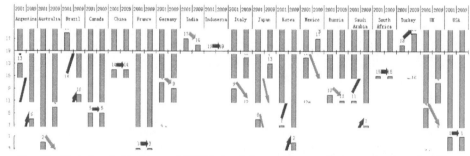

Fig. 40   Variations in Rankings of G20 National Competitiveness in Innovation Sustainability during 2001-2009

(III) Analysis on the Across-Array Variations and Motivation of G20 National Competitiveness in Innovation Sustainability

As for G20 national competitiveness in innovation sustainability in 2009, the following countries were in the first array (No. 1-5): US, Korea, France, Australia, Canada; the following in the second array (No. 6-10): Argentina, Saudi Arabia, the UK, Germany, Brazil; the following in the third array (No. 11-15): Russia, Italy, Japan, China, South Africa; and the following in the fourth array (No. 16-19): Turkey, Mexico, India, Indonesia.

As for G20 national competitiveness in innovation sustainability in 2001, the following countries were in the first array (No. 1-5): US, Australia, France, the UK, Canada; the following in the second array (No. 6-10): Japan, Korea, Germany, Italy, Russia; the following in the third array (No. 11-15): Saudi Arabia, Mexico, Argentina, China, South Africa; and the following in the fourth array (No. 16-19): Brazil, India, Turkey, Indonesia.

During the evaluation period, some countries acrossarray in competitiveness in innovation sustainability. The UK fell from the first array to the second array, Italy and Russia from the second array to the third array, Japan from the second array to the fourth array, and Mexico from the third array to the fourth array. Korea rose from the second array to the first array, Argentina and Saudi Arabia from the third array to the second array, and Brazil from the fourth array to the second array.

As for national competitiveness in innovation sustainability as the secondary indicator, its variation is synthetically caused by the variations of tertiary indicators. Tab. 14 also lists the variations of seven tertiary indicators.

According to the above countries in the rankings of competitiveness in innovation sustainability, the UK declined by 4 places in the ranking of competitiveness in innovation sustainability mainly from the in the rankings of growth rate of sci-tech funds, per capita expenditure on public education and growth rate of sci-tech personnel; Russia declined by 1 place mainly from the in the rankings of the growth rate of R&D funds and the proportion of scientists and engineers; Japan declined by 7 places mainly from the in the rankings of the proportion of gross expenditure on public education to GDP and the proportion of persons of higher education as well as the   in the rankings of the proportion of scientists and engineers, the growth rate of sci-tech personnel and the growth rate of sci-tech funds; Mexico declined by 5 places mainly from the in the rankings of the growth rate of sci-tech funds, per capita expenditure on public education and gross expenditure on public education.

Korea rose by 5 places mainly from the in rankings of the proportion of scientists and engineers and the growth rate of sci-tech personnel; Argentina rose by 7 places mainly from the in rankings of the growth rate of sci-tech funds, the growth rate of sci-tech personnel and per capita expenditure on public education; Saudi Arabia rose by 4 places mainly from in ranking of the growth rate of sci-tech funds; Brazil rose by 6 places mainly from the in rankings of the growth rate of sci-tech funds and per capita expenditure on public education.

It is from the above analysis that the growth rate of sci-tech funds, the growth rate of sci-tech personnel and per capita expenditure on public education have the greatest influence on competitiveness in innovation sustainability and just these three indicators mainly embody the gaps of the countries in competitiveness in innovation sustainability.

VIII. Principal Features and Variation Tendency of G20 NIC

The evaluation indicator system of NIC is composed of 1 primary indicator, 5 secondary indicators and 35 tertiary indicators, competitiveness in innovation base, competitiveness in innovation environment, competitiveness in innovation input, competitiveness in innovation output and competitiveness in innovation sustainability. It is a comprehensive evaluation system, in which, each part is closely connectedunique Accordingly, the evaluation results of NIC comprehensively represent the overall competitiveness and technological development level in five aspects innovation base, innovation environment, innovation input, innovation output and innovation sustainability. innovation competitiveness of each country show characteristics of variation and law of development, both the general rules universally existing in each country and the special rules determined by the different national conditions.

Through evaluation on G20 NIC during 2001-2009, this report objectively and comprehensively analyses the level, gap and situation of G20 NIC, profoundly understands and grasps these rules and characteristics, recognizes the essence and inherent features of the variations of NIC. It is of great significance to research and find out the right approach, method and countermeasure to enhance NICcountries to enhance their NIC and take corresponding measures as per the specific conditions and special national conditions of countr.

(I) NIC is Affected by a Variety of Innovation Factors

NIC is a comprehensive concept with rich connotation,integrating many concepts of national innovation, and is also a comprehensive indicator covering five aspects: innovation base, innovation environment, innovation input, innovation output and innovation sustainability. These five factorsto enhance the labor productivity, reduce resource consumption and production cost, and realize sustainable development of the econom comprehensively reflect and influence NIC by multiple means of economics and administration.

Tab. 15 lists the rankings and variations of G20 NIC during 2001-2009. Based on it, we conclude that, during 2001-2009, the overall rankings of the countries in innovation competitiveness (primary indicator) are relatively steady with minor fluctuation. Out of the five countries in the first array, four. The case is similar the second, third and fourth arrays. Most countries always   The of the ranking in NIC indicates to some degree that innovation competitiveness advantage of a country is affected by many innovation factors.

Tab. 15   Variations in Rankings of G20 NIC during 2001-2009

Regions	2009	2001	Section	Regions	2009	2001	Section	Regions	2009	2001	Section	Regions	2009	2001	Section
USA	1	1	First array	UK	6	3	Second array	Saudi Arabia	11	11	Third array	Mexico	16	14	Fourth array
Japan	2	2		Canada	7	7		Russia	12	10		Argentina	17	17	
Germany	3	4		Australia	8	8		Brazil	13	15		India	18	18	
France	4	5		Italy	9	9		Turkey	14	16		Indonesia	19	19	
Korea	5	6		China	10	12		South Africa	15	13					

During the evaluation period, there was no major fluctuation for the overall variation in rankings of NIC. No country Relative to primary indicators, there were greater variations for secondary indicators, for instance, in rankings of competitiveness in innovation environment, Saudi Arabia   up by 8 places; in ranking of competitiveness in innovation sustainability, Argentina and Japan Argentina up by 7 places Japan down by 7 places.

According to the variations in rankings of the secondary indicators, Russia rose by 2 places in both te competitiveness in innovation base and competitiveness in innovation environment; unchanged in competitiveness in innovation output; but by 2 places and 1 place in competitiveness in innovation input and competitiveness in innovation sustainability respectively thus overall ranking dropped greatly and innovation competitiveness by 2 places. China, rose by 3, 5and 6 places in competitiveness in innovation base, competitiveness in innovation input and competitiveness in innovation output; but by 1 place in competitiveness in innovation environment and unchanged in competitiveness in innovation sustainability thus the overall ranking only by 2 places. that innovation competitiveness was affected by five secondary indicators, all of which should be paidattention. The fluctuation of one secondary indicator may not be reflected in the primary indicators, but competitiveness and result in the of overall NIC. Only when the indicatorsoverall advantage in competition stand out. crucial importance for the analysis of secondary and tertiary indicators. Because, merely the primary indicators, we may not analyze the internal factors and fluctuation characteristics whose essence and fluctuation are likely to be hidden by the appearance. However, by strengthening the analysis of secondary and tertiary indicators, we make further analysis on the essential characteristics of innovation competitivenessreal reason

To sum up, is a process of long-term accumulation, which Of course, ach country should make constant effort. Those ranked front should keep up the good work, their competitive advantages, and avoid any dropping tendency; those ranked behind should take effective measures to modify the present situation and strive for more advantages in competition.

(II) The Integral Level of NIC Shows a Rising Tendency with Greater Gaps Among the Sections

During 2001-2009, the integral level of G20 NIC showed a rising overall average score 36.8 points from 35.0 points (as shown in Fig. 41). level of G20 NIC rose to some extent, which closely connected with the increasing attention and unremitting effort of in sci-tech innovation.

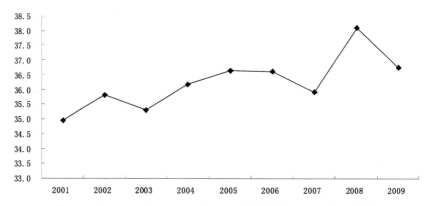

Fig. 41   Variation in Average Scores of G20 NIC during 2001-2009

According to the variations of secondary indicators in innovation competitiveness, the advancement of innovation competitiveness was mainly in scores in competitiveness in innovation base, competitiveness in innovation environment and competitiveness in innovation input. During 2001-2009, the average scores rose by 4.5 points, 6.7 points and 1.3 points respectively. these countries did well in the aspects of innovation base, innovation environment and innovation input and thus the level. three indicators, though the scores in competitiveness in innovation output and competitiveness in innovation sustainability, the overall scores of innovation competitiveness rose.

According to the fluctuation of countries in innovation competitiveness, out of the G20 nations, only by 3.2 points on average; fourteen by 3.6 points on average. Overall, the number of rising countries was than that of countries and the overall average rising score exceeded the overall score. Consequently, the overall score of innovation competitiveness showed a rising tendency.

Another characteristic of the variations for G20 NIC is the greater gaps of innovation competitiveness among the regions. Tab. 16 lists the average scores of G20 in the six continents in NIC as well as the numbers of the countries in the first and second arrays.

Based on the scores, among the countries of G20 in North America, South America, Europe, Asia, Africa and Oceania, those in North America scored the highest point and Africa scored the lowest the former 2.4 times of the latter.

According to the of the countries in the first and second arrays, in 2009, there are more countries Europe and Asia, two countries of both continents stayed in the first array and one in the second array, holding a bigger share in the total number. However, according to the proportions of the total countries of each continent in the arrays, in the first array, Europe held the biggest proportion, then North America and Asia, and South America, Africa and Oceania all in the second array, Oceania held the biggest proportion, then North America, Europe and Asia, and South America and Africa both   Consequently, on the whole, North America was the most competitive in innovation, Oceania, and then Europe, Asia, South America and Africa.

Tab. 16   Average Scores of G20 in the Six Continents in NIC as well as the Numbers and Proportions of the Countries in the First and Second Arrays

Indicators Regions	Average Scores		Numbers and proportions of the countries in the first array		Numbers and proportions of the countries in the second array	
	2009	2001	2009	2001	2009	2001
North America (3 countries)	50.6	52.3	1(33.3%)	1(33.3%)	1(33.3%)	1(33.3%)
South America (2 countries)	22.4	17.5	0(0.0%)	0(0.0%)	0(0.0%)	0(0.0%)
Europe (5 countries)	39.8	38.6	2(40.0%)	3(60.0%)	1(20.0%)	2(40.0%)
Asia (6 countries)	32.5	28.3	2(33.3%)	1(16.7%)	1(16.7%)	0(0.0%)
Africa (1 country)	20.7	21.9	0(0.0%)	0(0.0%)	0(0.0%)	0(0.0%)
Oceania (1 country)	46.9	44.2	0(0.0%)	0(0.0%)	1(100.0%)	1(100.0%)

Note: The figures in parenthesis are the proportions of the countries in the first or the second arrays of the total countries in each continent.

(III) Competitiveness in Innovation Base is the Most Direct Embodiment of NIC

Tab. 17 lists the relative coefficients of the scores in G20 NIC and the scores of the five secondary indicators competitiveness during 2001-2009.

Tab. 17   Relative Coefficients of the Scores in Innovation Competitiveness and the Elements

Years	Competitiveness in innovation base	Competitiveness in innovation environment	Competitiveness in innovation input	Competitiveness in innovation output	Competitiveness in innovation sustainability
2001	0.964	0.920	0.959	0.942	0.948
2002	0.964	0.922	0.960	0.936	0.947
2003	0.956	0.917	0.960	0.929	0.928
2004	0.954	0.925	0.956	0.908	0.932
2005	0.951	0.917	0.941	0.910	0.934
2006	0.953	0.914	0.935	0.903	0.881
2007	0.947	0.900	0.933	0.893	0.857
2008	0.948	0.851	0.928	0.899	0.818
2009	0.949	0.806	0.933	0.883	0.843

Based on Tab. 17, the secondary indicator with the biggest relative coefficient to the scores of innovation competitiveness was competitiveness in innovation base, competitiveness in innovation input, far beyond the other three secondary indicators. Based on the variations in each year, the relative coefficients of each indicator all, but competitiveness in innovation environment, competitiveness in innovation output and competitiveness in innovation sustainability at very high rates, all below 90%, and competitiveness in innovation base even reached 0.95. It indicated that competitiveness in innovation base is the most direct embodiment as well as the foundation of innovation competitiveness. That is to say, in the process of sci-tech innovation in future, countries should lay solid foundation of innovation, provide basic guarantee, and enhance competitiveness in innovation base, which is the root to improve the innovation competitiveness level.

Fig. 42 and Fig. 43 show the relation in scores between G20 NIC and competitiveness in innovation base in 2001 and 2009 respectively. In the figures, letters are used to mark the positions of the countries in the two-dimensional diagram: AR: Argentina; AU: Australia; BR: Brazil; CA: Canada; CN: China; FR: France; DE: Germany; IN: India; ID: Indonesia; IT: Italy; JP: Japan; KR: Korea; MX: Mexico; RU: Russia; SA: Saudi Arabia; ZA: South Africa; TR: Turkey; UK: the UK; US: the US (similar hereinafter).

According to Fig. 42 and Fig. 43, a strong positive was reflected between the scores of competitiveness in innovation base and innovation competitiveness. ountries with higher scores of competitiveness in innovation base also score higher in innovation competitiveness. It be   that the G20 nations were divided into three groups. The first group was the US, high in the scores of both competitiveness in innovation base and innovation competitiveness far beyond the other countries. The second group included seven developed countriesUK, France, Germany, etc., whose scores in the competitiveness in innovation base were, far beyond the developing countries and far below USinnovation competitiveness were also. The third group included 11 developing countries China, Korea, etc., whose scores were relatively low in both competitiveness in innovation base and innovation competitiveness (except for Korea). It also indicate that competitiveness in innovation base was the foundation and the most direct embodiment of innovation competitiveness.

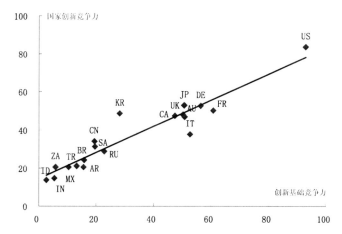

Fig. 42 Relational Graph of Scores between Competitiveness in Innovation Base and Innovation Competitiveness in 2001

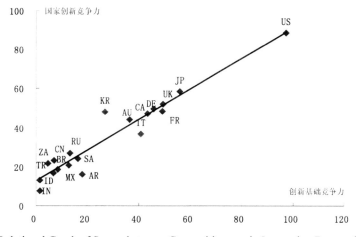

Fig. 43 Relational Graph of Scores between Competitiveness in Innovation Base and Innovation Competitiveness in 2009

(IV) NIC is Closely Related to the Economic Development Level of a Country

Since development stages, therather big gaps in economic and social development level and huge gaps in NIC. conomic development and innovation competitiveness are closely related.

Fig. 44 shows the relation between G20 NIC and GDP in 2009; Fig. 45 shows the relation between G20 NIC and per capita GDP in 2009.

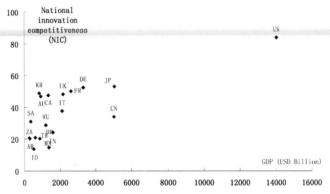

Fig. 44   Relation between NIC and GDP

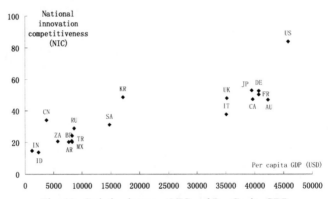

Fig. 45   Relation between NIC and Per Capita GDP

Fig. 44 shows between economic scale (GDP) and innovation competitiveness. innovation competitiveness economic strength was the important foundation of innovation competitiveness. Among them, the US GDP and score in innovation competitiveness were all far beyond the other countries. However, this For instance, the GDP of China ranked No. 3, close to Japan No. 2, but the innovation competitiveness of was far below Japan and even below countries with GDP the UK, France and Germany. On the contrary, Korea,

Australia and Canada, though GDP, boasts high innovation competitiveness, far beyond many other countries GDP, such as China, Russia, Brazil and Italy.

Fig. 45 shows the relation between NIC and economic development level more clearly. It from this figure that there is a linear relation between NIC and per capita GDP. The more per capita GDP, the higher the economic development level is and the higher the score in innovation competitiveness is. his figure naturally divide G20 nations into two groups: oneeight developed countriesthe US and Japan, all with per capita GDPs exceeding USD 35,000 and higher scores in the innovation competitiveness; the other eleven developing countries in Asia and South America, Korea and Saudi Arabia, all   per capita GDPs below USD 10,000 and lower scores in innovation competitiveness.

(V) by Constantly Optimizing the Indicator Structure, Consolidating the Strength and Supporting the Advantage Indicators, Increasing the Rising and Decreasing the Dropping Indicators.

Tab. 18 lists the strength and weakness of the tertiary indicators of G20 NIC in 2009 to reflect the strength and weakness of the indicators for competitiveness as well as the influence of theon the innovation competitiveness. Tab. 8-5 lists the variation tendency in rankings of the tertiary indicators of G20 NIC in 2009 to reflect the influence of the fluctuations in rankings and the competitiveness indicators on the ranking of innovation competitiveness.

According to Tab. 18, countries in the first array hold large proportion of the strength and advantage indicators, the proportions of the US and France over 90%, and the average proportion of the first array is 85.1%; in the second array, the UK and Canada also hold rather large proportion, both over 80%, and the average proportion of the second array is 69.1%; in the third array, the proportions are rather low in strength and advantage indicators, all below 50%, and the average proportion is 31.4%; in the fourth array, the proportions are very low, all below 25%, and the average proportion is 17.9%.

Generally speaking, the countries with larger proportions of strength and advantage indicators higher competitive advantage in innovation competitiveness, e.g. the US. Of course, there are also special cases Italy. The proportion of Italy is 68.6%, but the proportion of it weakness indicators is also high11.4%, far beyond other developed countries, dragging the overall ranking of it. Accordingly, besides the proportions of strength and advantage indicators, the proportion of weakness indicators should also be taken into consideration. During the development process in future, countries should take pointed and effective measures, continue consolidating strength indicators and actively supporting and transforming medium indicators and advantage indicators to strength indicators, constantly optimiz the composition structure of indicators, to consolidate and enhance the innovation competitiveness and maintain innovation competitiveness.

Tab. 18　Structure in Strength and Weakness of the Tertiary Indicators of G20 NIC in 2009

Items Regions	Numbers and proportions of strength indicators	Numbers and proportions of advantage indicators	Numbers and proportions of medium indicators	Numbers and proportions of weakness indicators	Totals and proportions of strength and advantage indicators	Overall rankings	Sections
USA	28	5	2	0	33	1	
	80.0%	14.3%	5.7%	0.0%	94.3%		
Japan	17	9	8	1	26	2	
	48.6%	25.7%	22.9%	2.9%	74.3%		
Germany	19	10	5	1	29	3	First array
	54.3%	28.6%	14.3%	2.9%	82.9%		
France	15	17	2	1	32	4	
	42.9%	48.6%	5.7%	2.9%	91.4%		
Korea	14	15	5	1	29	5	
	40.0%	42.9%	14.3%	2.9%	82.9%		
UK	13	17	3	2	30	6	
	37.1%	48.6%	8.6%	5.7%	85.7%		
Canada	13	16	5	1	29	7	
	37.1%	45.7%	14.3%	2.9%	82.9%		
Australia	13	10	11	1	23	8	Second array
	37.1%	28.6%	31.4%	2.9%	65.7%		
Italy	5	19	7	4	24	9	
	14.3%	54.3%	20.0%	11.4%	68.6%		
China	14	1	8	12	15	10	
	40.0%	2.9%	22.9%	34.3%	42.9%		
Saudi Arabia	6	8	6	15	14	11	
	17.1%	22.9%	17.1%	42.9%	40.0%		
Russia	5	12	13	5	17	12	
	14.3%	34.3%	37.1%	14.3%	48.6%		
Brazil	2	9	22	2	11	13	Third array
	5.7%	25.7%	62.9%	5.7%	31.4%		
Turkey	2	4	21	8	6	14	
	5.7%	11.4%	60.0%	22.9%	17.1%		
South Africa	1	6	10	18	7	15	
	2.9%	17.1%	28.6%	51.4%	20.0%		
Mexico	0	8	18	9	8	16	
	0.0%	22.9%	51.4%	25.7%	22.9%		
Argentina	6	0	11	18	6	17	Fourth array
	17.1%	0.0%	31.4%	51.4%	17.1%		
India	2	5	14	14	7	18	
	5.7%	14.3%	40.0%	40.0%	20.0%		
Indonesia	4	0	5	26	4	19	
	11.4%	0.0%	14.3%	74.3%	11.4%		

Note: As for the two lines of numbers corresponding to each region, the upper line refers to the numbers of the indicators and the lower line refers to the proportions of the indicators to the total indicators.

Similarly, according to Tab. 19, we conclude that, as for the countries the proportion

Tab. 19 Structure of the Variation Tendency in Rankings of the Tertiary Indicators of G20 NIC in 2009

Items Regions	Numbers of rising indicators	Numbers of staying indicators	Numbers of dropping indicators	Variation tendency	Overall rankings	Variations in overall rankings	Arrays
USA	5	15	15	Unchanged	1	0	First array
	14.3%	42.9%	42.9%				
Japan	5	13	17	Unchanged	2	0	
	14.3%	37.1%	48.6%				
Germany	12	11	12	Rising	3	1	
	34.3%	31.4%	34.3%				
France	11	7	17	Rising	4	1	
	31.4%	20.0%	48.6%				
Korea	13	10	12	Rising	5	1	
	37.1%	28.6%	34.3%				
UK	9	1	25	Dropping	6	-3	Second array
	25.7%	2.9%	71.4%				
Canada	8	6	21	Unchanged	7	0	
	22.9%	17.1%	60.0%				
Australia	10	12	13	Unchanged	8	0	
	28.6%	34.3%	37.1%				
Italy	8	15	12	Unchanged	9	0	
	22.9%	42.9%	34.3%				
China	22	6	7	Rising	10	2	
	62.9%	17.1%	20.0%				
Saudi Arabia	10	18	7	Unchanged	11	0	Third array
	28.6%	51.4%	20.0%				
Russia	17	5	13	Dropping	12	-2	
	48.6%	14.3%	37.1%				
Brazil	18	7	10	Rising	13	2	
	51.4%	20.0%	28.6%				
Turkey	18	11	6	Rising	14	2	
	51.4%	31.4%	17.1%				
South Africa	8	10	17	Dropping	15	-2	
	22.9%	28.6%	48.6%				
Mexico	6	10	19	Dropping	16	-2	Fourth array
	17.1%	28.6%	54.3%				
Argentina	10	9	16	Unchanged	17	0	
	28.6%	25.7%	45.7%				
India	16	10	9	Unchanged	18	0	
	45.7%	28.6%	25.7%				
Indonesia	15	12	8	Unchanged	19	0	
	42.9%	34.3%	22.9%				

Note: As for the two lines of numbers corresponding to each region, the upper line refers to the numbers of the indicators and the lower line refers to the proportions of the indicators to the total indicators.

of rising indicators larger than thindicators, innovation competitiveness will show rising tendency; Of course, there are also special cases, The proportion of rising indicators is only 14.3% and the one of dropping indicators is 42.9%, with a difference of 28.6%. However, because many of its indicators unchanged in the rankings,up to 42.9%, and theand the other countries, the USOn the whole, countries with larger proportion of rising indicators will in the ranking of innovation competitiveness, but concrete analysis should be made according to specific circumstances. For instance, the rising or dropping fluctuation in the rankings of indicators should be taken into consideration to analyze the rise and drop in the ranking of innovation competitiveness. During the development process in future, countries should exert to increase the numbers of the rising indicators and decrease the numbers of the dropping indicators, and thus they effectively facilitate the enhancement of level of innovation competitiveness.

IX. Strategic Principles, Strategic Orientation and Strategic Countermeasures to Enhance Innovation Competitiveness of G20 Countries

(I) Strategic Principles

1. Integration of technology innovation and institutional innovation. We give full play to the fundamental role of focus on the establishment of business-technological R&D and innovation, deepen sci-tech institutional reform, enhance the internationalization level of technolog development, promote independent innovation in a more open environment, technolog innovation with institutional innovation, establishment of new systems and mechanisms catering to the needs of market economy and the development of world technolog innovation, eliminate institutional barriers inhibiting the enhancement of NIC, further narrow the gap between technology and economy, optimize the allocation of technolog innovation resources, and further enhance national competitiveness in technology innovation.

2. Government guidance and the integration of research. We national innovation capability as the strategic base for sci-tech development, further strengthen government guidance and coordination, integrate technolog innovation with green development, coordinated development, harmonious development and inclusive development, embark on the track of innovation and endogenous-growth-driven economic and social development, address bottleneck problems encounterzed during the integration of research, coordinate the integration of innovation resources, and facilitate the formation of national technolog

innovation system on business and

3. Integration of independent innovation and technology. We target the edge of world sci-tech development, implement fundamental research and studies on   technologies, encourage continue to increase technolog accumulations, further enhance national independent innovation capability, take independent innovation as a key part to adjustoptimize our industrial structure and transform the development model, enhance the technical level of industries through independent innovation, achieve effective integration of independent innovation and technology, scientifically select the model of technology innovation, address key scientific and technological challenges which are crucial to the future development of our country, take technology as an important approach to enhance the capability of independent innovation, and emphasize further innovation and integrated innovation the digestion and absorption of introduced technologies.

4. Integration of key breakthroughs and overall advancement. According to the key needs of economic and social development, we must resolve and acquire key technologies, promote the commercialization of new technologies, accelerate the culture and development of strategic and emerging industries, and support the revival of key industries and the upgrade of traditional industries. In line with giving priority to leading industries and critical common technologies and highlighting technology and product innovation, we must select key technologies which can best demonstrate the comparative and competitive advantage of the country and great market potential and potential   industrial development and achiev development, promote the breakthrough in key technologies, and make breakthrough in common and core technologies. We also properly organize and centralize technological resources to tackle key technological challenges and achieve development of technological level and industrial scale, comprehensively enhance NIC.

5. Integration of -centered and market-oriented. The market must be considered as the basic starting point to enhance NIC and   must play principal role in industrial technology innovation activities, truly make business thetechnolog innovation, investment, R&D and benefits. This will help improve the market allocation of technolog innovation resources, facilitate the advancement of technological capacity and significantly enhance NIC.

(II) Strategic Orientation

Currently, technolog maintaining swift development throughout the world, ontemporary technologtrend of integration, internationalizationand accelerated development and changing the world economic structure and social development landscape, and pushing the world into a new era economic and social development is driven by technologies. Given the new situation, G20 countries must further and properly identify the objectives of their technology development strategy from the perspective of national strategy, improve national innovation policies, address prominent problems during technolog development, and give full play to the supporting and leading role of technology in economic and social development.

1. Inaugurate a new era of knowledge economy and innovation economy in the 21st entury

Without doubt, technolog development will certainly profound human society in the 21st entury. At this historical stage of great transitions, all nations, particularly G20 countries, will be faced with a great development opportunity. In the meantime, technolog development will also bring great changes to worldwide economic and social development. Since the global financial crisis in 2008, technolog innovation has increasingly play critical role in supporting the revival of key industries and effectively respond to international financial crisis. Technology will become the   social development and growth of knowledge economy and innovation economy, thus leading to the reform of social structure and the sustainable development human society. Therefore, fac the new situation, we must closely rely on the latest technologies and knowledge to give full play to their power. iffusion and penetration of knowledge into economy will help establish and inaugurate the new era of knowledge economy and innovation economy, so that the conflicts and disputes between people, between countries and between human and nature will be resolved and new and advanced human civilization will be built.

2. Strengthen innovation and industrialization capability with respect to strategic high-end technologies

Currently, world technolog development continual rise of emerging disciplines and inter-disciplines, continual acceleration of technolog upgrade, continual shortening of industrialization of scientific and technological achievements, and continual emergence of high and new technologies, products and industries. Nowadays, with abundant intelligence resources and technological basis, G20 nations can significantly increase R&D inputs, strengthen R&D deployment of core and key technologies, win over technolog innovation talents, and take the preemptive opportunity and initiative to develop strategic emerging industries. On the basis of absorbing technological achievements, G20 nations must greater breakthroughs in key fields with comparative advantages, allow development of social technology and social productive force. In the G20 countries, by following the pulse of world technology development and systematically integrating and optimizing sci-tech resources, strengthen innovation and industrialization capability with respect to strategic high-In the field of information technology, greater efforts be made by G20 nations to develop the new operating systems, the corresponding software platforms and embedded CPU chips, promptly enhance the core competitiveness of their information industry. In the field of biotechnology, the allocation of biological species resources shall be fully optimized and R&D on functional gene sequences, biological information, biological pharmaceuticals, and biological breeding be carried out, a place in the biotechnology and bio-pharmaceutical. In the field of modern transportation, we must accelerate the industrialization and scale demonstration of complete vehicle system and technological achievements and quicken the R&D and promotion of new-energy vehicles.

3. Coordinate the development of population, resources and environment

We must coordinate the relation between human and nature and pursue the co-evolution of human and nature. This is the for resolving contradictions between human development and nature, as well as the premise for standardizing technolog development. Since science is a "double-edged sword" to achieve sustainable development of technology, economy and society, a development strategy must be established. We must not only consider the way of human development, but also strictly control technological inventions and their applications according to the assimilative capacity of resources and environment. New technological inventions must consider impact on the sustainable development of society, while the application of technological achievements must also consider the capacity of ecological environment and adhere to the unification of technical, economic, ecological and social benefits.

At present, the world is at an important stage of in-depth industrialization, informatization, urbanization, marketization, and internationalization. Assuring and promoting sustainable economic and social development will become a vital objective in the development strategy of all nations. Energy is of important significance to all nationshave taken technolog development related to energy supply and energy consumption as an important development strategy. In particular, "9.11" incident, to meet the growing need for energy and to assure national security, all nations are paying closer attention to energy. G20 nations, according to their actual energy reserves, focus on the development and promotion of clean coal technology, raw coal liquefaction technologyAccording to the present status and trend of lake and water pollution, key efforts be made to develop polluted water restoration technologies, safe drinking water technologies, and sewage treatment technologies and facilities, so as to provide technical support for addressing critical water pollution problems. In the future, G20 nations pay further attention to the crucial technological challenges in the fields of population and health, resource development and utilization, environmental protection and ecological rectification, disaster relief and prevention, urban-rural construction and dwelling environment, comprehensively enhance the living standard and lay a solid technological foundation for the harmonious development between human and nature/environment.

4. Strengthen talent strategy and nurture a great number of innovative and high-class technical talents

Schultz, a famous development economist believes that "the decisive factors of production in improving the welfare of poor people are NOT space, energy, and; the decisive factor is improvement in population quality" alent development strategy everything is done by human. Technolog cannot achieve greater progress without talents, which come first. To become invincible in scientific research and technological competition, there must be a group of top-class scientists and engineering experts who can master and control new technologies. While paying special attention to the accelerated nurture of professional talents, we must also train composite talents who can operation, managementhigh and new technologies. For G20 nations, the most imminent need is to give full play to the role of existing talents by constantly improving "talent environment" establishing the mechanisms for attracting and nurturing talents, and encouraging more and better talents to participate in technological innovation. A favorable environment attractive to high-class talents is critical to the development of intellectual and non-intellectual factors. Innovative talents are not born naturally. There must be a scientific innovation talent nurturing systemOnly by implementing a strategy to nurture innovation talents can we occupy a commanding achieve development of economy and society.

5. Deepen technological institutional reform and establish a sound national innovation system

China's former president Jiang Zeming pointed out that "innovation is the soul for the progress of a nation and the inexhaustible driver to national prosperity and growth" The national economy in the 21st entury will certainly be dominated by technolog innovation. G20 is the important carrier of developed countries and emerging market countries in the world, its member countries must acquire new advantages and a leading competitive position through continual innovation. At present, the main conflict in the supply and demand of technolog is the scant demand for technologies in the field of social production. Therefore, the focus of technological institutional reform target instead of merely improving technology supply and the technological circle itself. We must promote institutional and organizational innovation which may help increase the need for technolog, continue to improve technology supply, and deepen the reform inside the technological circle, truly promote coordinated development of construction and technology.

An important strategic to occupy the commanding technolog development is to deepen and improve the national innovation system, which is a network system consisting of knowledge innovation and technolog innovation related institutions and organizations. The technolog innovation system is the core of national innovation system. intended to transform scientific and technological achievements into real productivity. In the near future, G20 nations must, promote the tight integration of research, accelerate the circulation of innovation resources among respective countries, jointly tackle key technological challenges through international sci-tech projects, vigorously promote integration and sharing of technological resources, and enhance sustainable technology innovation capability.

(III) Strategic Countermeasures

Innovation is the core of national competitiveness, key choice of all nations to respond to future challenges and the main strategy for future technology development. The experiences of world sci-tech development us that: only with robust innovation capability can one nation take the   international competition. Nowadays, technologies are experiencing booming development and innovations emerge quickly. The world is preparing for new and key breakthroughs. ompetition in overall national strength among countries has turned out to be competition in innovation competitiveness, which has become the main driver economic development and the progress of human civilization. In the present world, those who master advanced technologies and accumulate greater innovation competitiveness will take the lead in economic and social development. Therefore, to deepen the strategic of G20 NIC, we must start from the levels of international, national, industrial

1. International level

nnovation competition between countries or regions appears mainly as the competition to take the in the new round of sci-tech revolution and to international status. The conflicting but unified relationship of both cooperation and competition has jointly promoted the progressive development of economy and society. Therefore, facing key challenges in technology development, the only choice to strengthen international cooperation on innovation, actively build the carrier and promote the free circulation of knowledge and innovation resources.

(1) To establish innovation and promote the free circulation and sharing of innovation resources

The "Innovation Union" is one of the seven flagship initiatives of the Europe 2020 strategy. As a new model to continuously carry out innovation activities in the era of increasingly global competition, it represents an aggressive, comprehensive and strategic innovation aim to sustain the economic base and support the original living standard and social pattern through more strategic innovation while shrinking public budget, population aging and increasingly global competition. transform the way of development, rebuild advantage in international competition and elevat international status have become the important strategic tasks of countries and regions, while innovation is undoubtedly the most important strategic choice. With the deepening of innovation exchanges and cooperation between countries and regions, gradual unification of innovation and the increasing possibility of innovation resource sharing, establishing "Innovation Union" has become an important choice for respective countries and regions to enhance their NIC. "Innovation Union" can be jointly formed by countries or regions which are connected in innovation based on the same innovation objectives and the idea of innovation resource sharing, such as the win-win union between technologically developed countries, the complementary union between developed countries and underdeveloped countries, the improvement union between underdeveloped countries, and the catch-up union between emerging countries. Inside the innovation union, all countries/regions will strengthen the connection between their innovation systems, jointly invest in education, R&D, innovation and information communication technologies, freely circulate innovation resources and knowledge within the union, gather advantageous resources to jointly tackle key social challenges related to energy security, transportation, climate change, and resource utilization efficiency, and jointly promote innovation commercialization. Efficient and simplified intra-union coordination mechanism and the unified policy framework be formed to facilitate the flexible operation of

(2) To enhance the internationalization level of research activities

Strengthening international innovation cooperation and exchange and embarking on the track of innovation internationalization certainly be the strategic choice of all nations global technolog development. Only by building a cooperative innovation platform with a global view, building a more open innovation environment and introducing global innovation resources can innovation activities better adapt to the trend of international innovation development. At present, global challenges as climate change, energy, environment, food safety, and the prevention control of major diseases are testing the innovation capability of respective countries and regions. International sci-tech researchneeded to tackle the bottleneck problems inhibiting the growth of world economy. We proactively enhance the internationalization level of scientific innovation activities, encourage local R&D institutes to enter partnerships with world-leading R&D institutions, and actively promote the construction of international sci-tech cooperation bases, regional sci-tech cooperation centers and We must adhere to the organic integration of "going abroad" and "attracting in" by encouraging local enterprises or R&D institutes to set up R&D institutionsproactively attract world-leading scientists to support local innovation initiatives. We take an active part in multilateral sci-tech cooperation and key research projects and constantly improve our international innovation status and discourse in innovation standard formulation. We also consolidate and deepen inter-government sci-tech cooperation, expand the fields of cooperation and implement key innovation initiatives under a flexible and cooperation mechanism. Through international innovation exchange and cooperation, the capacity of respective countries and regions in original innovation, integrated innovation and introduction-absorption innovation will be enhanced significantly and new innovation advantages will be developed.

(3) To actively nurture world-leading multinational companies and educational institutions and build influential international innovation carriers

   and educational institutions are the fundamental carriers for countries and regions to carry out innovation. As the key player of innovation, the most active factor in the innovation initiative of a country/region. In the international innovation competition, multinational companies are undoubtedly playing an important role. The strength of multinational companies in innovation not only indicates the innovation level of a country, but also to innovation trend in certain fields. For example, the have benefited from the support of extensive multinational companies, such as Dell, Microsoft, Apple and Intel in the high-tech industry, Boeing, 3M and GE in the traditional manufacturing industry, FedEx, McDonald's and Starbucks. Innovation is the core competitiveness of these renowned multinational companies and has underpinned their development for over a century. All countries and regions are expected to vigorously nurture multinational companies (especially large-sized ones) and encourage/support them to carry out innovation initiatives. World-leading education system and institutions are important carriers for nurturing innovation talents and attracting elite respective industries. All countries and regions manage to build universities with international influence, proactively promote the reform of education system, construct an open education system, attract outstanding talent throughout the world, and develop a favorable circulation mechanism for innovation and talent nurturing, to provide inexhaustible talent resources for carrying out sustainable innovation.

2. National level

(1) To improve the innovation system and strengthen innovation inputs

echnical advancements contribut over 70% of GDP, innovation productivity contribut over 50% of GDP, R&D spending account for over 2% of GDP, and less than 30% dependence on foreign technologies. Taking 2007 as the example, the R&D spending of Ureached USD 368.27 billion, 2.68% of GDP, with per capita R&D spending hitting USD 1265.7. contrary, China's R&D spending reached USD 48.77 billion, 1.49% of GDP, with per capita R&D spending USD 37. According to the proportion of R&D spending to GDP in China's R&D spending must increase by USD 39.2 billion to keep up with and the per capita R&D spending USD 66.6. According to the per capita R&D spending in China's R&D spending must increase by USD 1,623.6 billion to keep up with and the proportion of R&D spending to GDP exceed 50% .

R&D spending assures the smooth implementation of innovation activities, and gradually increasing the proportion of R&D spending to GDP be the primary goal of G20 nations in sci-tech development. To accomplish this goal, we must first give full play to the guiding role of national policies, promulgate laws the innovation policies and various industrial/financial policies, and assure normal implementation of innovation activities from both legislation and policy. Further, we must attach greater importance to research activities and increase capital inputs. Not only we increase the funding of fundamental researches carried out universities/colleges, but also strengthen the support and encouragement of innovative enterprises and the construction of intermediary service institutions. In addition, we broaden innovation funding from multiple aspects, try to utilize the capital market to construct diversified investment and financ models, and establish

(2) To promote the construction of national innovation system and develop the mechanism for organic integration of research

The national innovation system requires businesses, universities/colleges, R&D institutions, and government to interact around technolog innovation, to promote the production, dissemination and application of knowledge and innovation and eventually enhance national innovation capability and comprehensive strength. Therefore, at the national level, cooperation between universit/college, R&D institution and business has become particularly important. First, we must further recognize the dominant role of businesses and the important supportive role of universities/colleges and R&D institutions in the innovation system. Universities/colleges, R&D institutions and businesses must give play to their respective advantages in fundamental research, application study and experimental development and improve their capability to transform knowledge and innovation into real productivity. Second, we must improve the innovation evaluation system, improve the quality of innovation outputs, increase per capita number of scientific papers and patents handled and authorized, increase the frequency of scientific paper and patent quotation, and inspect the application, development and input-output ratio of knowledge and innovation. Third, we must give play to the organization and coordination role of government departments and the advantages of universities/colleges in disciplines and profound fundamental researches, theoretical breakthroughs in high-end and emerging subject. Besides guiding universities/colleges to participate in industrial practices in order to enhance the efficiency of transforming scientific and technological achievements into productivity, we also give play to the advantages of in market-oriented R&D, direct to exchange and cooperate with and support universities/colleges and scientific institutions, and enable closer between universities/colleges, scientific institutions and.

(3) Improve innovation environment and vigorously nurture and introduce innovation talents

The lack of high-level talents, talents, talents, professional talents, and composite talents has become major bottleneck to the future development of innovation activities. Human the key to innovation initiatives, which must adhere to the philosophy of "human-oriented" First, we must provide a favorable innovation environment for talents, so as to attract and keep talents. Innovation environment covers working environment, learning environment, environment, and environment. ood innovation atmosphere, continual learning opportunities, convenient face-to-face exchange, comfortable living, flexible working system, and impartial scientific research environment can stimulate innovation potential and enhance innovation capability of talents. Second, we must further increase the input for talent nurturing, improve the structure for talent nurturing and encourage external exchange and cooperation. As the key place for nurturing and talents, universities/colleges not only nurture talents according to the needs of society, but also provide students/teachers with the opportunity to participate in innovation initiatives. Third, we must strengthen the encouragement of innovation achievements and stimulate the enthusiasm, initiative and creativity of innovation talents. try to apply a flexible remuneration system and incentive system to encourage innovation, while universities/colleges and scientific institutions implement talent policies to encourage talent flow. The government foreign invest to indirectly introduce foreign talents.

3. Industrial level

well as an important part original innovation and economic development. We must accelerate the nurture and development of strategic emerging industries, facilitate the transformation and upgrade of industrial structure, and quicken the industrialized application of sci-tech achievements, respond to the challenges of industrial competition and the innovation challenges behind them.

(1) To accelerate the nurture and development of strategic emerging industries and facilitate the internationalization of strategic emerging industries

The and transform the way of economic development has become the strategic choice of all countries and regions to reshape their international competitiveness after the financial crisis. Currently, the global economic competition is experiencing profound changes, and technolog development preparing for new revolutionary breakthroughs. To embark on the track of economic revival, it respective countries/regions to accelerate the nurture and development of emerging industries as energy conservation, environmental protection, new energy, information, biology etc. This will deeply change the existing track and landscape of worldwide economic growth. Developing strategic emerging industries is the new route for innovation industrialization. It is not only an important approach to upgrade the industrial structure, but also an important opportunity to elevate the level of industrial competitiveness and take the lead in the new round of international competition. Therefore, all countries and regions must strengthen international cooperation. Besides vigorously enhancing their independent innovation capability and consolidating the domestic foundation of strategic emerging industries, they must promote the internationalization of strategic emerging industries from the perspective of internationalization, take opportunities, strengthen R&D, make innovation, take the lead in the industry, and continuously inject vigor into economic development through industrial innovation initiatives. The internationalization of strategic emerging industries requires us to enhance the international development level of R&D, manufacturing, marketing, etc., to elevate the competitiveness of entire industrial chain, to improve the international development capability of industrial unions and talents, to enhance the competitiveness of market players, and to organically integrate the domestic market with international market.

(2) To deepen industrial innovation and promote the transformation and upgrade of

industrial structure

To deepen industrial innovation, based on the development of existing industries and driven by innovation, further promote high-end development of industries and propel the transformation and upgrade of industrial structure. Since the financial crisis, the concept of "reindustrialization" has As the reflection by developed countries likon the former development model of "de-industrialization" it implies people's wish to return to real economy. Reindustrialization is the secondary industrialization on the basis of primary industrialization, and is actually relying on high and new technologies to develop the advanced manufacturing industry, so as to have an industry with strong competitiveness and to lead and reshape other industries through a new round of technological revolution, especially new energy, information, biology, healthcare, environmental protection, and space. This shows that the development of industries, especially the real industries, is the important source of national competitiveness, while innovation is the fundamental route and impetus to explore space and elevate the level of industrial development. Therefore, countries/regions implement "reindustrialization" in order to promote in-depth development of industries and further consolidate the foundation of economic development through innovation. Countries/regions are currently in the middle of industrialization shall further rely on technology innovation to embark on track of new-type industrialization as China does, so as to promote the transformation and upgrade of traditional industries and the development of emerging high-tech industries. The experiences of developed countries also indicate that industrial cluster is an important configuration of organization to promote in-depth industrial innovation and enhance the core competitiveness of industries. We must promote the development of innovation industrial clusters through policy guidance and lay a solid micro-foundation for building a newnational innovation system.

(3) To step up the industrialization of sci-tech achievements and achieve organic integration of fundamental research and applied research

Technolog innovation is mainly done in the lab, but this is only half of the innovation mission. To truly realize the significance of innovation, we must transform technology into productivity, promote industrial development, further propel the transformation of sci-tech achievements, apply sci-tech achievements in industrial development, and produce products and commoditiessocial needs, thus truly realizing the social benefits and economic benefits of sci-tech achievements. For example, according to the Global Innovation Index launched by INSEAD Business School in June 2011, China ranks 29th among 125 appraised countries, and is the only developing country top 30. However, China perform well in sci-tech achievement transformation rate (around 25%), and the industrialization rate is even less than 5%, which is far below the 80% transformation rate in developed countries. With respect to the industrialized application of innovation, China's innovation competitiveness is indeed not strong. Therefore, all countries and regions must pay attention to and organically integrate fundamental research with applied research, and continuously explore the approaches and ways of technolog. We must develop effective means and mechanism for the industrialized application of sci-tech achievements, construction of national innovation system, actively promote the organic integration of research, improve the innovation service system, fully mobilize the enthusiasm of intermediary agencies, and pave the way for smooth industrialization of sci-tech achievements. Only by transforming high technologies into the impetus driving economic growth through industrialization can we truly call it innovation and acquire the competitive advantage in innovation.

4. level

(1) To make the key players of national innovation

Currently, given the new tendency and new requirements of sci-tech development, how to enhance the independent innovation capability of businesses and make them key players in independent innovation. For they must first develop the development philosophy of independent innovation, develop stage-specific goals and strategic planning for enterprise development according to their own situations, and reserve innovation space for future development. Second they must properly handle the relationship between independent innovation and technology utilization and transformation. Besides increasing the investment on innovation initiatives and talent nurturing, mastering key technologies related to product manufacturing and utilizing their own innovation capability to establish and build their own brands, must also study advanced production techniques, operation philosophies and management systems, so as to enhance production innovation capability and management innovation capability. Second, the exchange and cooperation with universities/colleges and research institutes can also be strengthened through talent nurturing, cooperation, technical exchange etc., so as to acquire -edge technologies and enhance the innovation capability. In addition, the formulation of government's industrial development policies and market competition policies, construction of knowledge innovation and productivity transformation platform and the construction of intermediary service institutions.

(2) To improve the innovation vigor of SMs

Constrained by small size, weak technological capacity and weak policy support, SMs' innovation capability has been weak for years. However, in recent years, SMs have experienced booming development by leveraging on their efficient technical application, flexible production model and sharp market sense, and become an important part of national economic development in G20 nations, while high-tech SMs are even requisite part of technology innovation.

Policy and funding are crucial to the innovation initiatives of SMs. From the perspective of the government, developing corresponding preferential policies on taxation, finance, talent and intellectual property right and establishing the corresponding market and productivity transformation platform are important steps to construct a favorable external environment for the development of SMs. From the perspective of SMs, first, they give play to their strong enthusiasm for independent innovation and adjust the development strategy according to their existing innovation conditions and market changes in order to implement product innovation and market expansion; secondly, SMs utilize the flexible remuneration system to attract innovation talents and utilize the but aggressive corporate culture to keep innovation talents and give full play to the subjectivity and creativity of those talents; third, on the premise of mutual trust, SMs strengthen technical exchanges with related enterprises and jointly implement R&D projects in which substantial funding is needed.

Part 3 Sub Report

Chapter 1

Evaluation and Analysis Report n the NIC of Argentina

Situated in the south of Latin America, Argentina borders Chile, Bolivia, Paraguay, and Brazil, and Atlantic Ocean. The country covers a total area of 2.77 million square kilometers, with coastline extending 4,989 kilometers. As of late 2010, the gross population was 40.09 million, with GDP reaching USD 368.7 billion, 9.16%. After the outbreak of the international financial crisis, all countries now giv high priority to technology innovation in order to secure a pioneering role in the global economic competition. Innovation has become the common and key strategic choice of countries to address the development problem. 2001 2009, there was no much change to the NIC ranking of Argentina. In 2001, the NIC of Argentina ranked 17th among G20 nations. In 2009, Argentina still ranked 17th. By analyzing the variations in the rankings of its NIC and respective elements there of among G20 nations 2001 2009, this chapter to the driving and influencing factors the NIC of Argentina.

I. Summary of Argentina's NIC

ariations in the ranking and of Argentina's NIC are shown in Figure 1-1, and variations in the of 5 secondary indicators are shown in Figure 1-2 and Table 1-1.

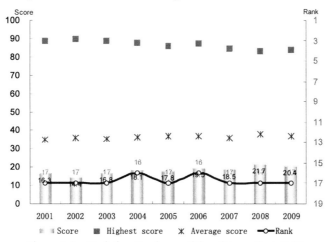

Figure 1-1   Variation Tendency of the of Argentina's NIC

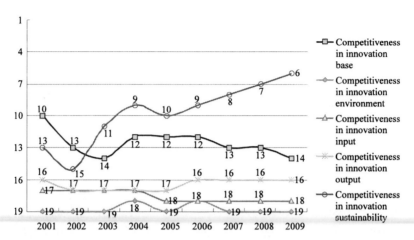

Figure 1-2　Variation Tendencies of the Rankings of the Secondary Indicators of Argentina's NIC

Table 1-1　Scores and Rankings of the Secondary Indicators of Argentina's NIC

Item Year	Competitiveness in innovation base		Competitiveness in innovation environment		Competitiveness in innovation input		Competitiveness in innovation output		Competitiveness in innovation sustainability		Innovation competitiveness	
	Score	Rank	Score	Rank	Score	Rank	Score	Rank	Score	Rank	Score	Rank
2001	17.9	10	14.2	19	8.1	17	9.1	16	32.2	13	16.3	17
2002	12.5	13	13.7	19	8.6	17	8.9	17	28.3	15	14.4	17
2003	13.4	14	16.8	19	8.4	17	8.5	17	36.9	11	16.8	17
2004	14.4	12	19.0	18	9.3	17	7.6	17	40.3	9	18.1	16
2005	16.1	12	21.1	19	8.0	18	7.4	17	36.2	10	17.8	17
2006	14.8	12	23.3	18	7.4	18	7.2	16	44.5	9	19.5	16
2007	14.5	13	24.9	19	7.0	18	7.4	16	38.6	8	18.5	17
2008	15.8	13	26.3	19	7.4	18	8.3	16	50.6	7	21.7	17
2009	15.7	14	25.3	19	7.8	18	8.1	16	45.2	6	20.4	17
Variance	-2.2		11.1		-0.3		-1.0		13.0		4.1	
Variance		-4		0		-1		0		7		0
Quality		Medium		Weakness		Weakness		Weakness		Weakness		Weakness

(1) With respect to overall ranking, Argentina's NIC ranked 17th among G20 nations in 2009, compared to 2001. The ranking of Argentina rose slightly in 2004 and 2006. Generally speaking, minor fluctuations were observed in the evaluation period.

(2) With respect to the points of indicators, Argentina's NIC scored 20.4 points in 2009, which is 63.4 points lower than the highest score and 16.3 points lower than the average score. Compared to 2001, Argentina's score rose by 4.1 points, narrowing its gap with the

highest score in 2001 by 9.1 points and the average score in 2001 by 2.3 points.

(3) With respect to the ranking sections, in 2009, among the 5 secondary indicators of Argentina's NIC, there was no strength indicator. The competitiveness in innovation sustainability was an advantage indicator, while the competitiveness in innovation environment, the competitiveness in innovation input and the competitiveness in innovation output were weakness indicators.

(4) With respect to the variation tendency of indicator rankings, among the 5 secondary indicators, there were one rising indicator (the competitiveness in innovation sustainability) and two dropping indicators (the competitiveness in innovation base and the competitiveness in innovation input), which were the main of the decline in Argentina's NIC. Rankings of the competitiveness in innovation environment and the competitiveness in innovation output remained unchanged.

(5) With respect to the of such variations, secondary indicator in ranking, while 2 secondary indicators in rankings. Due to the combined influence of ranking fluctuations, the overall ranking of Argentina's NIC remained unchanged in 2009 (17th).

II. Dynamic Variations of All Levels of Indicators of Argentina's NIC

Dynamic variations of all levels indicators of Argentina's NIC and the structure there of during 2001-2009 are shown in Figure 1-3 and Table 1-2.

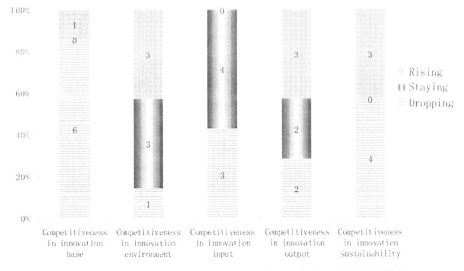

Figure 1-3   Dynamic Variation Structure of Argentina's NIC (2001-2009)

Secondary indicators	Number of tertiary indicators	Rising		Staying		Dropping		Variation tendency
		Number	Ratio (%)	Number	Ratio (%)	Number	Ratio (%)	
Innovation base	7	1	14.3	0	0.0	6	85.7	Dropping
Innovation environment	7	3	42.9	3	42.9	1	14.3	Staying
Innovation input	7	0	0.0	4	57.1	3	42.9	Dropping
Innovation output	7	3	42.9	2	28.6	2	28.6	Staying
Innovation sustainability	7	3	42.9	0	0.0	4	57.1	Rising
Total	35	10	28.6	9	25.7	16	45.7	Staying

According to Figure 1-3, the number of rising tertiary indicators is less than the number of dropping ones, indicating that dropping indicators are dominating. The figures in Table 1-2 further demonstrate that, among the 35 tertiary indicators of Argentina's NIC, there are 10 rising indicators (28.6%), 9 staying indicators (25.7%) and 16 dropping indicators (45.7%). The number of dropping indicators is greater than the number of rising indicators, but the rising is Therefore, the ranking of Argentina's NIC remained in 17th place among G20 nations in 2009.

III. Driver Analysis on the Variations of All Levels of Indicators of Argentina's NIC

Quality variations of all levels indicators of Argentina's NIC and the structure there of during 2001-2009 are shown in Table 1-3.

Table 1-3   Comparison of the Quality of All Levels of Indicators of Argentina's NIC (2001-2009)

Secondary indicators	Number of tertiary indicators	Strength		Advantage		Medium		Weakness		Quality
		Number	Ratio (%)	Number	Ratio (%)	Number	Ratio (%)	Number	Ratio (%)	
Innovation base	7	1	14.3	0	0.0	3	42.9	3	42.9	Medium
Innovation environment	7	1	14.3	0	0.0	2	28.6	4	57.1	Weakness
Innovation input	7	0	0.0	0	0.0	2	28.6	5	71.4	Weakness
Innovation output	7	0	0.0	0	0.0	2	28.6	5	71.4	Weakness
Innovation sustainability	7	4	57.1	0	0.0	2	28.6	1	14.3	Advantage
Total	35	6	17.1	0	0.0	11	31.4	18	51.4	Weakness

According to Figure 1-3, among the 35 tertiary indicators of Argentina's NIC, there are 6 strength indicators (17.1%), 0 advantage indicator, 11 medium indicators (31.4%), and 18 weakness indicators (51.4%). The sum of strength indicators and advantage indicators accounts for 17.1% of total indicators, which is smaller than the sum of medium indicators and weakness indicators. Among secondary indicators, there are   strength indicator, 1 advantage indicator (20%), 1 medium indicator (20%), and 3 weakness indicators (60%). Since the indicator system is dominated by weakness indicators, Argentina's NIC wasduring 2001-2009.

Evaluation and Analysis Reportn the NIC
of Australia

Facing Pacific Ocean on the east and Indian Ocean on the west, Australia consists of mainland and proximate islands including Tasmania. The country covers a total area of 7.69 million square, 70% of which are with coastline extending 36,735. As of late 2010, the gross population was 22.73 million, with GDP reaching USD up 2.75% year-on-year. 2001 2009, there was no much change to the NIC ranking of Australia. In 2001, the NIC of Australia ranked 8th among G20 nations. In 2009, Australia still ranked 8th. By the variations in the rankings of its NIC and respective elements there of among G20 nations 2001 2009, Australia.

I. Summary of Australia's NIC

of Australia's NIC are shown in Figure 2-1, and 5 secondary indicators are shown in Figure 2-2 and Table 2-1.

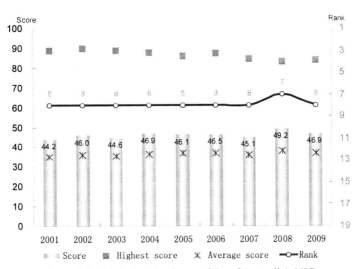

Figure 2-1   Variation Tendency of the of Australia's NIC

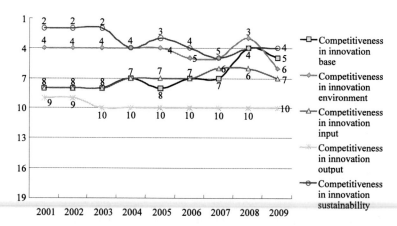

Figure 2-2　Variation Tendencies of the Rankings of the Secondary Indicators of Australia's NIC

Table 2-1　Scores and Rankings of the Secondary Indicators of Australia's NIC

Item Year	Competitiveness in innovation base		Competitiveness in innovation environment		Competitiveness in innovation input		Competitiveness in innovation output		Competitiveness in innovation sustainability		Innovation competitiveness	
	Score	Rank	Score	Rank	Score	Rank	Score	Rank	Score	Rank	Score	Rank
2001	36.5	8	70.2	4	38.2	8	20.7	9	55.3	2	44.2	8
2002	40.5	8	69.8	4	40.9	8	21.8	9	57.1	2	46.0	8
2003	40.6	8	70.2	4	41.2	8	19.8	10	51.3	2	44.6	8
2004	47.9	7	70.1	4	42.3	7	18.9	10	55.1	4	46.9	8
2005	45.3	8	69.8	4	42.7	7	18.8	10	53.7	3	46.1	8
2006	47.2	7	68.9	5	43.9	7	18.4	10	53.9	4	46.5	8
2007	48.9	7	68.3	5	44.8	6	18.3	10	45.2	5	45.1	8
2008	52.5	4	71.5	3	46.7	6	18.4	10	56.8	4	49.2	7
2009	50.8	5	67.7	6	47.0	7	20.3	10	48.7	4	46.9	8
Variance	14.3		-2.5		8.8		-0.4		-6.6		2.7	
Variance		3		-2		1		-1		-2		0
Quality		Strength		Advantage		Advantage		Advantage		Strength		Advantage

(1) With respect to overall ranking, Australia's NIC ranked 8th among G20 nations in 2009, compared to 2001. The ranking of Australia rose to 7th in 2008. Generally speaking, minor fluctuations were observed in the evaluation period.

(2) With respect to the points of indicators, Australia's NIC scored 46.9 points in 2009,

which is 36.9 points lower than the highest score and 10.1 points lower than the average score. Compared to 2001, Australia's score rose by 2.7 points, narrowing its gap with the highest score in 2001 by 7.7 points and the average score in 2001 by 0.9 points.

(3) With respect to the ranking sections, in 2009, among the 5 secondary indicators of Australia's NIC, the competitiveness in innovation base and the competitiveness in innovation sustainability were strength indicators, while the competitiveness in innovation environment, the competitiveness in innovation input and the competitiveness in innovation output were advantage indicators. There was no weakness indicator.

(4) With respect to the variation tendency of indicator rankings, among the 5 secondary indicators, there were two rising indicators (the competitiveness in innovation base and the competitiveness in innovation input) and two dropping indicators (the competitiveness in innovation environment and the competitiveness in innovation output).

(5) With respect to the driver of such variations, 2 secondary indicators ranking, while 2 secondary indicators drop in rankings. Due to the combined influence of ranking fluctuations, the overall ranking of Australia's NIC remained unchanged in 2009 (8th).

II. Dynamic Variations of All Levels of Indicators of Australia's NIC

Dynamic variations of all levels indicators of Australia's NIC and the structure there of during 2001-2009 are shown in Figure 2-3 and Table 2-2.

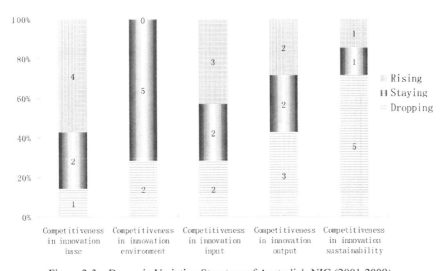

Figure 2-3　Dynamic Variation Structure of Australia's NIC (2001-2009)

Table 2-2 Comparison of the Variations in Rankings of All Levels of Indicators of Australia's NIC (2001-2009)

Secondary indicators	Number of tertiary indicators	Rising		Staying		Dropping		Variation tendency
		Number	Ratio (%)	Number	Ratio (%)	Number	Ratio (%)	
Innovation base	7	4	57.1	2	28.6	1	14.3	Rising
Innovation environment	7	0	0.0	5	71.4	2	28.6	Dropping
Innovation input	7	3	42.9	2	28.6	2	28.6	Rising
Innovation output	7	2	28.6	2	28.6	3	42.9	Dropping
Innovation sustainability	7	1	14.3	1	14.3	5	71.4	Dropping
Total	35	10	28.6	12	34.3	13	37.1	Staying

According to Figure 2-3, the number of rising tertiary indicators is slightly less than the number of dropping ones. The figures in Table 2-2 further demonstrate that, among the 35 tertiary indicators of Argentina's NIC, there are 10 rising indicators (28.6%), 12 staying indicators (34.3%) and 13 dropping indicators (37.1%). The rising is slightly weaker than the dropping, but there are quite a number of staying indicators. Therefore, the ranking of Australia's NIC remained in 8th place among G20 nations in 2009.

III. Driver Analysis on the Variations of All Levels of Indicators of Australia's NIC

Quality variations of all levels indicators of Australia's NIC and the structure there of during 2001-2009 are shown in Table 2-3.

Table 2-3 Comparison of the Quality of All Levels of Indicators of Australia's NIC (2001-2009)

Secondary indicators	Number of tertiary indicators	Strength		Advantage		Medium		Weakness		Quality
		Number	Ratio (%)	Number	Ratio (%)	Number	Ratio (%)	Number	Ratio (%)	
Innovation base	7	4	57.1	1	14.3	2	28.6	0	0.0	Strength
Innovation environment	7	2	28.6	5	71.4	0	0.0	0	0.0	Advantage
Innovation input	7	3	42.9	1	14.3	2	28.6	1	14.3	Advantage
Innovation output	7	1	14.3	3	42.9	3	42.9	0	0.0	Advantage
Innovation sustainability	7	3	42.9	0	0.0	4	57.1	0	0.0	Strength
Total	35	13	37.1	10	28.6	11	31.4	1	2.9	Advantage

According to Figure 2-3, among the 35 tertiary indicators of Australia's NIC, there are 13 strength indicators (37.1%), 10 advantage indicators (28.6%), 11 medium indicators (31.4%), and 1 weakness indicator (2.9%). The sum of strength indicators and advantage indicators accounts for 55.7% of total indicators, which is far greater than the sum of medium indicators and weakness indicators. Among secondary indicators, there are 2 strength indicator (40%), 3 advantage indicator (60%) and medium/weakness indicator. Since the indicator system is dominated by strength indicators and advantage indicators, Australia's NIC was during 2001-2009.

Chapter 3

Evaluation and Analysis Report n the NIC of Brazil

Situated in the east of Latin America and facing the Atlantic Ocean, Brazil borders Uruguay, Argentina, Paraguay, Bolivia, Peru, Colombia, Venezuela, Guyana, Surinam and French Guiana. The country covers a total area of 8.51 million square kilometers, with coastline extending 7,400 kilometers. As of late 2010, the gross population was 190.7 million, with GDP reaching USD 2087.89 billion, up 7.49% year-on-year. After the break of international financial crisis, there substantial change to the NIC ranking of Brazil. In 2001, the NIC of Brazil ranked 15th among G20 nations. In 2009, Brazil climbed up two places to 13th. By analyzing the variations in the rankings of its NIC and respective elements there of among G20 nations 2001 2009, NIC of Brazil.

I. Summary of Brazil's NIC

The variations in the ranking and of Brazil's NIC are shown in Figure 3-1, and the variations in the 5 secondary indicators are shown in Figure 3-2 and Table 3-1.

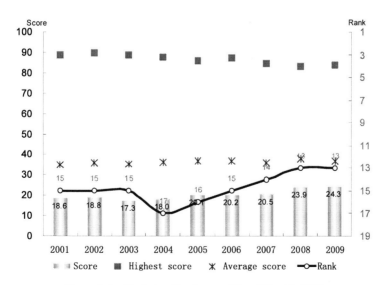

Figure 3-1   Variation Tendency of the of Brazil's NIC

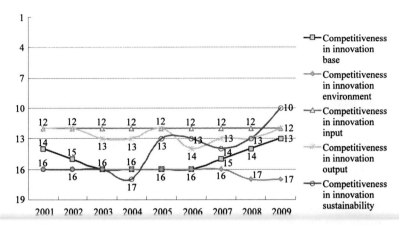

Figure 3-2　Variation Tendencies of the Rankings of the Secondary Indicators of Brazil's NIC

Table 3-1　Scores and Rankings of the Secondary Indicators of Brazil's NIC

Item Year	Competitiveness in innovation base		Competitiveness in innovation environment		Competitiveness in innovation input		Competitiveness in innovation output		Competitiveness in innovation sustainability		Innovation competitiveness	
	Score	Rank	Score	Rank	Score	Rank	Score	Rank	Score	Rank	Score	Rank
2001	8.3	14	23.0	16	22.2	12	13.0	12	26.5	16	18.6	15
2002	8.9	15	24.1	16	21.9	12	13.0	12	26.1	16	18.8	15
2003	8.5	16	24.2	16	20.5	12	10.0	13	23.5	16	17.3	15
2004	9.3	16	26.1	16	19.8	12	10.0	13	25.0	17	18.0	17
2005	11.7	16	26.6	16	20.7	12	10.8	12	30.7	13	20.1	16
2006	10.9	16	27.3	16	20.3	12	10.2	14	32.2	13	20.2	15
2007	12.4	15	28.5	16	19.5	12	10.8	13	31.0	14	20.5	14
2008	14.6	14	34.9	17	20.1	12	11.1	13	38.9	13	23.9	13
2009	15.8	13	35.0	17	20.3	12	12.2	12	38.2	10	24.3	13
Variance	7.5		12.0		-1.9		-0.8		11.7		5.7	
Variance		1		-1		0		0		6		2
Quality		Medium		Weakness		Medium		Medium		Advantage		Medium

(1) With respect to overall ranking, Brazil's NIC ranked 13th among G20 nations in 2009, rising by two places compared to 2001. The ranking rose steadily from 2005 through 2009. Generally speaking, upward fluctuations were observed in the evaluation period.

(2) With respect to the points of indicators, Brazil's NIC scored 24.3 points in 2009, which is 59.5 points lower than the highest score and 12.5 points lower than the average score. Compared to 2001, Brazil's score rose by 5.7 points, narrowing its gap with the highest score in 2001 by 10.7 points and the average score in 2001 by 3.9 points.

(3) With respect to the ranking sections, in 2009, among the 5 secondary indicators of Brazil's NIC, there was no strength indicator. The competitiveness in innovation sustainability was an advantage indicator, while the competitiveness in innovation environment was a weakness indicator.

(4) With respect to the variation tendency of indicator rankings, among the 5 secondary indicators, there were two rising indicators (the competitiveness in innovation base and the competitiveness in innovation sustainability); the competitiveness in innovation sustainability and was the main driver of the growth in Brazil's innovation competitiveness ranking. There was one dropping indicator (the competitiveness in innovation environment) and two staying indicators (the competitiveness in innovation input and the competitiveness in innovation output).

(5) With respect to the driver of such variations, 2 secondary indicators in ranking compared to the decline of dropping indicator. Due to the influence of rising indicators, the overall ranking of Brazil's NIC rose to 13th in 2009.

II. Dynamic Variations of All Levels of Indicators of Brazil's NIC

Dynamic variations of all levels indicators of Brazil's NIC and the structure there of during 2001-2009 are shown in Figure 3-3 and Table 3-2.

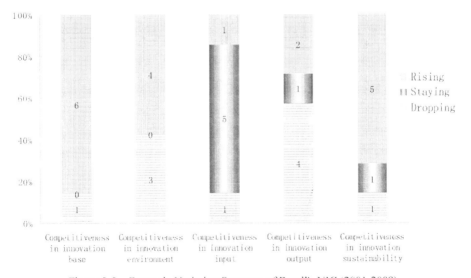

Figure 3-3　Dynamic Variation Structure of Brazil's NIC (2001-2009)

Table 3-2   Comparison of the Variations in Rankings of All Levels of Indicators of Brazil's NIC (2001-2009)

Secondary indicators	Number of tertiary indicators	Rising		Staying		Dropping		Variation tendency
		Number	Ratio (%)	Number	Ratio (%)	Number	Ratio (%)	
Innovation base	7	6	85.7	0	0.0	1	14.3	Rising
Innovation environment	7	4	57.1	0	0.0	3	42.9	Dropping
Innovation input	7	1	14.3	5	71.4	1	14.3	Staying
Innovation output	7	2	28.6	1	14.3	4	57.1	Staying
Innovation sustainability	7	5	71.4	1	14.3	1	14.3	Rising
Total	35	18	51.4	7	20.0	10	28.6	Rising

According to Figure 3-3, the number of rising tertiary indicators is greater than the number of dropping ones, indicating that rising indicators are dominating. The figures in Table 3-2 further demonstrate that, among the 35 tertiary indicators of Brazil's NIC, there are 18 rising indicators (51.4%), 7 staying indicators (20.0%) and 10 dropping indicators (28.6%). The rising is stronger than the dropping momentum. Therefore, the ranking of Brazil's NIC rose two places to 13th among G20 nations in 2009.

III. Driver Analysis on the Variations of All Levels of Indicators of Brazil's NIC

Quality variations of all levels indicators of Brazil's NIC and the structure there of during 2001-2009 are shown in Table 3-3.

Table 3-3   Comparison of the Quality of All Levels of Indicators of Brazil's NIC (2001-2009)

Secondary indicators	Number of tertiary indicators	Strength		Advantage		Medium		Weakness		Quality
		Number	Ratio (%)	Number	Ratio (%)	Number	Ratio (%)	Number	Ratio (%)	
Innovation base	7	0	0.0	3	42.9	4	57.1	0	0.0	Medium
Innovation environment	7	1	14.3	0	0.0	4	57.1	2	28.6	Weakness
Innovation input	7	0	0.0	2	28.6	5	71.4	0	0.0	Medium
Innovation output	7	0	0.0	1	14.3	6	85.7	0	0.0	Medium
Innovation sustainability	7	1	14.3	3	42.9	3	42.9	0	0.0	Advantage
Total	35	2	5.7	9	25.7	22	62.9	2	5.7	Medium

According to Figure 3-3, among the 35 tertiary indicators of Brazil's NIC, there are 2 strength indicators (5.7%), 9 advantage indicators (25.7%), 22 medium indicators (62.9%), and 2 weakness indicators (5.7%). The sum of strength indicators and advantage indicators accounts for 34.4% of total indicators, which is greater than weakness indicators, and the medium indicators are dominating. Among secondary indicators, there are strength indicator, 1 advantage indicator (20%), 3 medium indicator (60%), and 1 weakness indicators (20%). Since the indicator system is dominated by medium indicators, Brazil's NIC was average during 2001-2009.

Chapter 4

Evaluation and Analysis Report n the NIC of Canada

Situated in the north of North America, Atlantic Ocean on the east Pacific Ocean on the west, border Alaska on the northwest, fac Greenland of Denmark to the northeast, borders United States. The country covers a total area of 9.98 million square kilometers, with borderline extending 8,892 kilometers, which is the longest unguarded borderline in the world. The coastline extends 240,000 kilometers, which is also the longest one in the world. As of late 2010, the gross population was 34.61 million, with GDP reaching USD 1574.05 billion, up 3.07% year-on-year. After the break of international financial crisis, there was no much change to the NIC ranking of Canada. In 2001, the NIC of Canada ranked 7th among G20 nations. In 2009, Canada still ranked 7th. By analyzing the variations in the rankings of its NIC and respective elements there of among G20 nations 2001 2009.

I. Summary of Canada's NIC

The variations in the ranking and of Canada's NIC are shown in Figure 4-1, and the variations in 5 secondary indicators are shown in Figure 4-2 and Table 4-1.

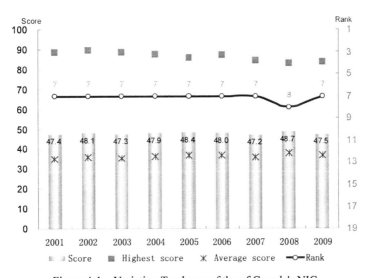

Figure 4-1   Variation Tendency of the of Canada's NIC

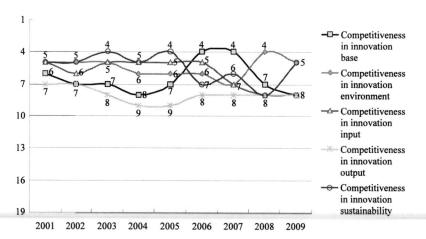

Figure 4-2   Variation Tendencies of the Rankings of the Secondary Indicators of Canada's NIC

Table 4-1   Scores and Rankings of the Secondary Indicators of Canada's NIC

Item Year	Competitiveness in innovation base		Competitiveness in innovation environment		Competitiveness in innovation input		Competitiveness in innovation output		Competitiveness in innovation sustainability		Innovation competitiveness	
	Score		Rank		Score		Rank		Score		Rank	
2001	43.4	6	64.8	5	50.3	5	27.6	7	50.8	5	47.4	7
2002	44.5	7	67.3	5	50.4	6	27.1	7	51.6	5	48.1	7
2003	44.2	7	67.2	5	49.2	5	26.0	8	49.9	4	47.3	7
2004	44.6	8	66.7	6	49.9	5	23.3	9	54.8	5	47.9	7
2005	50.6	7	67.2	6	48.1	5	24.6	9	51.4	4	48.4	7
2006	52.6	4	67.2	6	46.7	5	24.8	8	48.3	7	48.0	7
2007	55.8	4	66.6	7	44.8	7	25.2	8	43.6	6	47.2	7
2008	50.5	7	71.3	4	44.9	8	26.2	8	50.3	8	48.7	8
2009	47.4	8	69.9	5	44.3	8	27.8	8	47.8	5	47.5	7
Variance	4.1		5.1		-6.0		0.2		-3.0		0.1	
Variance		-2		0		-3		-1		0		0
Quality		Advantage		Strength		Advantage		Advantage		Strength		Advantage

(1) With respect to overall ranking, Canada's NIC ranked 7th among G20 nations in 2009, compared to 2001. The ranking of Canada dropped to 8th in 2008. Generally speaking, minor fluctuations were observed in the evaluation period.

(2) With respect to the points of indicators, Canada's NIC scored 47.5 points in 2009, which is 36.3 points lower than the highest score and 10.7 points higher than the average

score. Compared to 2001, Canada's score rose by 0.1 point, narrowing its gap with the highest score in 2001 by 5.1 points and the average score in 2001 by 1.7 points.

(3) With respect to the ranking sections, in 2009, among the 5 secondary indicators of Canada's NIC, the competitiveness in innovation environment and the competitiveness in innovation sustainability were strength indicators, while the competitiveness in innovation base, the competitiveness in innovation input and the competitiveness in innovation output were advantage indicators. There was no weakness indicator.

(4) With respect to the variation tendency of indicator rankings, among the 5 secondary indicators, there no rising indicators, but there were three dropping indicators (the competitiveness in innovation base, the competitiveness in innovation input and the competitiveness in innovation output) and two staying indicators (the competitiveness in innovation environment and the competitiveness in innovation sustainability).

(5) With respect to the driver of such variations, 3 secondary indicators in rankings. Due to the combined influence of external factors, the overall ranking of Australia's NIC remained unchanged in 2009 (7th).

II. Dynamic Variations of All Levels of Indicators of Canada's NIC

Dynamic variations of all levels indicators of Canada's NIC and the structure there of during 2001-2009 are shown in Figure 4-3 and Table 4-2.

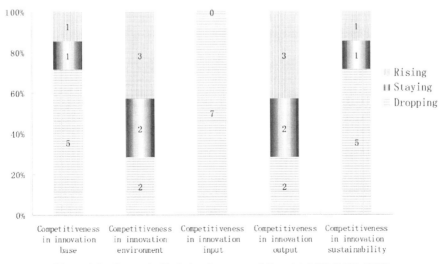

Figure 4-3   Dynamic Variation Structure of Canada's NIC (2001-2009)

Table 4-2   Comparison of the Variations in Rankings of All Levels of Indicators of Canada's NIC (2001-2009)

Secondary indicators	Number of tertiary indicators	Rising		Staying		Dropping		Variation tendency
		Number	Ratio (%)	Number	Ratio (%)	Number	Ratio (%)	
Innovation base	7	1	14.3	1	14.3	5	71.4	Dropping
Innovation environment	7	3	42.9	2	28.6	2	28.6	Staying
Innovation input	7	0	0.0	0	0.0	7	100.0	Dropping
Innovation output	7	3	42.9	2	28.6	2	28.6	Dropping
Innovation sustainability	7	1	14.3	1	14.3	5	71.4	Staying
Total	35	8	22.9	6	17.1	21	60.0	Staying

According to Figure 4-3, the number of rising tertiary indicators is less than the number of dropping ones, indicating that dropping indicators are dominating. The figures in Table 4-2 further demonstrate that, among the 35 tertiary indicators of Canada's NIC, there are 8 rising indicators (22.9%), 6 staying indicators (17.1%) and 21 dropping indicators (60.0%). The rising is weaker than the dropping momentum. However, due to the combined influence of external factors, the ranking of Canada's NIC remained in 7th place among G20 nations in 2009.

III. Driver Analysis on the Variations of All Levels of Indicators of Canada's NIC

Quality variations of all levels indicators of Canada's NIC and the structure there of during 2001-2009 are shown in Table 4-3.

Table 4-3   Comparison of the Quality of All Levels of Indicators of Canada's NIC (2001-2009)

Secondary indicators	Number of tertiary indicators	Strength		Advantage		Medium		Weakness		Quality
		Number	Ratio (%)	Number	Ratio (%)	Number	Ratio (%)	Number	Ratio (%)	
Innovation base	7	2	28.6	4	57.1	1	14.3	0	0.0	Advantage
Innovation environment	7	6	85.7	0	0.0	0	0.0	1	14.3	Strength
Innovation input	7	1	14.3	4	57.1	2	28.6	0	0.0	Advantage
Innovation output	7	2	28.6	5	71.4	0	0.0	0	0.0	Advantage
Innovation sustainability	7	2	28.6	3	42.9	2	28.6	0	0.0	Strength
Total	35	13	37.1	16	45.7	5	14.3	1	2.9	Advantage

According to Figure 4-3, among the 35 tertiary indicators of Canada's NIC, there are 13 strength indicators (37.1%), 16 advantage indicators (45.7%), 5 medium indicators (14.3%), and 1 weakness indicator (2.9%). The sum of strength indicators and advantage indicators accounts for 82.8% of total indicators, which is far greater than the sum of medium indicators and weakness indicators. Among secondary indicators, there are 2 strength indicator (40%), 3 advantage indicator (60%) and medium/weakness indicator. Since the indicator system is dominated by strength indicators and advantage indicators, Canada's NIC was during 2001-2009.

Chapter 5

Evaluation and Analysis Report On the NIC of China

Situated in the east of Asian continent and on the western shore of the Pacific Ocean, the People's Republic of China (PRC) has a land area of about 9.6 million square kilometers, land boundary of some 22,800 kilometers, a total maritime area of 4.73 million square kilometers, and a continental coastline of about 18,000 kilometers. As of late 2010, the gross population was 1.3397 billion, with GDP reaching USD 58786 billion, up 10.3% year-on-year., there substantial change to the NIC ranking of China. In 2001, the NIC of China ranked 12th among G20 nations. In 2009, China rose two places to 10th. By analyzing the variations in the rankings of its NIC and respective elements there of among G20 nations 2001 2009.

I. Summary of China's NIC

The variations in the ranking and of China's NIC are shown in Figure 5-1, and the variations in the of 5 secondary indicators are shown in Figure 5-2 and Table 5-1.

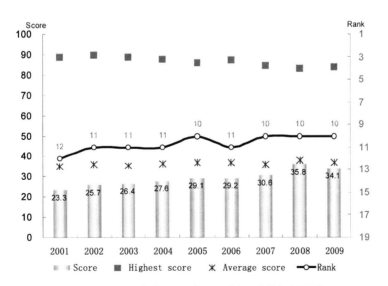

Figure 5-1   Variation Tendency of the of China's NIC

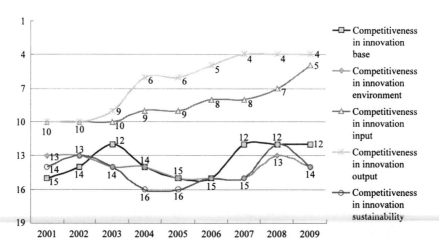

Figure 5-2　Variation Tendencies of the Rankings of the Secondary Indicators of China's NIC

Table 5-1　Scores and Rankings of the Secondary Indicators of China's NIC

Item Year	Competitiveness in innovation base		Competitiveness in innovation environment		Competitiveness in innovation input		Competitiveness in innovation output		Competitiveness in innovation sustainability		Innovation competitiveness	
	Score	Rank	Score	Rank	Score	Rank	Score	Rank	Score	Rank	Score	Rank
2001	6.9	15	31.5	13	30.4	10	16.1	10	31.7	14	23.3	12
2002	12.1	14	32.4	13	32.6	10	19.6	10	32.0	13	25.7	11
2003	14.9	12	32.7	14	33.7	10	25.1	9	25.4	14	26.4	11
2004	10.9	14	33.0	14	36.4	9	29.7	6	27.8	16	27.6	11
2005	13.3	15	34.1	15	38.9	9	32.2	6	27.1	16	29.1	10
2006	11.3	15	33.8	15	40.5	8	31.7	5	28.9	15	29.2	11
2007	14.9	12	34.1	15	42.6	8	32.7	4	28.6	15	30.6	10
2008	16.1	12	44.4	13	45.4	7	33.8	4	39.3	12	35.8	10
2009	19.5	12	41.5	14	48.0	5	34.8	4	26.9	14	34.1	10
Variance	12.6		10.0		17.6		18.7		-4.8		10.8	
Variance		3		-1		5		6		0		2
Quality		Medium		Medium		Strength		Strength		Medium		Advantage

(1) With respect to overall ranking, China's NIC ranked 10th among G20 nations in 2009, by two places compared to 2001. The ranking rose with fluctuations from 2005 through 2009. Generally speaking, upward fluctuations were observed in the evaluation period.

(2) With respect to the points of indicators, China's NIC scored 34.1 points in 2009, which is 49.6 points lower than the highest score and 2.6 points lower than the average

score. Compared to 2001, China's score rose by 10.8 points, narrowing its gap with the highest score in 2001 by 15.8 points and the average score in 2001 by 9.0 points.

(3) With respect to the ranking sections, in 2009, among the 5 secondary indicators of China's NIC, the competitiveness in innovation input and the competitiveness in innovation output were strength indicators. There was no advantage indicator or weakness indicator. The remaining indicators were medium indicators.

(4) With respect to the variation tendency of indicator rankings, among the 5 secondary indicators, there were three rising indicators (the competitiveness in innovation base, the competitiveness in innovation input and the competitiveness in innovation output), one dropping indicator (the competitiveness in innovation environment, the main driver of the decline in China's NIC ranking). The ranking of the competitiveness in innovation sustainability remained unchanged.

(5) With respect to the driver of such variations, 3 secondary indicators in rankings compared to the decline of dropping indicator. Due to such influence, the overall ranking of China's NIC rose to 10th in 2009.

II. Dynamic Variations of All Levels of Indicators of China's NIC

Dynamic variations of all levels indicators of China's NIC and the structure there of during 2001-2009 are shown in Figure 5-3 and Table 5-2.

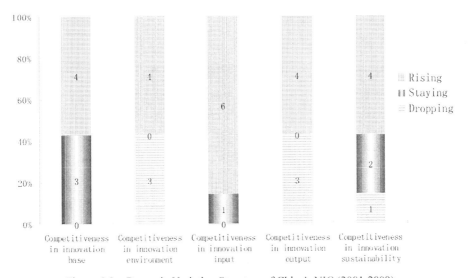

Figure 5-3   Dynamic Variation Structure of China's NIC (2001-2009)

Table 5-2   Comparison of the Variations in Rankings of All Levels of Indicators of China's NIC (2001-2009)

Secondary indicators	Number of tertiary indicators	Rising		Staying		Dropping		Variation tendency
		Number	Ratio (%)	Number	Ratio (%)	Number	Ratio (%)	
Innovation base	7	4	57.1	3	42.9	0	0.0	Rising
Innovation environment	7	4	57.1	0	0.0	3	42.9	Dropping
Innovation input	7	6	85.7	1	14.3	0	0.0	Rising
Innovation output	7	4	57.1	0	0.0	3	42.9	Rising
Innovation sustainability	7	4	57.1	2	28.6	1	14.3	Staying
Total	35	22	62.9	6	17.1	7	20.0	Rising

According to Figure 5-3, the number of rising tertiary indicators is greater than the number of dropping ones, indicating that rising indicators are dominating. The figures in Table 5-2 further demonstrate that, among the 35 tertiary indicators of China's NIC, there are 22 rising indicators (62.9%), 6 staying indicators (17.1%) and 7 dropping indicators (20.0%). The rising is stronger the dropping momentum. Therefore, the ranking of China's NIC rose by two places to 10th place among G20 nations in 2009.

III. Driver Analysis on the Variations of All Levels of Indicators of China's NIC

Quality variations of all levels indicators of China's NIC and the structure there of during 2001-2009 are shown in Table 5-3.

Table 5-3   Comparison of the Quality of All Levels of Indicators of China's NIC (2001-2009)

Secondary indicators	Number of tertiary indicators	Strength		Advantage		Medium		Weakness		Quality
		Number	Ratio (%)	Number	Ratio (%)	Number	Ratio (%)	Number	Ratio (%)	
Innovation base	7	3	42.9	0	0.0	0	0.0	4	57.1	Medium
Innovation environment	7	1	14.3	0	0.0	3	42.9	3	42.9	Medium
Innovation input	7	4	57.1	1	14.3	2	28.6	0	0.0	Strength
Innovation output	7	3	42.9	0	0.0	2	28.6	2	28.6	Strength
Innovation sustainability	7	3	42.9	0	0.0	1	14.3	3	42.9	Medium
Total	35	14	40.0	1	2.9	8	22.9	12	34.3	Advantage

According to Figure 5-3, among the 35 tertiary indicators of China's NIC, there are 14 strength indicators (40%), 1 advantage indicators (2.9%), 8 medium indicators (22.9%), and 12 weakness indicator (34.3%). The sum of strength indicators and advantage indicators accounts for 42.9% of total indicators, which is smaller than the sum of medium indicators and weakness indicators. Among secondary indicators, there are 2 strength indicator (40%), advantage indicator, 3 medium indicators (60%), and weakness indicator. Since the indicator system is dominated by strength indicators and medium indicators, due to their combined influence, China's NIC was during 2001-2009.

Chapter 6

Evaluation and Analysis Report n the NIC of France

Situated in the west of Europe and facing United Kingdom across English Channel, France borders Belgium, Luxemburg, Germany, Switzerland, Italy, Monaco, Andorra, and Spain. The country covers a total area of 550,000 square kilometers, with coastline extending 7,000 kilometers. As of late 2010, the gross population was 65.82 million, with GDP reaching USD 2,560 billion, up 1.49% year-on-year., there a minor change to the NIC ranking of France. In 2001, the NIC of France ranked 5th among G20 nations. In 2009, France rose by one place to 4th. By analyzing the variations in the rankings of its NIC and respective elements there of among G20 nations 2001 2009.

I. Summary of France's NIC

The variations in the ranking and of France's NIC are shown in Figure 6-1, and the variations in the of 5 secondary indicators are shown in Figure 6-2 and Table 6-1.

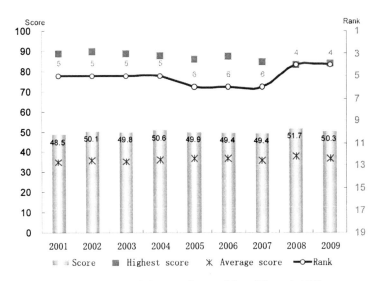

Figure 6-1   Variation Tendency of the of France's NIC

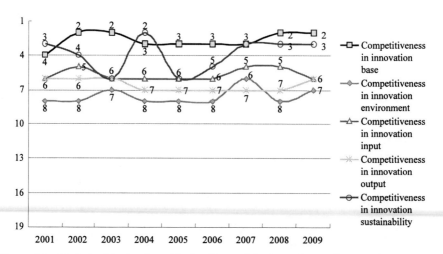

Figure 6-2   Variation Tendencies of the Rankings of the Secondary Indicators of France's NIC

Table 6-1   Scores and Rankings of the Secondary Indicators of France's NIC

Item Year	Competitiveness in innovation base		Competitiveness in innovation environment		Competitiveness in innovation input		Competitiveness in innovation output		Competitiveness in innovation sustainability		Innovation competitiveness	
	Score	Rank	Score	Rank	Score	Rank	Score	Rank	Score	Rank	Score	Rank
2001	49.2	4	60.7	8	49.9	6	29.1	6	53.7	3	48.5	5
2002	55.5	2	60.3	8	51.0	5	29.3	6	54.5	4	50.1	5
2003	61.2	2	64.2	7	48.8	6	27.9	6	46.7	6	49.8	5
2004	57.5	3	64.0	8	49.0	6	27.3	7	55.4	2	50.6	5
2005	60.7	3	63.9	8	46.7	6	27.9	7	50.0	6	49.9	6
2006	56.7	3	63.7	8	46.7	6	27.6	7	52.5	5	49.4	6
2007	59.3	3	66.7	6	46.9	5	26.3	7	47.6	3	49.4	6
2008	57.9	2	68.2	8	47.7	5	27.7	7	57.3	3	51.7	4
2009	60.7	2	64.0	7	47.2	6	28.5	6	51.1	3	50.3	4
Variance	11.5		3.3		-2.7		-0.6		-2.6		1.8	
Variance		2		1		0		0		0		1
Quality		Strength		Advantage		Advantage		Advantage		Strength		Strength

(1) With respect to overall ranking, France's NIC ranked 4th among G20 nations in 2009, rising by one place compared to 2001. The ranking rose steadily from 2005 through 2009. Generally speaking, upward fluctuations were observed in the evaluation period.

(2) With respect to the points of indicators, France's NIC scored 50.3 points in 2009,

which is 33.5 points lower than the highest score and 13.5 points higher than the average score. Compared to 2001, France's score rose by 1.8 point, narrowing its gap with the highest score in 2001 by 6.8 points and the average score in 2001 by 0 points.

(3) With respect to the ranking sections, in 2009, among the 5 secondary indicators of France's NIC, the competitiveness in innovation base and the competitiveness in innovation sustainability were strength indicators, while the competitiveness in innovation environment, the competitiveness in innovation input and the competitiveness in innovation output were advantage indicators. There was no weakness indicator.

(4) With respect to the variation tendency of indicator rankings, among the 5 secondary indicators, there were two rising indicators (the competitiveness in innovation base and the competitiveness in innovation environment) and no dropping indicators.

(5) With respect to the driver of such variations, 3 secondary indicators in rankings. Due to the influence of rising indicators, the overall ranking of France's NIC rose to 4th in 2009.

II. Dynamic Variations of All Levels of Indicators of France's NIC

Dynamic variations of all levels indicators of France's NIC and the structure there of during 2001-2009 are shown in Figure 6-3 and Table 6-2.

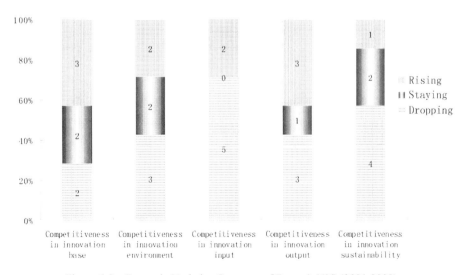

Figure 6-3   Dynamic Variation Structure of France's NIC (2001-2009)

Table 6-2   Comparison of the Variations in Rankings of All Levels of Indicators of France's NIC (2001-2009)

Secondary indicators	Number of tertiary indicators	Rising		Staying		Dropping		Variation tendency
		Number	Ratio (%)	Number	Ratio (%)	Number	Ratio (%)	
Innovation base	7	3	42.9	2	28.6	2	28.6	Rising
Innovation environment	7	2	28.6	2	28.6	3	42.9	Rising
Innovation input	7	2	28.6	0	0.0	5	71.4	Staying
Innovation output	7	3	42.9	1	14.3	3	42.9	Staying
Innovation sustainability	7	1	14.3	2	28.6	4	57.1	Staying
Total	35	11	31.4	7	20.0	17	48.6	Rising

According to Figure 6-3, the number of rising tertiary indicators is less than the number of dropping ones, indicating that dropping indicators are dominating. The figures in Table 6-2 further demonstrate that, among the 35 tertiary indicators of France's NIC, there are 11 rising indicators (31.4%), 7 staying indicators (20.0%) and 17 dropping indicators (48.6%). The number of rising indicators is greater than the number of dropping indicators. However, due to the combined influence of external factors, the ranking of France's NIC rose by one place to 4th place among G20 nations in 2009.

III. Driver Analysis on the Variations of All Levels of Indicators of France's NIC

Quality variations of all levels indicators of France's NIC and the structure there of during 2001-2009 are shown in Table 6-3.

Table 6-3   Comparison of the Quality of All Levels of Indicators of France's NIC (2001-2009)

Secondary indicators	Number of tertiary indicators	Strength		Advantage		Medium		Weakness		Quality
		Number	Ratio (%)	Number	Ratio (%)	Number	Ratio (%)	Number	Ratio (%)	
Innovation base	7	6	85.7	1	14.3	0	0.0	0	0.0	Strength
Innovation environment	7	1	14.3	5	71.4	0	0.0	1	14.3	Advantage
Innovation input	7	1	14.3	6	85.7	0	0.0	0	0.0	Advantage
Innovation output	7	4	57.1	3	42.9	0	0.0	0	0.0	Advantage
Innovation sustainability	7	3	42.9	2	28.6	2	28.6	0	0.0	Strength
Total	35	15	42.9	17	48.6	2	5.7	1	2.9	Strength

According to Figure 6-3, among the 35 tertiary indicators of France's NIC, there are 15 strength indicators (42.9%), 17 advantage indicators (48.6%), 2 medium indicators (5.7%), and 1 weakness indicator (2.9%). The sum of strength indicators and advantage indicators accounts for 91.5% of total indicators, which is far greater than the sum of medium indicators and weakness indicators. Among secondary indicators, there are 2 strength indicators (40%), 3 advantage indicators (60%) and   medium/weakness indicator. Since the indicator system is dominated by strength indicators and advantage indicators, France's NIC was during 2001-2009.

Chapter 7

Evaluation and Analysis Report n the NIC of Germany

Situated in the middle of Europe, Germany borders Poland and Czech Republic the east, Austria and Switzerland the south, Netherlands, Belgium, Luxemburg and France the west, and Denmark, North Sea and Baltic Sea the north, and faces Northern European countries across the ocean. The country covers a total area of 357,000 square kilometers, with coastline extending 2,389 kilometers. As of late 2010, the gross population was 81.75 million, with GDP reaching USD 3,309.7 billion, up 3.5% year-on-year., there minor change to the NIC ranking of Germany. In 2001, the NIC of Germany ranked 4th among G20 nations. In 2009, Germany rose by one place to 3rd. By analyzing the variations in the rankings of its NIC and respective elements there of among G20 nations 2001 2009, Germany.

I. Summary of Germany's NIC

The variations in the ranking and of Germany's NIC are shown in Figure 7-1, and the variations in the of 5 secondary indicators are shown in Figure 7-2 and Table 7-1.

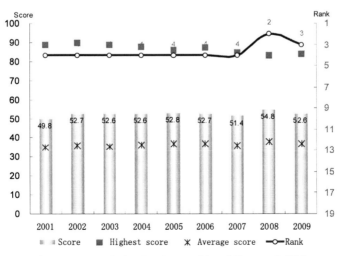

Figure 7-1   Variation Tendency of the of Germany's NIC

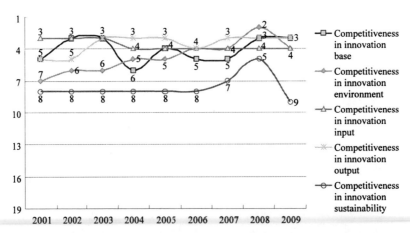

Figure 7-2   Variation Tendencies of the Rankings of the Secondary Indicators of Germany's NIC

Table 7-1   Scores and Rankings of the Secondary Indicators of Germany's NIC

Item Year	Competitiveness in innovation base		Competitiveness in innovation environment		Competitiveness in innovation input		Competitiveness in innovation output		Competitiveness in innovation sustainability		Innovation competitiveness	
	Score	Rank	Score	Rank	Score	Rank	Score	Rank	Score	Rank	Score	Rank
2001	45.8	5	62.2	7	58.2	3	34.9	5	47.6	8	49.8	4
2002	54.8	3	65.0	6	58.7	3	36.9	5	48.3	8	52.7	4
2003	56.9	3	65.6	6	58.5	3	37.2	3	44.7	8	52.6	4
2004	51.0	6	68.3	5	58.4	4	38.3	3	47.3	8	52.6	4
2005	54.5	4	69.5	5	57.1	4	39.4	3	43.6	8	52.8	4
2006	52.3	5	69.5	4	57.2	4	38.3	4	46.2	8	52.7	4
2007	55.3	5	69.2	4	56.9	4	35.1	3	40.4	7	51.4	4
2008	53.8	3	72.6	2	58.7	4	34.6	3	54.4	5	54.8	2
2009	56.3	3	70.0	4	58.0	4	35.3	3	43.6	9	52.6	3
Variance	10.5		7.8		-0.2		0.3		-4.1		2.9	
Variance		2		3		-1		2		-1		1
Quality		Strength		Strength		Strength		Strength		Advantage		Strength

(1) With respect to overall ranking, Germany's NIC ranked 3rd among G20 nations in 2009, rising by one places compared to 2001. The ranking was maintained continuously from 2001 through 2007. Generally speaking, upward fluctuations were observed in the evaluation period.

(2) With respect to the points of indicators, Germany's NIC scored 52.6 points in 2009, which is 31.2 points lower than the highest score and 15.9 points higher than the average score. Compared to 2001, Germany's score rose by 2.9 points, narrowing its gap with the

highest score in 2001 by 7.8 points and expanding gap with the average score in 2001 by 1.1 points.

(3) With respect to the ranking sections, in 2009, among the 5 secondary indicators of Germany's NIC, the competitiveness in innovation base, the competitiveness in innovation environment, the competitiveness in innovation input, and the competitiveness in innovation output were strength indicators, while the competitiveness in innovation sustainability was advantage indicators. There was no weakness indicator.

(4) With respect to the variation tendency of indicator rankings, among the 5 secondary indicators, there were three rising indicators (the competitiveness in innovation base, the competitiveness in innovation environment and the competitiveness in innovation output), which were the main drivers of the growth in Germany's NIC. There were two dropping indicators (the competitiveness in innovation input and the competitiveness in innovation sustainability).

(5) With respect to the driver of such variations, 3 secondary indicators in rankings compared to the decline of dropping indicators. Due to the influence of rising indicators, the overall ranking of Germany's NIC rose to 3rd in 2009.

II. Dynamic Variations of All Levels of Indicators of Germany's NIC

Dynamic variations of all levels indicators of Germany's NIC and the structure there of during 2001-2009 are shown in Figure 7-3 and Table 7-2.

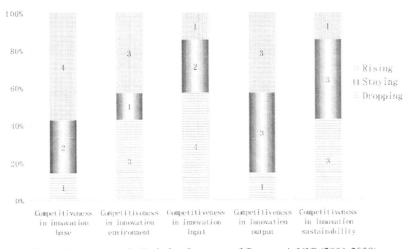

Figure 7-3   Dynamic Variation Structure of Germany's NIC (2001-2009)

Table 7-2　Comparison of the Variations in Rankings of All Levels of Indicators of Germany's NIC (2001-2009)

Secondary indicators	Number of tertiary indicators	Rising		Staying		Dropping		Variation tendency
		Number	Ratio (%)	Number	Ratio (%)	Number	Ratio (%)	
Innovation base	7	4	57.1	2	28.6	1	14.3	Rising
Innovation environment	7	3	42.9	1	14.3	3	42.9	Rising
Innovation input	7	1	14.3	2	28.6	4	57.1	Dropping
Innovation output	7	3	42.9	3	42.9	1	14.3	Rising
Innovation sustainability	7	1	14.3	3	42.9	3	42.9	Dropping
Total	35	12	34.3	11	31.4	12	34.3	Rising

According to Figure 7-3, the number of rising tertiary indicators is equal to the number of dropping ones. The figures in Table 7-2 further demonstrate that, among the 35 tertiary indicators of Germany's NIC, there are 12 rising indicators (34.3%), 11 staying indicators (31.4%) and 12 dropping indicators (34.3%). Although the number of rising indicators is equal to the number of dropping indicators, due to the combined influence of external factors, the ranking of Germany's NIC rose by one place to 3rd among G20 nations in 2009.

III. Driver Analysis on the Variations of All Levels of Indicators of Germany's NIC

Quality variations of all levels indicators of Germany's NIC and the structure there of during 2001-2009 are shown in Table 7-3.

Table 7-3　Comparison of the Quality of All Levels of Indicators of Germany's NIC (2001-2009)

Secondary indicators	Number of tertiary indicators	Strength		Advantage		Medium		Weakness		Quality
		Number	Ratio (%)	Number	Ratio (%)	Number	Ratio (%)	Number	Ratio (%)	
Innovation base	7	6	85.7	0	0.0	1	14.3	0	0.0	Strength
Innovation environment	7	3	42.9	2	28.6	2	28.6	0	0.0	Strength
Innovation input	7	4	57.1	3	42.9	0	0.0	0	0.0	Strength
Innovation output	7	5	71.4	2	28.6	0	0.0	0	0.0	Strength
Innovation sustainability	7	1	14.3	3	42.9	2	28.6	1	14.3	Advantage
Total	35	19	54.3	10	28.6	5	14.3	1	2.9	Strength

According to Figure 7-3, among the 35 tertiary indicators of Germany's NIC, there are 19 strength indicators (54.3%), 10 advantage indicators (28.6%), 5 medium indicators (14.3%), and 1 weakness indicator (2.9%). The sum of strength indicators and advantage indicators accounts for 82.9% of total indicators, which is far greater than the sum of medium indicators and weakness indicators. Among secondary indicators, there are 4 strength indicator (80%), 1 advantage indicator (20%) and medium/weakness indicator. Since the indicator system is dominated by strength indicators, Germany's NIC was during 2001-2009.

Chapter 8

Evaluation and Analysis Report n the NIC of India

Situated in the south of Asia and being the largest country on South Asi ub-ontinent, India borders Bangladesh, Burma, China, Bhutan, Nepal and Pakistan, and faces Sri Lanka and Maldives across the ocean. The country covers a total area of 3.2876 million square kilometers, measures 3,214 kilometers from north to south and 2,993 kilometers from east to west, with coastline extending more than 7,000 kilometers. As of late 2010, the gross population was 1.21 billion, with GDP reaching USD 1,729 billion, up 11.1% year-on-year., there was no much change to the NIC ranking of India. In 2001, the NIC of India ranked 18th among G20 nations. In 2009, India still ranked 18th. By analyzing the variations in the rankings of its NIC and respective elements there of among G20 nations 2001 2009, India.

I. Summary of India's NIC

The variations in the ranking and point of India's NIC are shown in Figure 8-1, and the variations in the of 5 secondary indicators are shown in Figure 8-2 and Table 8-1.

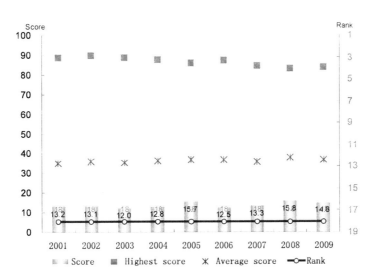

Figure 8-1   Variation Tendency of the of India's NIC

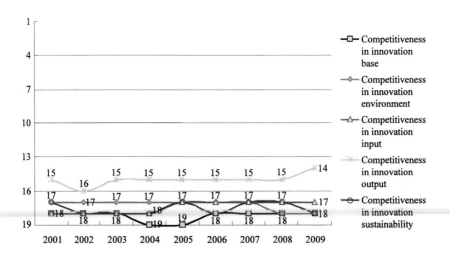

Figure 8-2   Variation Tendencies of the Rankings of the Secondary Indicators of India's NIC

Table 8-1   Scores and Rankings of the Secondary Indicators of India's NIC

Item Year	Competitiveness in innovation base		Competitiveness in innovation environment		Competitiveness in innovation input		Competitiveness in innovation output		Competitiveness in innovation sustainability		Innovation competitiveness	
	Score	Rank	Score	Rank	Score	Rank	Score	Rank	Score	Rank	Score	Rank
2001	1.4	18	22.6	17	7.7	18	9.8	15	24.5	17	13.2	18
2002	1.9	18	22.6	17	7.5	18	9.7	16	23.9	18	13.1	18
2003	2.0	18	21.8	17	7.4	18	8.8	15	20.2	18	12.0	18
2004	2.5	19	23.5	17	7.4	18	8.4	15	22.5	18	12.8	18
2005	4.0	19	25.8	17	13.6	17	7.9	15	27.0	17	15.7	18
2006	2.7	18	25.8	17	7.5	17	8.0	15	18.4	18	12.5	18
2007	2.8	18	27.1	17	7.5	17	8.0	15	21.1	17	13.3	18
2008	3.1	18	31.2	18	9.3	17	8.7	15	26.8	17	15.8	18
2009	5.3	18	29.1	18	9.8	17	10.1	14	19.7	18	14.8	18
Variance	3.9		6.6		2.1		0.2		-4.8		1.6	
Variance		0		-1		1		1		-1		0
Quality		Weakness		Weakness		Weakness		Medium		Weakness		Weakness

(1) With respect to overall ranking, India's NIC ranked 18th among G20 nations in 2009, compared to 2001. Generally speaking, there is no change to the ranking in the evaluation period.

(2) With respect to the points of indicators, India's NIC scored 14.8 points in 2009,

which is 69 points lower than the highest score and 22 points higher than the average score. Compared to 2001, India's score rose by 1.6 points, narrowing its gap with the highest score in 2001 and expanding its gap with the average score in 2001 to a certain extent.

(3) With respect to the ranking sections, in 2009, among the 5 secondary indicators of India's NIC, there no strength indicator or advantage indicator. Except for the competitiveness in innovation output which was a medium indicator he remaining four indicators were weakness indicators.

(4) With respect to the variation tendency of indicator rankings, among the 5 secondary indicators, there were two rising indicators (the competitiveness in innovation input and the competitiveness in innovation output) and two dropping indicators (the competitiveness in innovation environment and the competitiveness in innovation sustainability), which were the main drivers of the decline in India's NIC.

(5) With respect to the driver of such variations, 2 secondary indicators The overall ranking of India's NIC remained unchanged in 2009 (18th).

II. Dynamic Variations of All Levels of Indicators of India's NIC

Dynamic variations of all levels indicators of India's NIC and the structure there of during 2001-2009 are shown in Figure 8-3 and Table 8-2.

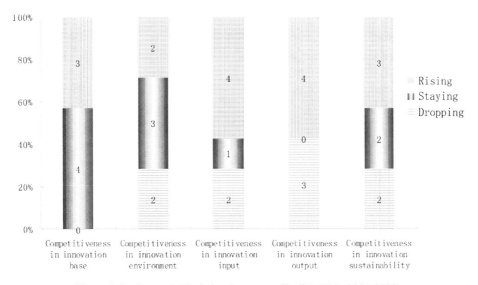

Figure 8-3   Dynamic Variation Structure of India's NIC (2001-2009)

Table 8-2 **Comparison of the Variations in Rankings of All Levels of Indicators of India's NIC (2001-2009)**

Secondary indicators	Number of tertiary indicators	Rising		Staying		Dropping		Variation tendency
		Number	Ratio (%)	Number	Ratio (%)	Number	Ratio (%)	
Innovation base	7	3	42.9	4	57.1	0	0.0	Staying
Innovation environment	7	2	28.6	3	42.9	2	28.6	Dropping
Innovation input	7	4	57.1	1	14.3	2	28.6	Rising
Innovation output	7	4	57.1	0	0.0	3	42.9	Rising
Innovation sustainability	7	3	42.9	2	28.6	2	28.6	Dropping
Total	35	16	45.7	10	28.6	9	25.7	Staying

According to Figure 8-3, the number of rising tertiary indicators is greater than the number of dropping ones, indicating that rising indicators are dominating. The figures in Table 8-2 further demonstrate that, among the 35 tertiary indicators of India's NIC, there are 16 rising indicators (45.7%), 10 staying indicators (28.6%) and 9 dropping indicators (25.7%). The rising is stronger than the dropping momentum. However, due to the combined influence of external factors, the ranking of India's NIC remained in 18th place among G20 nations in 2009.

III. Driver Analysis on the Variations of All Levels of Indicators of India's NIC

Quality variations of all levels indicators of India's NIC and the structure there of during 2001-2009 are shown in Table 8-3.

Table 8-3 **Comparison of the Quality of All Levels of Indicators of India's NIC (2001-2009)**

Secondary indicators	Number of tertiary indicators	Strength		Advantage		Medium		Weakness		Quality
		Number	Ratio (%)	Number	Ratio (%)	Number	Ratio (%)	Number	Ratio (%)	
Innovation base	7	0	0.0	2	28.6	1	14.3	4	57.1	Weakness
Innovation environment	7	0	0.0	0	0.0	5	71.4	2	28.6	Weakness
Innovation input	7	1	14.3	1	14.3	1	14.3	4	57.1	Weakness
Innovation output	7	0	0.0	1	14.3	6	85.7	0	0.0	Medium
Innovation sustainability	7	1	14.3	1	14.3	1	14.3	4	57.1	Weakness
Total	35	2	5.7	5	14.3	14	40.0	14	40.0	Weakness

According to Figure 8-3, among the 35 tertiary indicators of India's NIC, there are 2 strength indicators (5.7%), 5 advantage indicators (14.3%), 14 medium indicators (40%), and 14 weakness indicators (40.0%). The sum of strength indicators and advantage indicators accounts for 20% of total indicators, which is smaller than the sum of medium indicators and weakness indicators. Among secondary indicators, there are strength/advantage indicator, 1 medium indicator (20%) and 4 weakness indicators (80%). Since the indicator system is dominated by weakness indicators, India's NIC was during 2001-2009.

Chapter 9

Evaluation and Analysis Report n the NIC of Indonesia

Situated in Southeast Asia, Indonesia consists of thousands of islands, with territory spanning Asia and Oceania. The country covers a total area of 1.911 million square kilometers, with coastline extending 35,000 kilometers. As of late 2010, the gross population was 245 million, with GDP reaching USD 706.56 billion, up 6.1% year-on-year., there was no much change to the NIC ranking of Indonesia. In 2001, the NIC of Indonesia ranked 19th among G20 nations. In 2009, Indonesia still ranked 19th. By analyzing the variations in the rankings of its NIC and respective elements there of among G20 nations, Indonesia.

I. Summary of Indonesia's NIC

The variations in the ranking and of Indonesia's NIC are shown in Figure 9-1, and the variations in the of 5 secondary indicators are shown in Figure 9-2 and Table 9-2.

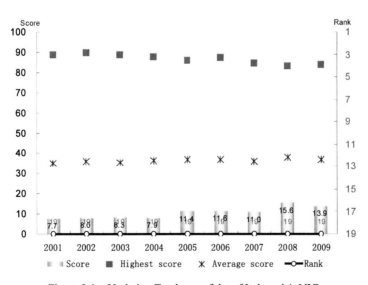

Figure 9-1   Variation Tendency of the of Indonesia's NIC

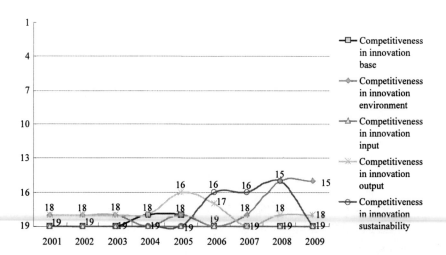

Figure 9-2   Variation Tendencies of the Rankings of the Secondary Indicators of Indonesia's NIC

Table 9-1   Scores and Rankings of the Secondary Indicators of Indonesia's NIC

Item Year	Competitiveness in innovation base		Competitiveness in innovation environment		Competitiveness in innovation input		Competitiveness in innovation output		Competitiveness in innovation sustainability		Innovation competitiveness	
	Score	Rank	Score	Rank	Score	Rank	Score	Rank	Score	Rank	Score	Rank
2001	1.3	19	16.9	18	0.7	19	6.2	18	13.3	19	7.7	19
2002	1.7	19	17.1	18	0.7	19	7.6	18	12.8	19	8.0	19
2003	1.7	19	17.4	18	0.6	19	6.4	18	15.2	19	8.3	19
2004	2.7	18	17.7	19	0.6	19	7.4	18	11.2	19	7.9	19
2005	4.6	18	23.4	18	0.7	19	7.6	16	20.6	19	11.4	19
2006	2.4	19	22.8	19	0.7	19	5.5	17	26.8	16	11.6	19
2007	1.8	19	26.2	18	0.6	19	4.9	19	21.3	16	11.0	19
2008	2.6	19	39.1	15	2.3	19	5.1	18	28.7	15	15.6	19
2009	2.7	19	39.6	15	2.8	19	5.9	18	18.7	19	13.9	19
Variance	1.4		22.7		2.1		-0.3		5.4		6.2	
Variance		0		3		0		0		0		0
Quality		Weakness		Medium		Weakness		Weakness		Weakness		Weakness

(1) With respect to overall ranking, Indonesia's NIC ranked 19th among G20 nations in 2009, unchanged compared to 2001. Generally speaking, bottom ranking was maintained in the evaluation period.

(2) With respect to the points of indicators, Indonesia's NIC scored 13.9 points in 2009,

which is 69.9 points lower than the highest score and 22.8 points higher than the average score. Compared to 2001, Indonesia's score rose by 6.2 point, narrowing its gap with the highest score in 2001 and the average score in 2001 to a certain extent.

(3) With respect to the ranking sections, in 2009, among the 5 secondary indicators of Indonesia's NIC, there no strength indicator or advantage indicator. The competitiveness in innovation base, the competitiveness in innovation input, the competitiveness in innovation output, and the competitiveness in innovation sustainability were weakness indicators.

(4) With respect to the variation tendency of indicator rankings, among the 5 secondary indicators, there was one rising indicator (the competitiveness in innovation environment) and no dropping indicator. Rankings of the other four indicators remained unchanged.

(5) With respect to the driver of such variations, secondary indicator in ranking compared to the decline of dropping indicator. However, due to the influence of external factors, the overall ranking of Indonesia's NIC remained unchanged in 2009 (19th).

II. Dynamic Variations of All Levels of Indicators of Indonesia's NIC

Dynamic variations of all levels indicators of Indonesia's NIC and the structure there of during 2001-2009 are shown in Figure 9-3 and Table 9-2.

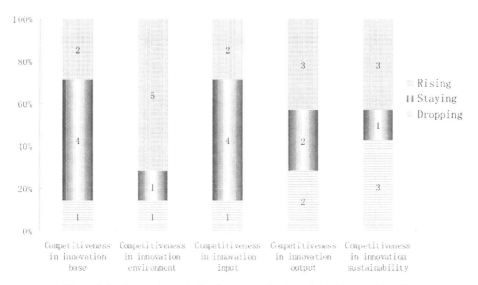

Figure 9-3   Dynamic Variation Structure of Indonesia's NIC (2001-2009)

Table 9-2　Comparison of the Variations in Rankings of All Levels of Indicators of Indonesia's NIC (2001-2009)

Secondary indicators	Number of tertiary indicators	Rising		Staying		Dropping		Variation tendency
		Number	Ratio (%)	Number	Ratio (%)	Number	Ratio (%)	
Innovation base	7	2	28.6	4	57.1	1	14.3	Staying
Innovation environment	7	5	71.4	1	14.3	1	14.3	Rising
Innovation input	7	2	28.6	4	57.1	1	14.3	Staying
Innovation output	7	3	42.9	2	28.6	2	28.6	Staying
Innovation sustainability	7	3	42.9	1	14.3	3	42.9	Staying
Total	35	15	42.9	12	34.3	8	22.9	Staying

According to Figure 9-3, the number of rising tertiary indicators is greater than the number of dropping ones, indicating that rising indicators are dominating. The figures in Table 9-2 further demonstrate that, among the 35 tertiary indicators of Indonesia's NIC, there are 15 rising indicators (42.9%), 12 staying indicators (34.3%) and 8 dropping indicators (22.9%). The rising is stronger than the dropping momentum. However, due to the combined influence of external factors, the ranking of Indonesia's NIC remained in the last place among G20 nations in 2009.

III. Driver Analysis on the Variations of All Levels of Indicators of Indonesia's NIC

Quality variations of all levels indicators of Indonesia's NIC and the structure there of during 2001-2009 are shown in Table 9-3.

Table 9-3　Comparison of the Quality of All Levels of Indicators of Indonesia's NIC (2001-2009)

Secondary indicators	Number of tertiary indicators	Strength		Advantage		Medium		Weakness		Quality
		Number	Ratio (%)	Number	Ratio (%)	Number	Ratio (%)	Number	Ratio (%)	
Innovation base	7	0	0.0	0	0.0	0	0.0	7	100.0	Weakness
Innovation environment	7	2	28.6	0	0.0	2	28.6	3	42.9	Medium
Innovation input	7	0	0.0	0	0.0	1	14.3	6	85.7	Weakness
Innovation output	7	0	0.0	0	0.0	2	28.6	5	71.4	Weakness
Innovation sustainability	7	2	28.6	0	0.0	0	0.0	5	71.4	Weakness
Total	35	4	11.4	0	0.0	5	14.3	26	74.3	Weakness

According to Figure 9-3, among the 35 tertiary indicators of Indonesia's NIC, there are 4 strength indicators (11.4%), advantage indicator, 5 medium indicators (14.3%), and 26 weakness indicators (74.3%). The sum of strength indicators and advantage indicators accounts for 11.4% of total indicators, which is smaller than the sum of medium indicators and weakness indicators. Among secondary indicators, there strength/advantage indicator, 1 medium indicator (20%) and 4 weakness indicators (80%). Since the indicator system is dominated by weakness indicators, Indonesia's NIC was during 2001-2009.

Chapter 10

Evaluation and Analysis Report n the NIC of Italy

Situated in the south of Europe, Italy mainly consists of the boot-shaped Apennine Peninsula and two Mediterranean islandsSicily and Sardinia. The country covers a total area of 301,300 square kilometers, with 80% of its borderline being coastline, which extends more than 7,200 kilometers. As of late 2010, the gross population was 60.62 million, with GDP reaching USD 2,051.4 billion, up 1.3% year-on-year., there was no much change to the NIC ranking of Italy. In 2001, the NIC of Italy ranked 9th among G20 nations. In 2009, Italy still ranked 9th. By analyzing the variations in the rankings of its NIC and respective elements there of among G20 nations 2001 2009, Italy.

I. Summary of Italy's NIC

The variations in the ranking and of Italy's NIC are shown in Figure 10-1, and the variations in the of 5 secondary indicators are shown in Figure 10-2 and Table 10-1.

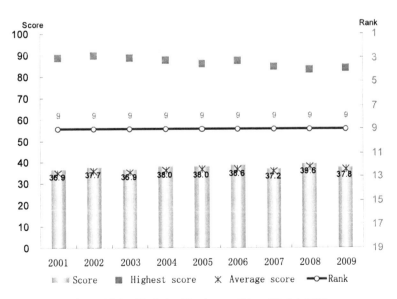

Figure 10-1   Variation Tendency of the of Italy's NIC

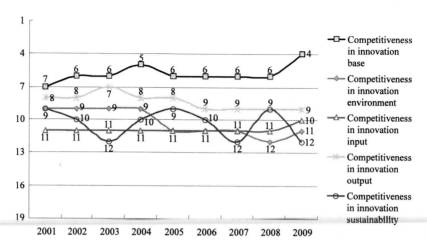

Figure 10-2　Variation Tendencies of the Rankings of the Secondary Indicators of Italy's NIC

Table 10-1　Scores and Rankings of the Secondary Indicators of Italy's NIC

Item Year	Competitiveness in innovation base		Competitiveness in innovation environment		Competitiveness in innovation input		Competitiveness in innovation output		Competitiveness in innovation sustainability		Innovation competitiveness	
	Score	Rank	Score	Rank	Score	Rank	Score	Rank	Score	Rank	Score	Rank
2001	40.8	7	48.4	9	26.0	11	26.1	8	43.3	9	36.9	9
2002	44.7	6	47.4	9	27.0	11	26.7	8	42.5	10	37.7	9
2003	50.6	6	47.9	9	25.8	11	26.1	7	34.1	12	36.9	9
2004	51.1	5	48.1	9	25.6	11	26.2	8	39.1	10	38.0	9
2005	51.2	6	48.9	11	24.2	11	25.6	8	40.1	9	38.0	9
2006	50.3	6	49.1	11	24.6	11	24.7	9	44.1	10	38.6	9
2007	52.0	6	49.9	11	25.4	11	24.8	9	33.9	12	37.2	9
2008	50.6	6	48.8	12	28.1	11	24.8	9	45.7	9	39.6	9
2009	52.7	4	47.7	11	28.3	10	24.9	9	35.4	12	37.8	9
Variance	11.8		-0.7		2.3		-1.1		-7.9		0.9	
Variance		3		-2		1		-1		-3		0
Quality		Strength		Medium		Advantage		Advantage		Medium		Advantage

(1) With respect to overall ranking, Italy's NIC ranked 9th among G20 nations in 2009, unchanged compared to 2001. Generally speaking, there is no change to the ranking in the evaluation period.

(2) With respect to the points of indicators, Italy's NIC scored 37.8 points in 2009, which is 46 points lower than the highest score and 1 point higher than the average score.

Compared to 2001, Italy's score rose by 0.9 point, narrowing its gap with the highest score in 2001 but remaining at the average score in 2001.

(3) With respect to the ranking sections, in 2009, among the 5 secondary indicators of Italy's NIC, the competitiveness in innovation base was a strength indicator, while the competitiveness in innovation input and the competitiveness in innovation output were advantage indicators. There no weakness indicator.

(4) With respect to the variation tendency of indicator rankings, among the 5 secondary indicators, there were two rising indicators (the competitiveness in innovation base and the competitiveness in innovation input) and three dropping indicators (the competitiveness in innovation environment, the competitiveness in innovation output and the competitiveness in innovation sustainability), which were the main driver of the decline in Italy's NIC.

(5) With respect to the driver of such variations, 2 secondary indicators in rankings compared to the decline of dropping indicators. Due to the combined influence of other external factors, the overall ranking of Italy's NIC remained unchanged in 2009 (9th).

II. Dynamic Variations of All Levels of Indicators of Italy's NIC

Dynamic variations of all levels indicators of Italy's NIC and the structure there of during 2001-2009 are shown in Figure 10-3 and Table 10-2.

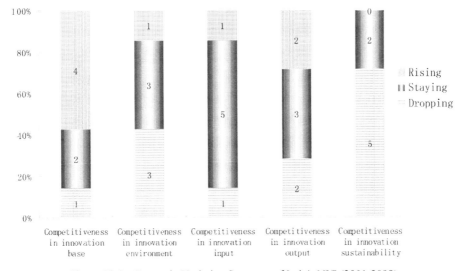

Figure 10-3   Dynamic Variation Structure of Italy's NIC (2001-2009)

Table 10-2 Comparison of the Variations in Rankings of All Levels of Indicators
of Italy's NIC (2001-2009)

Secondary indicators	Number of tertiary indicators	Rising		Staying		Dropping		Variation tendency
		Number	Ratio (%)	Number	Ratio (%)	Number	Ratio (%)	
Innovation base	7	4	57.1	2	28.6	1	14.3	Rising
Innovation environment	7	1	14.3	3	42.9	3	42.9	Dropping
Innovation input	7	1	14.3	5	71.4	1	14.3	Rising
Innovation output	7	2	28.6	3	42.9	2	28.6	Dropping
Innovation sustainability	7	0	0.0	2	28.6	5	71.4	Dropping
Total	35	8	22.9	15	42.9	12	34.3	Staying

According to Figure 10-3, the number of rising tertiary indicators is less than the number of dropping ones. The figures in Table 10-2 further demonstrate that, among the 35 tertiary indicators of Italy's NIC, there are 8 rising indicators (22.9%), 15 staying indicators (42.9%) and 12 dropping indicators (34.3%). The rising is weaker than the dropping momentum. However, due to the combined influence of external factors, the ranking of Italy's NIC remained in 9th place among G20 nations in 2009.

III. Driver Analysis on the Variations of All Levels of Indicators of Italy's NIC

Quality variations of all levels indicators of Italy's NIC and the structure there of during 2001-2009 are shown in Table 10-3.

Table 10-3   Comparison of the Quality of All Levels of Indicators of Italy's NIC (2001-2009)

Secondary indicators	Number of tertiary indicators	Strength		Advantage		Medium		Weakness		Quality
		Number	Ratio (%)	Number	Ratio (%)	Number	Ratio (%)	Number	Ratio (%)	
Innovation base	7	2	28.6	5	71.4	0	0.0	0	0.0	Strength
Innovation environment	7	2	28.6	2	28.6	1	14.3	2	28.6	Medium
Innovation input	7	0	0.0	3	42.9	4	57.1	0	0.0	Advantage
Innovation output	7	1	14.3	5	71.4	0	0.0	1	14.3	Advantage
Innovation sustainability	7	0	0.0	4	57.1	2	28.6	1	14.3	Medium
Total	35	5	14.3	19	54.3	7	20.0	4	11.4	Advantage

According to Figure 10-3, among the 35 tertiary indicators of Italy's NIC, there are 5 strength indicators (14.3%), 19 advantage indicators (54.3%), 7 medium indicators (20.0%), and 4 weakness indicator (11.4%). The sum of strength indicators and advantage indicators accounts for 68.6% of total indicators, which is far greater than the sum of medium indicators and weakness indicators. Among secondary indicators, there are 1 strength indicator (20%), 2 advantage indicators (40%), 2 medium indicators (40%), and   weakness indicator. Since the indicator system is dominated by strength indicators and advantage indicators, Italy's NIC was during 2001-2009.

Chapter 11

Evaluation and Analysis Report n the NIC of Japan

Situated off the eastern edge of the Asian continent, Japan consists of Hokkaido, Honshu, Shikoku, Kyushu, and over 3,000 small islands. The country covers a total area of 378,000 square kilometers, 70% of which are mountainous areas. Japan measures 3,800 kilometers from south to north, with coastline extending 33,889 kilometers and territorial sea area reaching 310,000 square kilometers. As of late 2010, the gross population was 128 million, with GDP reaching USD 5,497.8 billion, up 3.94% year-on-year., there was no much change to the NIC ranking of Japan. In 2001, the NIC of Japan ranked 2nd among G20 nations. In 2009, Japan still ranked 2nd. By analyzing the variations in the rankings of its NIC and respective elements there of among G20 nations 2001 2009.

I. Summary of Japan's NIC

The variations in the ranking and of Japan's NIC are shown in Figure 11-1, and the variations in theof 5 secondary indicators are shown in Figure 11-2 and Table 11-1.

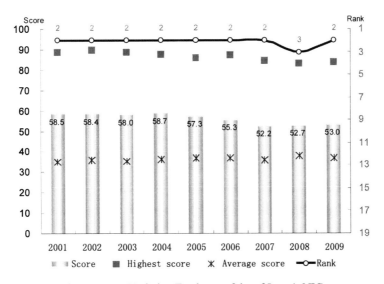

Figure 11-1　Variation Tendency of the of Japan's NIC

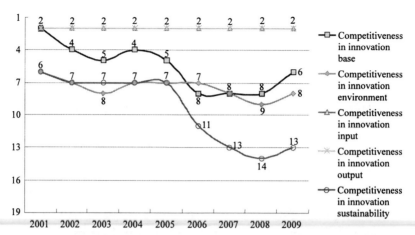

Figure 11-2   Variation Tendencies of the Rankings of the Secondary Indicators of Japan's NIC

Table 11-1   Scores and Rankings of the Secondary Indicators of Japan's NIC

Item Year	Competitiveness in innovation base		Competitiveness in innovation environment		Competitiveness in innovation input		Competitiveness in innovation output		Competitiveness in innovation sustainability		Innovation competitiveness	
	Score	Rank	Score	Rank	Score	Rank	Score	Rank	Score	Rank	Score	Rank
2001	55.9	2	62.5	6	75.2	2	48.5	2	50.2	6	58.5	2
2002	53.7	4	63.1	7	76.4	2	50.1	2	48.8	7	58.4	2
2003	53.5	5	62.7	8	76.5	2	50.5	2	46.6	7	58.0	2
2004	53.9	4	64.6	7	76.7	2	49.6	2	49.0	7	58.7	2
2005	52.4	5	65.1	7	77.5	2	46.5	2	44.8	7	57.3	2
2006	46.5	8	64.6	7	77.4	2	45.3	2	42.8	11	55.3	2
2007	45.1	8	63.3	8	77.4	2	41.9	2	33.3	13	52.2	2
2008	47.1	8	64.3	9	77.2	2	41.9	2	33.1	14	52.7	3
2009	50.6	6	62.9	8	78.1	2	41.3	2	32.0	13	53.0	2
Variance	-5.3		0.4		2.9		-7.2		-18.3		-5.5	
Variance		-4		-2		0		0		-7		0
Quality		Advantage		Advantage		Strength		Strength		Medium		Strength

(1) With respect to overall ranking, Japan's NIC ranked 2nd among G20 nations in 2009, compared to 2001. Generally speaking, minor fluctuations were observed in the evaluation period.

(2) With respect to the points of indicators, Japan's NIC scored 53 points in 2009, which is 30.8 points lower than the highest score and 16.2 points higher than the average score. Compared to 2001, Japan's score rose by 5.5 points, expanding its gap with the

highest score in 2001 and the average score in 2001 to a certain extent.

(3) With respect to the ranking sections, in 2009, among the 5 secondary indicators of Japan's NIC, the competitiveness in innovation input and the competitiveness in innovation output were strength indicators, while the competitiveness in innovation base and the competitiveness in innovation environment were advantage indicators. There no weakness indicator.

(4) With respect to the variation tendency of indicator rankings, among the 5 secondary indicators, there no rising indicator, but there were three dropping indicators (the competitiveness in innovation base, the competitiveness in innovation environment and the competitiveness in innovation sustainability), which were the main drivers of the decline in Japan's NIC. Rankings of the competitiveness in innovation input and the competitiveness in innovation output remained unchanged.

(5) With respect to the driver of such variations, no secondary indicator in ranking, yet certain indicatorsin ranking. Due to the combined influence of other factors, the overall ranking of Japan's NIC remained unchanged in 2009 (2nd).

II. Dynamic Variations of All Levels of Indicators of Japan's NIC

Dynamic variations of all levels indicators of Japan's NIC and the structure there of during 2001-2009 are shown in Figure 11-3 and Table 11-2.

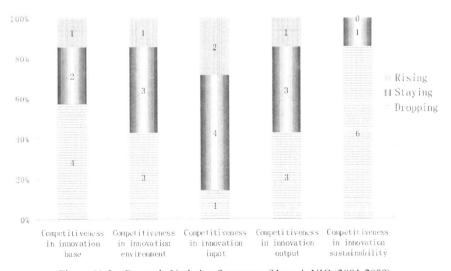

Figure 11-3   Dynamic Variation Structure of Japan's NIC (2001-2009)

Table 11-2 Comparison of the Variations in Rankings of All Levels of Indicators of Japan's NIC (2001-2009)

Secondary indicators	Number of tertiary indicators	Rising		Staying		Dropping		Variation tendency
		Number	Ratio (%)	Number	Ratio (%)	Number	Ratio (%)	
Innovation base	7	1	14.3	2	28.6	4	57.1	Dropping
Innovation environment	7	1	14.3	3	42.9	3	42.9	Dropping
Innovation input	7	2	28.6	4	57.1	1	14.3	Staying
Innovation output	7	1	14.3	3	42.9	3	42.9	Staying
Innovation sustainability	7	0	0.0	1	14.3	6	85.7	Dropping
Total	35	5	14.3	13	37.1	17	48.6	Staying

According to Figure 11-3, the number of rising tertiary indicators is less than the number of dropping ones, indicating that dropping indicators are dominating. The figures in Table 11-2 further demonstrate that, among the 35 tertiary indicators of Japan's NIC, there are 5 rising indicators (14.3%), 13 staying indicators (37.1%) and 17 dropping indicators (48.6%). The rising is weaker than the dropping momentum. However, due to the combined influence of external factors, the ranking of Japan's NIC remained in 2nd place among G20 nations in 2009.

III. Driver Analysis on the Variations of All Levels of Indicators of Japan's NIC

Quality variations of all levels indicators of Japan's NIC and the structure there of during 2001-2009 are shown in Table 11-3.

Table 11-3 Comparison of the Quality of All Levels of Indicators of Japan's NIC (2001-2009)

Secondary indicators	Number of tertiary indicators	Strength		Advantage		Medium		Weakness		Quality
		Number	Ratio (%)	Number	Ratio (%)	Number	Ratio (%)	Number	Ratio (%)	
Innovation base	7	2	28.6	4	57.1	1	14.3	0	0.0	Advantage
Innovation environment	7	1	14.3	3	42.9	3	42.9	0	0.0	Advantage
Innovation input	7	7	100.0	0	0.0	0	0.0	0	0.0	Strength
Innovation output	7	5	71.4	1	14.3	1	14.3	0	0.0	Strength
Innovation sustainability	7	2	28.6	1	14.3	3	42.9	1	14.3	Medium
Total	35	17	48.6	9	25.7	8	22.9	1	2.9	Strength

According to Figure 11-3, among the 35 tertiary indicators of Japan's NIC, there are 17 strength indicators (48.6%), 9 advantage indicators (25.7%), 8 medium indicators (22.9%), and 1 weakness indicator (2.9%). The sum of strength indicators and advantage indicators accounts for 74.3% of total indicators, which is far greater than the sum of medium indicators and weakness indicators. Among secondary indicators, there are 2 strength indicators (40%), 2 advantage indicators (40%), 1 medium indicator (20%), and weakness indicator. Since the indicator system is dominated by strength indicators and advantage indicators, Japan's NIC was during 2001-2009.

Chapter 12

Evaluation and Analysis Report n the NIC
of South Korea

Located on the southern half of the Korean Peninsula in Northeast Asia, South Korea faces Yellow Sea the southwest, Korean Strait the southeast, and the Sea of Japan the east. The country covers a total area of 99,646 square kilometers, with coastline extending 5,259 kilometers. As of late 2010, the gross population was 48.99 million, with GDP reaching USD 1014.5 billion, up 6.11% year-on-year., there a minor change to the NIC ranking of South Korea. In 2001, the NIC of South Korea ranked 6th among G20 nations. In 2009, South Korea rose by one place to 5th. By analyzing the variations in the rankings of its NIC and respective elements there of among G20 nations 2001 2009.

I. Summary of South Korea's NIC

The variations in the ranking and of South Korea's NIC are shown in Figure 12-1, and the variations in the of 5 secondary indicators are shown in Figure 12-2and Table 12-1.

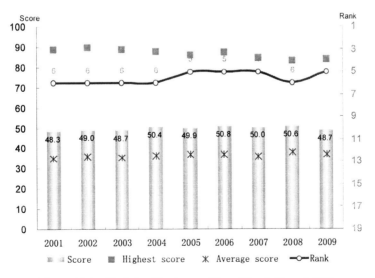

Figure 12-1   Variation Tendency of the of South Korea's NIC

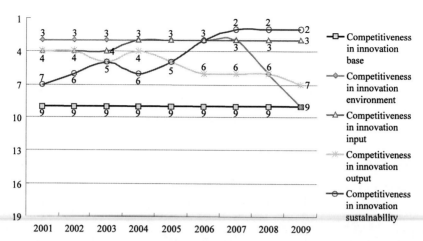

Figure 12-2　Variation Tendencies of the Rankings of the Secondary Indicators
of South Korea's NIC

Table 12-1　Scores and Rankings of the Secondary Indicators of South Korea's NIC

Item Year	Competitiveness in innovation base		Competitiveness in innovation environment		Competitiveness in innovation input		Competitiveness in innovation output		Competitiveness in innovation sustainability		Innovation competitiveness	
	Score	Rank	Score	Rank	Score	Rank	Score	Rank	Score	Rank	Score	Rank
2001	26.9	9	73.0	3	55.6	4	36.1	4	49.9	7	48.3	6
2002	28.4	9	73.3	3	55.9	4	37.2	4	50.4	6	49.0	6
2003	29.3	9	73.5	3	56.7	4	36.1	5	47.7	5	48.7	6
2004	30.5	9	73.4	3	59.2	3	34.7	4	54.0	6	50.4	6
2005	33.2	9	72.6	3	60.6	3	32.4	5	50.9	5	49.9	5
2006	32.2	9	72.4	3	63.0	3	29.8	6	56.3	3	50.8	5
2007	32.4	9	71.5	3	64.7	3	28.9	6	52.7	2	50.0	5
2008	29.1	9	69.2	6	67.1	3	28.5	6	59.3	2	50.6	6
2009	28.2	9	62.2	9	67.7	3	28.0	7	57.4	2	48.7	5
Variance	1.3		-10.8		12.2		-8.1		7.5		0.4	
Variance		0		-6		1		-3		5		1
Quality		Advantage		Advantage		Strength		Advantage		Strength		Strength

(1) With respect to overall ranking, South Korea's NIC ranked 5th among G20 nations in 2009, by one place compared to 2001. Generally speaking, upward fluctuations were observed in the evaluation period.

(2) With respect to the points of indicators, South Korea's NIC scored 48.7 points in 2009, which is 35.1 points lower than the highest score and 11.9 points higher than the average score. Compared to 2001, South Korea's score rose by 0.4 point, narrowing its gap with the highest score in 2001 and expanding its gap with the average score in 2001 to a

certain extent.

(3) With respect to the ranking sections, in 2009, among the 5 secondary indicators of South Korea's NIC, the competitiveness in innovation input and the competitiveness in innovation sustainability were strength indicators. The competitiveness in innovation base, the competitiveness in innovation environment and the competitiveness in innovation output were advantage indicators. There no weakness indicator.

(4) With respect to the variation tendency of indicator rankings, among the 5 secondary indicators, there were two rising indicators (the competitiveness in innovation input and the competitiveness in innovation sustainability) and two dropping indicators (the competitiveness in innovation environment and the competitiveness in innovation output), which were the main drivers of the decline in South Korea's NIC. Ranking of the competitiveness in innovation base remained unchanged.

(5) With respect to the driver of such variations, 2 secondary indicatorsin ranking compared to the decline of dropping indicators. However, due to the combined influence of external factors, the overall ranking of South Korea's NIC rose to 5th in 2009.

II. Dynamic Variations of All Levels of Indicators of South Korea's NIC

Dynamic variations of all levels indicators of South Korea's NIC and the structure there of during 2001-2009 are shown in Figure 12-3 and Table 12-2.

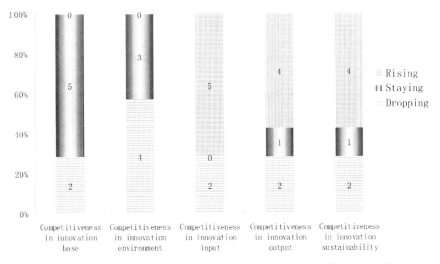

Figure 12-3   Dynamic Variation Structure of South Korea's NIC (2001-2009)

**Table 12-2   Comparison of the Variations in Rankings of All Levels of Indicators
of South Korea's NIC (2001-2009)**

Secondary indicators	Number of tertiary indicators	Rising		Staying		Dropping		Variation tendency
		Number	Ratio (%)	Number	Ratio (%)	Number	Ratio (%)	
Innovation base	7	0	0.0	5	71.4	2	28.6	Staying
Innovation environment	7	0	0.0	3	42.9	4	57.1	Dropping
Innovation input	7	5	71.4	0	0.0	2	28.6	Rising
Innovation output	7	4	57.1	1	14.3	2	28.6	Dropping
Innovation sustainability	7	4	57.1	1	14.3	2	28.6	Rising
Total	35	13	37.1	10	28.6	12	34.3	Rising

According to Figure 12-3, the number of rising tertiary indicators is greater than the number of dropping ones, indicating that rising indicators are dominating. The figures in Table 12-2 further demonstrate that, among the 35 tertiary indicators of South Korea's NIC, there are 13 rising indicators (47.1%), 10 staying indicators (28.6%) and 12 dropping indicators (34.3%). The rising is stronger than the dropping momentum. Therefore, the ranking of South Korea's NIC rose by one place to 5th among G20 nations in 2009.

III. Driver Analysis on the Variations of All Levels of Indicators of South Korea's NIC

Quality variations of all levels indicators of South Korea's NIC and the structure there of during 2001-2009 are shown in Table 12-3.

**Table 12-3   Comparison of the Quality of All Levels of Indicators
of South Korea's NIC (2001-2009)**

Secondary indicators	Number of tertiary indicators	Strength		Advantage		Medium		Weakness		Quality
		Number	Ratio (%)	Number	Ratio (%)	Number	Ratio (%)	Number	Ratio (%)	
Innovation base	7	1	14.3	3	42.9	2	28.6	1	14.3	Advantage
Innovation environment	7	2	28.6	4	57.1	1	14.3	0	0.0	Advantage
Innovation input	7	6	85.7	1	14.3	0	0.0	0	0.0	Strength
Innovation output	7	2	28.6	4	57.1	1	14.3	0	0.0	Advantage
Innovation sustainability	7	3	42.9	3	42.9	1	14.3	0	0.0	Strength
Total	35	14	40.0	15	42.9	5	14.3	1	2.9	Strength

According to Figure 12-3, among the 35 tertiary indicators of South Korea's NIC, there are 14 strength indicators (40.0%), 15 advantage indicators (42.9%), 5 medium indicators (14.3%), and 1 weakness indicator (2.9%). The sum of strength indicators and advantage indicators accounts for 82.9% of total indicators, which is far greater than the sum of medium indicators and weakness indicators. Among secondary indicators, there are 2 strength indicators (40%), 3 advantage indicators (60%)and   medium/weakness indicator. Since the indicator system is dominated by strength indicators and advantage indicators, South Korea's NIC was   during 2001-2009.

Chapter 13

Evaluation and Analysis Report the NIC of Mexico

Situated in North America, Mexico borders United States the north and Guatemala and Belize the southeast, faces Pacific Ocean the west, and the Gulf of Mexico and Caribbean the east. The country covers a total area of 1.97 million square kilometers, with coastline extending 9,330 kilometers. As of late 2010, the gross population was 110 million, with GDP reaching USD 1039.66 billion, up 5.52% year-on-year., there was no much change to the NIC ranking of Mexico. In 2001, the NIC of Mexico ranked 14th among G20 nations. In 2009, Mexico dropped two places to 16th. By analyzing the variations in the rankings of its NIC and respective elements there of among G20 nations 2001 2009, Mexico.

I. Summary of Mexico's NIC

The variations in the ranking and of Mexico's NIC are shown in Figure 13-1, and the variations in the of 5 secondary indicators are shown in Figure 13-2 and Table 13-1.

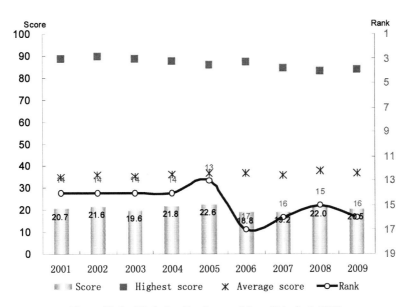

Figure 13-1   Variation Tendency of the of Mexico's NIC

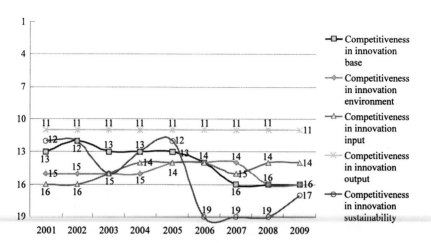

Figure 13-2　Variation Tendencies of the Rankings of the Secondary Indicators of Mexico's NIC

Table 13-1　Scores and Rankings of the Secondary Indicators of Mexico's NIC

Item Year	Competitiveness in innovation base		Competitiveness in innovation environment		Competitiveness in innovation input		Competitiveness in innovation output		Competitiveness in innovation sustainability		Innovation competitiveness	
	Score	Rank	Score	Rank	Score	Rank	Score	Rank	Score	Rank	Score	Rank
2001	12.7	13	28.7	15	11.3	16	15.6	11	35.5	12	20.7	14
2002	14.3	12	29.5	15	12.7	16	16.2	11	35.6	12	21.6	14
2003	13.9	13	30.1	15	12.3	15	16.8	11	25.2	15	19.6	14
2004	13.2	13	30.7	15	15.6	14	15.8	11	33.9	13	21.8	14
2005	14.5	13	34.4	14	16.3	14	15.4	11	32.4	12	22.6	13
2006	12.6	14	34.2	14	15.5	14	15.4	11	16.1	19	18.8	17
2007	12.2	16	34.4	14	15.4	15	14.6	11	19.4	19	19.2	16
2008	11.8	16	38.2	16	16.7	14	16.6	11	26.6	19	22.0	15
2009	10.4	16	37.4	16	16.7	14	18.0	11	19.9	17	20.5	16
Variance	-2.2		8.7		5.4		2.4		-15.6		-0.3	
Variance		-3		-1		2		0		-5		-2
Quality		Weakness		Weakness		Medium		Medium		Weakness		Weakness

(1) With respect to overall ranking, Mexico's NIC ranked 16th among G20 nations in 2009, two places compared to 2001. Generally speaking, downward fluctuations were observed in the evaluation period.

(2) With respect to the points of indicators, Mexico's NIC scored 20.5 points in 2009, which is 63.3 points lower than the highest score and 16.3 points lower than the average

score. Compared to 2001, Mexico's score dropped by 0.3 point, narrowing its gap with the highest score in 2001 and expanding its gap with the average score in 2001.

(3) With respect to the ranking sections, in 2009, among the 5 secondary indicators of Mexico's NIC, there no strength indicator or advantage indicator. The competitiveness in innovation base, the competitiveness in innovation environment and the competitiveness in innovation sustainability were weakness indicators.

(4) With respect to the variation tendency of indicator rankings, among the 5 secondary indicators, there were one rising indicator (the competitiveness in innovation input) and three dropping indicators (the competitiveness in innovation base, the competitiveness in innovation environment and the competitiveness in innovation sustainability), which were the main drivers of the decline in Mexico's NIC. Ranking of the competitiveness in innovation output remained unchanged.

(5) With respect to the driver of such variations, secondary indicator in ranking compared to the decline of dropping indicators. Due to the influence of dropping indicators, the overall ranking of Mexico's NIC dropped to 16th in 2009.

II. Dynamic Variations of All Levels of Indicators of Mexico's NIC

Dynamic variations of all levels indicators of Mexico's NIC and the structure there of during 2001-2009 are shown in Figure 13-3 and Table 13-2.

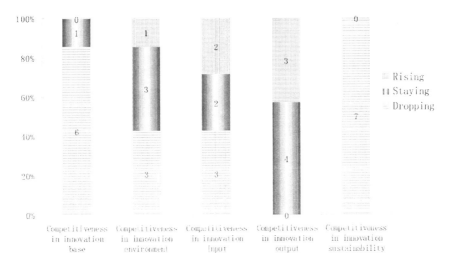

Figure 13-3   Dynamic Variation Structure of Mexico's NIC (2001-2009)

Table 13-2 Comparison of the Variations in Rankings of All Levels of Indicators of Mexico's NIC (2001-2009)

Secondary indicators	Number of tertiary indicators	Rising		Staying		Dropping		Variation tendency
		Number	Ratio (%)	Number	Ratio (%)	Number	Ratio (%)	
Innovation base	7	0	0.0	1	14.3	6	85.7	Dropping
Innovation environment	7	1	14.3	3	42.9	3	42.9	Dropping
Innovation input	7	2	28.6	2	28.6	3	42.9	Rising
Innovation output	7	3	42.9	4	57.1	0	0.0	Staying
Innovation sustainability	7	0	0.0	0	0.0	7	100.0	Dropping
Total	35	6	17.1	10	28.6	19	54.3	Dropping

According to Figure 13-3, the number of rising tertiary indicators is less than the number of dropping ones, indicating that dropping indicators are dominating. The figures in Table 13-2 further demonstrate that, among the 35 tertiary indicators of Mexico's NIC, there are 6 rising indicators (17.1%), 10 staying indicators (28.6%) and 19 dropping indicators (54.3%). The rising is weaker than the dropping momentum. Therefore, the ranking of Mexico's NIC dropped two places to 16th among G20 nations in 2009.

III. Driver Analysis on the Variations of All Levels of Indicators of Mexico's NIC

Quality variations of all levels indicators of Mexico's NIC and the structure there of during 2001-2009 are shown in Table 13-3.

Table 13-3 Comparison of the Quality of All Levels of Indicators of Mexico's NIC (2001-2009)

Secondary indicators	Number of tertiary indicators	Strength		Advantage		Medium		Weakness		Quality
		Number	Ratio (%)	Number	Ratio (%)	Number	Ratio (%)	Number	Ratio (%)	
Innovation base	7	0	0.0	0	0.0	7	100.0	0	0.0	Weakness
Innovation environment	7	0	0.0	1	14.3	4	57.1	2	28.6	Weakness
Innovation input	7	0	0.0	2	28.6	1	14.3	4	57.1	Medium
Innovation output	7	0	0.0	4	57.1	3	42.9	0	0.0	Medium
Innovation sustainability	7	0	0.0	1	14.3	3	42.9	3	42.9	Weakness
Total	35	0	0.0	8	22.9	18	51.4	9	25.7	Weakness

According to Figure 13-3, among the 35 tertiary indicators of Mexico's NIC, there are strength indicator, 8 advantage indicators (22.9%), 18 medium indicators (54.1%), and 9 weakness indicators (25.7%). The sum of strength indicators and advantage indicators accounts for 22.9% of total indicators, which is smaller than the sum of medium indicators and weakness indicators. Among secondary indicators, there are   strength/advantage indicator, 2 medium indicator (40%) and 3 weakness indicators (60%). Since the indicator system is dominated by weakness indicators, Mexico's NIC was during 2001-2009.

Chapter 14

Evaluation and Analysis Report n the NIC of Russia

Boasting the largest land area in the world, Russia crosses European and Asian continents and borders multiple countries, with coastline extending from Arctic Oceanto North Pacific, including Black Sea and Caspian Sea (continental sea). The country covers a total area of 17.07 million square kilometers and measures 9,000 kilometers from east to west and 4,000 kilometers from south to north, with coastline extending 37,653 kilometers. As of late 2010, the gross population was 140 million, with GDP reaching USD 1479.8 billion, up 4% year-on-year., there notable change to the NIC ranking of Russia. In 2001, the NIC of Russia ranked 10th among G20 nations. In 2009, Russia dropped two places to 12th. By analyzing the variations in the rankings of its NIC and respective elements there of among G20 nations 2001 2009.

I. Summary of Russia's NIC

The variations in the ranking and of Russia's NIC are shown in Figure 14-1, and the variations in the of 5 secondary indicators are shown in Figure 14-2 and Table 14-1.

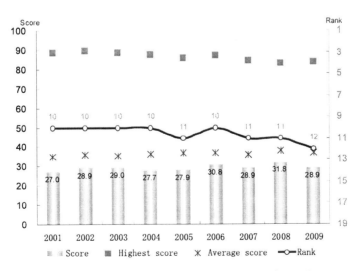

Figure 14-1   Variation Tendency of the of Russia's NIC

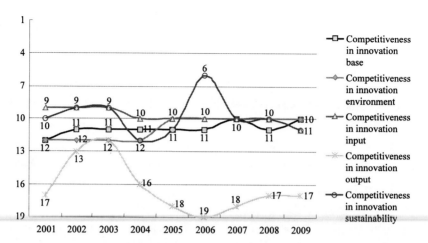

Figure 14-2　Variation Tendencies of the Rankings of the Secondary Indicators of Russia's NIC

Table 14-1　Scores and Rankings of the Secondary Indicators of Russia's NIC

Item Year	Competitiveness in innovation base		Competitiveness in innovation environment		Competitiveness in innovation input		Competitiveness in innovation output		Competitiveness in innovation sustainability		Innovation competitiveness	
	Score	Rank	Score	Rank	Score	Rank	Score	Rank	Score	Rank	Score	Rank
2001	13.2	12	36.2	12	35.7	9	8.0	17	41.9	10	27.0	10
2002	14.3	11	37.2	12	35.9	9	11.8	13	45.2	9	28.9	10
2003	15.6	11	39.8	12	34.2	9	11.0	12	44.6	9	29.0	10
2004	17.7	11	44.1	12	32.5	10	7.8	16	36.2	12	27.7	10
2005	20.3	11	49.6	10	28.9	10	5.5	18	35.2	11	27.9	11
2006	20.6	11	49.8	10	28.1	10	5.1	19	50.4	6	30.8	10
2007	23.2	10	50.8	10	28.1	10	5.0	18	37.2	10	28.9	11
2008	25.9	11	55.6	10	28.3	10	5.3	17	43.7	10	31.8	11
2009	22.8	10	51.5	10	27.8	11	6.3	17	35.8	11	28.9	12
Variance	9.6		15.4		-7.9		-1.8		-6.1		1.8	
Variance		2		2		-2		0		-1		-2
Quality		Advantage		Advantage		Medium		Weakness		Medium		Medium

(1) With respect to overall ranking, Russia's NIC ranked 12th among G20 nations in 2009, by two places compared to 2001. Generally speaking, downward fluctuations were observed in the evaluation period.

(2) With respect to the points of indicators, Russia's NIC scored 28.9 points in 2009, which is 54.9 points lower than the highest score and 7.9 points lower than the average

score. Compared to 2001, Russia's score rose by 1.8 points, narrowing its gap with the highest score in 2001 and the average score in 2001 to a certain extent.

(3) With respect to the ranking sections, in 2009, among the 5 secondary indicators of Russia's NIC, there no strength. The competitiveness in innovation base and the competitiveness in innovation environment were advantage indicators, while the competitiveness in innovation output was a weakness indicator.

(4) With respect to the variation tendency of indicator rankings, among the 5 secondary indicators, there were two rising indicators (the competitiveness in innovation base and the competitiveness in innovation environment) and two dropping indicators (the competitiveness in innovation input and the competitiveness in innovation sustainability), which were the main drivers of the decline in Russia's NIC. Ranking of the competitiveness in innovation output remained unchanged.

(5) With respect to the driver of such variations, 2 secondary indicators in rankings compared to the decline of dropping indicators. Due to such influence, the overall ranking of Russia's NIC dropped to 12th in 2009.

II. Dynamic Variations of All Levels of Indicators of Russia's NIC

Dynamic variations of all levels indicators of Russia's NIC and the structure there of during 2001-2009 are shown in Figure 14-3 and Table 14-2.

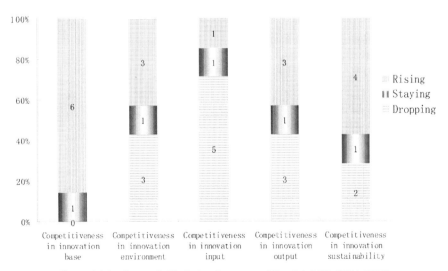

Figure 14-3　Dynamic Variation Structure of Russia's NIC (2001-2009)

Table 14-2 Comparison of the Variations in Rankings of All Levels of Indicators of Russia's NIC (2001-2009)

Secondary indicators	Number of tertiary indicators	Rising		Staying		Dropping		Variation tendency
		Number	Ratio (%)	Number	Ratio (%)	Number	Ratio (%)	
Innovation base	7	6	85.7	1	14.3	0	0.0	Rising
Innovation environment	7	3	42.9	1	14.3	3	42.9	Rising
Innovation input	7	1	14.3	1	14.3	5	71.4	Dropping
Innovation output	7	3	42.9	1	14.3	3	42.9	Staying
Innovation sustainability	7	4	57.1	1	14.3	2	28.6	Dropping
Total	35	17	48.6	5	14.3	13	37.1	Dropping

According to Figure 14-3, the number of rising tertiary indicators is greater than the number of dropping ones, indicating that rising indicators are dominating. The figures in Table 14-2 further demonstrate that, among the 35 tertiary indicators of Russia's NIC, there are 17 rising indicators (48.6%), 5 staying indicators (14.3%) and 13 dropping indicators (37.1%). The rising is stronger than the dropping momentum. However, due to the combined influence of external factors, the ranking of Russia's NIC dropped two places to 12th among G20 nations in 2009.

III. Driver Analysis on the Variations of All Levels of Indicators of Russia's NIC

Quality variations of all levels indicators of Russia's NIC and the structure there of during 2001-2009 are shown in Table 14-3.

Table 14-3 Comparison of the Quality of All Levels of Indicators of Russia's NIC (2001-2009)

Secondary indicators	Number of tertiary indicators	Strength		Advantage		Medium		Weakness		Quality
		Number	Ratio (%)	Number	Ratio (%)	Number	Ratio (%)	Number	Ratio (%)	
Innovation base	7	1	14.3	2	28.6	4	57.1	0	0.0	Advantage
Innovation environment	7	2	28.6	2	28.6	1	14.3	2	28.6	Advantage
Innovation input	7	1	14.3	4	57.1	1	14.3	1	14.3	Medium
Innovation output	7	0	0.0	1	14.3	5	71.4	1	14.3	Weakness
Innovation sustainability	7	1	14.3	3	42.9	2	28.6	1	14.3	Medium
Total	35	5	14.3	12	34.3	13	37.1	5	14.3	Medium

According to Figure 14-3, among the 35 tertiary indicators of Russia's NIC, there are 5 strength indicators (14.3%), 12 advantage indicators (34.3%), 13 medium indicators (37.1%), and 5 weakness indicator (14.3%). The sum of strength indicators and advantage indicators accounts for 48.6% of total indicators, which is smaller than the sum of medium indicators and weakness indicators. Among secondary indicators, there are 2 strength indicators (40%), 2 advantage indicators (40%), 1 medium indicator (20%), and   weakness indicator. Since the indicator system is dominated by medium indicators and weakness indicators, Russia's NIC was average during 2001-2009.

Chapter 15

Evaluation and Analysis Reportn the NIC
of Saudi Arabia

Located on Arabian Peninsula in the southwest of Asia, Saudi Arabia faces the gulf on the east and Red Sea on the west, and borders Jordan, Iraq, Kuwait, United Arab Emirates, Oman, and Yemen. The country covers a total area of 2.55 million square kilometers, with coastline extending 2,437 kilometers. As of late 2010, the gross population was 27.14 million, with GDP reaching USD 434.666 billion, up 3.74% year-on-year., there was no much change to the NIC ranking of Saudi Arabia. In 2001, the NIC of Saudi Arabia ranked 11th among G20 nations. In 2009, Saudi Arabia still ranked 11th. By analyzing the variations in the rankings of its NIC and respective elements there of among G20 nations 2001 2009, Saudi Arabia.

I. Summary of Saudi Arabia's NIC

The variations in the ranking and of Saudi Arabia's NIC are shown in Figure 15-1, and the variations in the of 5 secondary indicators are shown in Figure 15-2 and Table 15-1.

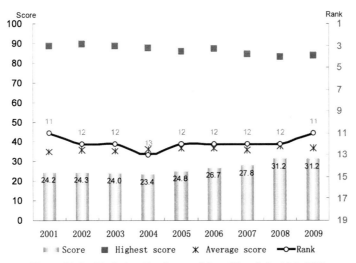

Figure 15-1   Variation Tendency of the of Saudi Arabia's NIC

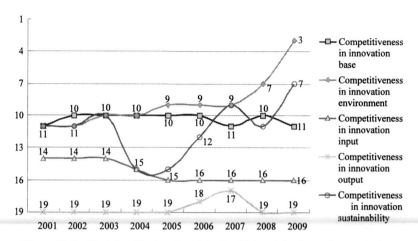

Figure 15-2   Variation Tendencies of the Rankings of the Secondary Indicators
of Saudi Arabia's NIC

Table 15-1   Scores and Rankings of the Secondary Indicators of Saudi Arabia's NIC

Item Year	Competitiveness in innovation base		Competitiveness in innovation environment		Competitiveness in innovation input		Competitiveness in innovation output		Competitiveness in innovation sustainability		Innovation competitiveness	
	Score	Rank	Score	Rank	Score	Rank	Score	Rank	Score	Rank	Score	Rank
2001	16.3	11	42.8	11	15.1	14	5.6	19	41.4	11	24.2	11
2002	15.2	10	44.5	11	15.1	14	6.2	19	40.8	11	24.3	12
2003	16.4	10	45.2	10	14.6	14	5.4	19	38.3	10	24.0	12
2004	18.9	10	46.8	10	14.6	15	4.9	19	31.9	15	23.4	13
2005	24.5	10	51.2	9	14.5	16	5.5	19	28.4	15	24.8	12
2006	23.9	10	56.1	9	14.0	16	5.4	18	34.3	12	26.7	12
2007	22.1	11	59.8	9	13.7	16	5.5	17	38.1	9	27.8	12
2008	27.3	10	68.4	7	14.4	16	4.9	19	41.2	11	31.2	12
2009	19.6	11	71.8	3	14.4	16	4.9	19	45.1	7	31.2	11
Variance	3.3		29.0		-0.7		-0.7		3.7		6.9	
Variance		0		8		-2		0		4		0
Quality		Medium		Strength		Weakness		Weakness		Advantage		Medium

(1) With respect to overall ranking, Saudi Arabia's NIC ranked 11th among G20 nations in 2009, compared to 2001. Generally speaking, minor fluctuations were observed in the evaluation period.

(2) With respect to the points of indicators, Saudi Arabia's NIC scored 31.2 points in 2009, which is 52.6 points lower than the highest score and 5.6 points lower than the average score. Compared to 2001, Saudi Arabia's score rose by 7 point, narrowing its gap

with the highest score in 2001 and the average score in 2001.

(3) With respect to the ranking sections, in 2009, among the 5 secondary indicators of Saudi Arabia's NIC, the competitiveness in innovation environment was a strength indicator, while the competitiveness in innovation sustainability was an advantage indicator. The competitiveness in innovation input and the competitiveness in innovation output were weakness indicators.

(4) With respect to the variation tendency of indicator rankings, among the 5 secondary indicators, there were two rising indicators (the competitiveness in innovation environment and the competitiveness in innovation sustainability) and one dropping indicator (the competitiveness in innovation input), which was the main driver of the decline in Saudi Arabia's NIC. Rankings of the competitiveness in innovation base and the competitiveness in innovation output remained unchanged.

(5) With respect to the driver of such variations, secondary indicators have seen a greater boost in ranking compared to the decline of dropping indicator. However, due to the combined influence of external factors, the overall ranking of Saudi Arabia's NIC remained unchanged in 2009 (11th).

II. Dynamic Variations of All Levels of Indicators of Saudi Arabia's NIC

Dynamic variations of all levels indicators of Saudi Arabia's NIC and the structure there of during 2001-2009 are shown in Figure 15-3 and Table 15-2.

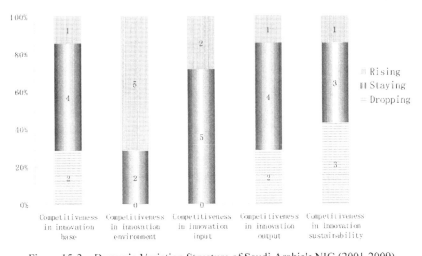

Figure 15-3   Dynamic Variation Structure of Saudi Arabia's NIC (2001-2009)

Table 15-2 Comparison of the Variations in Rankings of All Levels of Indicators of Saudi Arabia's NIC (2001-2009)

Secondary indicators	Number of tertiary indicators	Rising		Staying		Dropping		Variation tendency
		Rising	Staying	Dropping	Rising	Staying	Dropping	
Innovation base	7	1	14.3	4	57.1	2	28.6	Staying
Innovation environment	7	5	71.4	2	28.6	0	0.0	Rising
Innovation input	7	2	28.6	5	71.4	0	0.0	Dropping
Innovation output	7	1	14.3	4	57.1	2	28.6	Staying
Innovation sustainability	7	1	14.3	3	42.9	3	42.9	Rising
Total	35	10	28.6	18	51.4	7	20.0	Staying

According to Figure 15-3, the number of rising tertiary indicators is greater than the number of dropping ones. The figures in Table 15-2 further demonstrate that, among the 35 tertiary indicators of Saudi Arabia's NIC, there are 10 rising indicators (28.6%), 18 staying indicators (51.4%) and 7 dropping indicators (20.0%). The rising impetus is stronger than the dropping momentum. However, due to the combined influence of external factors, the ranking of Saudi Arabia's NIC remained in 11th place among G20 nations in 2009.

III. Driver Analysis on the Variations of All Levels of Indicators of Saudi Arabia's NIC

Quality variations of all levels indicators of Saudi Arabia's NIC and the structure there of during 2001-2009 are shown in Table 15-3.

Table 15-3 Comparison of the Quality of All Levels of Indicators of Saudi Arabia's NIC (2001-2009)

Secondary indicators	Number of tertiary indicators	Strength		Advantage		Medium		Weakness		Quality
		Number	Ratio (%)	Number	Ratio (%)	Number	Ratio (%)	Number	Ratio (%)	
Innovation base	7	0	0.0	3	42.9	2	28.6	2	28.6	Medium
Innovation environment	7	4	57.1	1	14.3	1	14.3	1	14.3	Strength
Innovation input	7	0	0.0	2	28.6	0	0.0	5	71.4	Weakness
Innovation output	7	0	0.0	0	0.0	1	14.3	6	85.7	Weakness
Innovation sustainability	7	2	28.6	2	28.6	2	28.6	1	14.3	Advantage
Total	35	6	17.1	8	22.9	6	17.1	15	42.9	Medium

According to Figure 15-3, among the 35 tertiary indicators of Saudi Arabia's NIC, there are 6 strength indicators (17.1%), 8 advantage indicators (22.9%), 6 medium indicators (17.1%), and 15 weakness indicator (42.9%). The sum of strength indicators and advantage indicators accounts for 40% of total indicators, which is smaller than the sum of medium indicators and weakness indicators. Among secondary indicators, there 1 strength indicator (20%), 1 advantage indicator (20%), 1 medium indicator (20%), and 2 weakness indicators (40%). Since the indicator system is dominated by medium indicators, Saudi Arabia's NIC was average during 2001-2009.

Chapter 16

Evaluation and Analysis Reportn
the NIC of South Africa

Located at the south end of African continent, South Africa faces Indian Ocean, Atlantic Ocean and Antarctic Ocean on east, west and south respectively, with coastline extending 3,000 kilometers. The country covers a total area of 1.219 million square kilometers, which is smaller than Xinjiang Uygur Autonomous Region but slightly larger than Inner Mongolia Autonomous Region of China. As of late 2010, the gross population was 50.58 million, with GDP reaching USD 363.7 billion, up 2.78% year-on-year., there minor change to the NIC ranking of South Africa. In 2001, the NIC of South Africa ranked 13th among G20 nations. In 2009, South Africa dropped two places to 15th. By analyzing the variations in the rankings of its NIC and respective elements there of among G20 nations 2001 2009, South Africa.

I. Summary of South Africa's NIC

The variations in the ranking and of South Africa's NIC are shown in Figure 16-1, and the variations in the of 5 secondary indicators are shown in Figure 16-2 and Table 16-1.

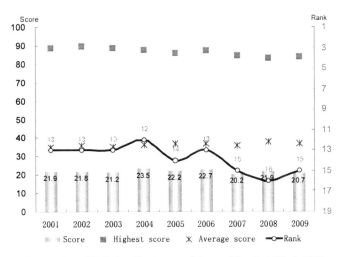

Figure 16-1   Variation Tendency of the   of South Africa's NIC

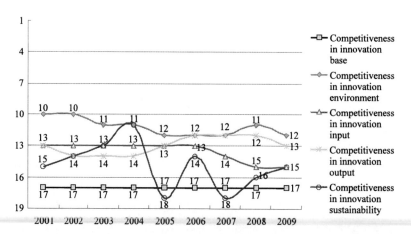

Figure 16-2　Variation Tendencies of the Rankings of the Secondary Indicators
of South Africa's NIC

Table 16-1　Scores and Rankings of the Secondary Indicators of South Africa's NIC

Item Year	Competitiveness in innovation base		Competitiveness in innovation environment		Competitiveness in innovation input		Competitiveness in innovation output		Competitiveness in innovation sustainability		Innovation competitiveness	
	Score	Rank	Score	Rank	Score	Rank	Score	Rank	Score	Rank	Score	Rank
2001	4.6	17	44.5	10	19.0	13	10.9	13	30.3	15	21.9	13
2002	3.8	17	44.9	10	19.6	13	11.2	14	29.6	14	21.8	13
2003	5.0	17	45.2	11	19.8	13	9.9	14	25.9	13	21.2	13
2004	6.6	17	46.2	11	18.5	13	9.0	14	37.3	11	23.5	12
2005	9.0	17	48.5	12	17.1	13	10.7	13	25.9	18	22.2	14
2006	6.4	17	48.7	12	16.9	13	10.3	12	31.3	14	22.7	13
2007	6.0	17	49.1	12	15.5	14	10.9	12	19.7	18	20.2	15
2008	5.6	17	49.5	11	16.0	15	11.1	12	27.5	16	21.9	16
2009	5.9	17	43.8	12	15.8	15	12.1	13	25.8	15	20.7	15
Variance	1.3		-0.7		-3.2		1.2		-4.5		-1.2	
Variance		0		-2		-2		0		0		-2
Quality		Weakness		Medium		Medium		Medium		Medium		Medium

(1) With respect to overall ranking, South Africa's NIC ranked 15th among G20 nations in 2009, compared to 2001. Generally speaking, downward fluctuations were observed in the evaluation period.

(2) With respect to the points of indicators, South Africa's NIC scored 20.7 points in 2009, which is 63.1 points lower than the highest score and 16.1 points lower than the

average score. Compared to 2001, South Africa's score dropped by 1.2 points, narrowing its gap with the highest score in 2001 and expanding its gap with the average score in 2001.

(3) With respect to the ranking sections, in 2009, among the 5 secondary indicators of South Africa's NIC, there no strength indicator or advantage indicator. The competitiveness in innovation base was a weakness indicator.

(4) With respect to the variation tendency of indicator rankings, among the 5 secondary indicators, there was no rising indicator, but there were two rising indicators (the competitiveness in innovation environment and the competitiveness in innovation input), which were the main drivers of the decline in South Africa's NIC. Rankings of the competitiveness in innovation base, the competitiveness in innovation output and the competitiveness in innovation sustainability remained unchanged.

(5) With respect to the driver of such variations, no secondary indicator has seen a boost in rankings, while 2 secondary indicators have experienced a drop in rankings. Due to the influence of dropping indicators, the overall ranking of South Africa's NIC dropped to 15th in 2009.

II. Dynamic Variations of All Levels of Indicators of South Africa's NIC

Dynamic variations of all levels indicators of South Africa's NIC and the structure there of during 2001-2009 are shown in Figure 16-3 and Table 16-2.

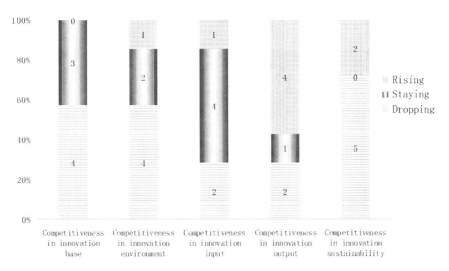

Figure 16-3   Dynamic Variation Structure of South Africa's NIC (2001-2009)

**Table 16-2   Comparison of the Variations in Rankings of All Levels of Indicators
of South Africa's NIC (2001-2009)**

Secondary indicators	Number of tertiary indicators	Rising		Staying		Dropping		Variation tendency
		Number	Ratio (%)	Number	Ratio (%)	Number	Ratio (%)	
Innovation base	7	0	0.0	3	42.9	4	57.1	Staying
Innovation environment	7	1	14.3	2	28.6	4	57.1	Dropping
Innovation input	7	1	14.3	4	57.1	2	28.6	Dropping
Innovation output	7	4	57.1	1	14.3	2	28.6	Staying
Innovation sustainability	7	2	28.6	0	0.0	5	71.4	Staying
Total	35	8	22.9	10	28.6	17	48.6	Dropping

According to Figure 16-3, the number of rising tertiary indicators is less than the number of dropping ones, indicating that dropping indicators are dominating. The figures in Table 16-2 further demonstrate that, among the 35 tertiary indicators of South Africa's NIC, there are 8 rising indicators (22.9%), 10 staying indicators (28.6%) and 17 dropping indicators (48.6%). The rising is weaker than the dropping momentum. Therefore, the ranking of South Africa's NIC dropped two places to 15th among G20 nations in 2009.

III. Driver Analysis on the Variations of All Levels of Indicators of South Africa's NIC

Quality variations of all levels indicators of South Africa's NIC and the structure there of during 2001-2009 are shown in Table 16-3.

**Table 16-3   Comparison of the Quality of All Levels of Indicators
of South Africa's NIC (2001-2009)**

Secondary indicators	Number of tertiary indicators	Strength		Advantage		Medium		Weakness		Quality
		Number	Ratio (%)	Number	Ratio (%)	Number	Ratio (%)	Number	Ratio (%)	
Innovation base	7	0	0.0	0	0.0	0	0.0	7	100.0	Weakness
Innovation environment	7	1	14.3	1	14.3	2	28.6	3	42.9	Medium
Innovation input	7	0	0.0	0	0.0	5	71.4	2	28.6	Medium
Innovation output	7	0	0.0	2	28.6	1	14.3	4	57.1	Medium
Innovation sustainability	7	0	0.0	3	42.9	2	28.6	2	28.6	Medium
Total	35	1	2.9	6	17.1	10	28.6	18	51.4	Medium

According to Figure 16-3, among the 35 tertiary indicators of South Africa's NIC, there are 1 strength indicator (2.9%), 6 advantage indicators (17.1%), 10 medium indicators (28.6%), and 18 weakness indicators (51.4%). The sum of strength indicators and advantage indicators accounts for 20.0% of total indicators, which is smaller than the sum of medium indicators and weakness indicators. Among secondary indicators, there are strength/advantage indicator, 4 medium indicators (80%) and 1 weakness indicators (20%). Since the indicator system is dominated by medium indicators, South Africa's NIC was average during 2001-2009.

Chapter 17

Evaluation and Analysis Reportn
the NIC of Turkey

Crossing European and Asian continents, Turkey consists of Anatolian Peninsula and the Thrace in the east of Balkan Peninsula. It borders Black Sea north and Mediterranean Sea south, Syria and Iraq southeast, Aegean Sea, Greece and Bulgaria west, and Georgia, Armenia, Azerbaijan and Iran east. The country covers a total area of 780,000 square kilometers, which is slightly smaller than Pakistan but larger than Qinghai Province of China, with coastline extending 8,046 kilometers. As of late 2010, the gross population was 73.72 million, with GDP reaching USD 735.2 billion, up 8.2% year-on-year., there a minor change to the NIC ranking of Turkey. In 2001, the NIC of Turkey ranked 16th among G20 nations. In 2009, Turkey rose by two places to 14th. By analyzing the variations in the rankings of its NIC and respective elements there of among G20 nations 2001 2009, Turkey.

I. Summary of Turkey's NIC

The variations in the ranking and of Turkey's NIC are shown in Figure 17-1, and the variations in the of 5 secondary indicators are shown in Figure 17-2 and Table 17-1.

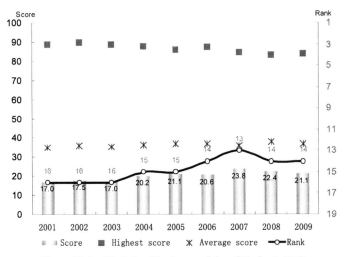

Figure 17-1   Variation Tendency of the of Turkey's NIC

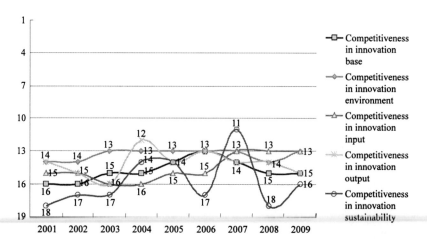

Figure 17-2 Variation Tendencies of the Rankings of the Secondary Indicators of Turkey's NIC

Table 17-1 Scores and Rankings of the Secondary Indicators of Turkey's NIC

Item Year	Competitiveness in innovation base		Competitiveness in innovation environment		Competitiveness in innovation input		Competitiveness in innovation output		Competitiveness in innovation sustainability		Innovation competitiveness	
	Score	Rank	Score	Rank	Score	Rank	Score	Rank	Score	Rank	Score	Rank
2001	6.7	16	29.9	14	14.4	15	9.9	14	24.3	18	17.0	16
2002	7.3	16	31.5	14	13.5	15	11.1	15	24.2	17	17.5	16
2003	9.1	15	34.8	13	11.7	16	8.7	16	21.0	17	17.0	16
2004	10.9	15	35.3	13	12.0	16	10.3	12	32.4	14	20.2	15
2005	14.3	14	36.3	13	14.5	15	10.5	14	29.9	14	21.1	15
2006	13.6	13	38.2	13	15.4	15	10.3	13	25.6	17	20.6	14
2007	14.0	14	40.0	13	17.8	13	9.8	14	37.1	11	23.8	13
2008	14.1	15	42.4	14	18.8	13	10.2	14	26.6	18	22.4	14
2009	13.1	15	41.7	13	18.0	13	10.0	15	22.8	16	21.1	14
Variance	6.4		11.8		3.6		0.2		-1.4		4.1	
Variance		1		1		2		-1		2		2
Quality		Medium		Medium		Medium		Medium		Weakness		Medium

(1) With respect to overall ranking, Turkey's NIC ranked 14th among G20 nations in 2009, by two places compared to 2001. The ranking rose with fluctuations from 2001 through 2007. Generally speaking, upward fluctuations were observed in the evaluation period.

(2) With respect to the points of indicators, Turkey's NIC scored 21.1 points in 2009,

which is 62.7 points lower than the highest score and 15.7 points lower than the average score. Compared to 2001, Turkey's score rose by 4.1 points, narrowing its gap with the highest score in 2001 and the average score in 2001.

(3) With respect to the ranking sections, in 2009, among the 5 secondary indicators of Turkey's NIC, there no strength indicator or advantage indicator. The competitiveness in innovation sustainability was a weakness indicator.

(4) With respect to the variation tendency of indicator rankings, among the 5 secondary indicators, there were four rising indicators (the competitiveness in innovation base, the competitiveness in innovation environment, the competitiveness in innovation input, and the competitiveness in innovation sustainability) and one dropping indicator (the competitiveness in innovation output), which was the main driver of the decline in Turkey's NIC.

(5) With respect to the driver of such variations, 4 secondary indicators have seen a greater boost in rankings compared to the decline of dropping indicator. Due to the influence of rising indicators, the overall ranking of Turkey's NIC rose to 14th in 2009.

II. Dynamic Variations of All Levels of Indicators of Turkey's NIC

Dynamic variations of all levels indicators of Turkey's NIC and the structure there of during 2001-2009 are shown in Figure 17-3 and Table 17-2.

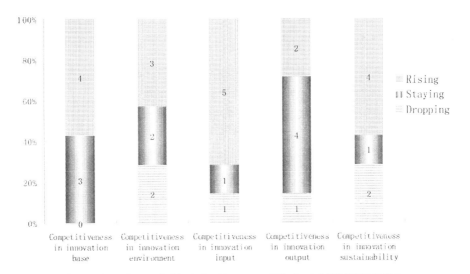

Figure 17-3   Dynamic Variation Structure of Turkey's NIC (2001-2009)

Table 17-2 Comparison of the Variations in Rankings of All Levels of Indicators of Turkey's NIC (2001-2009)

Secondary indicators	Number of tertiary indicators	Rising		Staying		Dropping		Variation tendency
		Number	Ratio (%)	Number	Ratio (%)	Number	Ratio (%)	
Innovation base	7	4	57.1	3	42.9	0	0.0	Rising
Innovation environment	7	3	42.9	2	28.6	2	28.6	Rising
Innovation input	7	5	71.4	1	14.3	1	14.3	Rising
Innovation output	7	2	28.6	4	57.1	1	14.3	Dropping
Innovation sustainability	7	4	57.1	1	14.3	2	28.6	Rising
Total	35	18	51.4	11	31.4	6	17.1	Rising

According to Figure 17-3, the number of rising tertiary indicators is greater than the number of dropping ones, indicating that rising indicators are dominating. The figures in Table 17-2 further demonstrate that, among the 35 tertiary indicators of Turkey's NIC, there are 18 rising indicators (51.4%), 11 staying indicators (31.4%) and 6 dropping indicators (17.1%). The rising is stronger than the dropping momentum. Therefore, the ranking of Turkey's NIC rose by two places to 14th among G20 nations in 2009.

III. Driver Analysis on the Variations of All Levels of Indicators of Turkey's NIC

Quality variations of all levels indicators of Turkey's NIC and the structure there of during 2001-2009 are shown in Table 17-3.

Table 17-3 Comparison of the Quality of All Levels of Indicators of Turkey's NIC (2001-2009)

Secondary indicators	Number of tertiary indicators	Strength		Advantage		Medium		Weakness		Quality
		Number	Ratio (%)	Number	Ratio (%)	Number	Ratio (%)	Number	Ratio (%)	
Innovation base	7	0	0.0	0	0.0	7	100.0	0	0.0	Medium
Innovation environment	7	1	14.3	1	14.3	4	57.1	1	14.3	Medium
Innovation input	7	0	0.0	0	0.0	7	100.0	0	0.0	Medium
Innovation output	7	1	14.3	0	0.0	2	28.6	4	57.1	Medium
Innovation sustainability	7	0	0.0	3	42.9	1	14.3	3	42.9	Weakness
Total	35	2	5.7	4	11.4	21	60.0	8	22.9	Medium

According to Figure 17-3, among the 35 tertiary indicators of Turkey's NIC, there are 2 strength indicators (5.7%), 4 advantage indicators (11.4%), 21 medium indicators (60.0%), and 8 weakness indicators (22.9%). The sum of strength indicators and advantage indicators accounts for 17.1% of total indicators, which is smaller than the sum of medium indicators and weakness indicators. Among secondary indicators, there are strength/advantage indicator, 4 medium indicator (80%), and 1 weakness indicators (20%). Since the indicator system is dominated by medium indicators, Turkey's NIC was average during 2001-2009.

Chapter 18

Evaluation and Analysis Report n the NIC
of the United Kingdom

Located in Western Europe, United Kingdom consists of England, Scotland and Wales on the island of Great Britain, North Ireland and a series of attached islands. The country covers a total area of 244,800 square kilometers, 1.34% of which are water areas, with coastline extending 11,450 kilometers. As of late 2010, the gross population was 62.43 million, with GDP reaching USD 2,246.1 billion, up 1.25% year-on-year., a downward trend was observed with respect to the NIC ranking of United Kingdom. In 2001, the NIC of United Kingdom ranked 3rd among G20 nations. In 2009, United Kingdom dropped three places to 6th. By analyzing the variations in the rankings of its NIC and respective elements there of among G20 nations 2001 2009, United Kingdom.

I. Summary of United Kingdom's NIC

The variations in the ranking and of United Kingdom's NIC are shown in Figure 18-1, and the variations in the of 5 secondary indicators are shown in Figure 18-2 and Table 18-1.

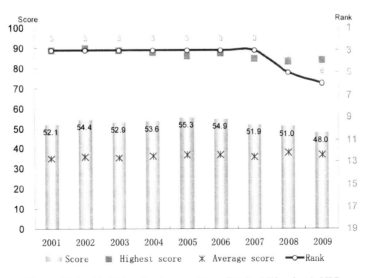

Figure 18-1　Variation Tendency of the of United Kingdom's NIC

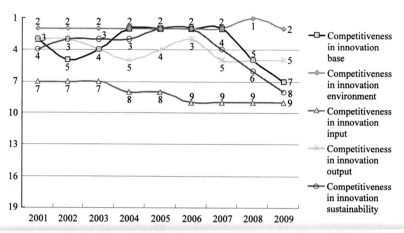

Figure 18-2　Variation Tendencies of the Rankings of the Secondary Indicators
of United Kingdom's NIC

Table 18-1　Scores and Rankings of the Secondary Indicators of United Kingdom's NIC

Item Year	Competitiveness in innovation base		Competitiveness in innovation environment		Competitiveness in innovation input		Competitiveness in innovation output		Competitiveness in innovation sustainability		Innovation competitiveness	
	Score	Rank	Score	Rank	Score	Rank	Score	Rank	Score	Rank	Score	Rank
2001	49.5	3	74.1	2	43.4	7	41.4	3	51.9	4	52.1	3
2002	52.1	5	78.3	2	44.0	7	40.6	3	57.0	3	54.4	3
2003	55.6	4	79.1	2	42.5	7	36.5	4	50.5	3	52.9	3
2004	58.5	2	78.7	2	41.8	8	33.7	5	55.3	3	53.6	3
2005	65.5	2	77.6	2	39.7	8	36.5	4	57.5	2	55.3	3
2006	60.9	2	76.8	2	40.1	9	39.0	3	57.5	2	54.9	3
2007	64.9	2	78.3	2	39.4	9	30.1	5	46.6	4	51.9	3
2008	52.2	5	80.2	1	39.5	9	30.0	5	53.2	6	51.0	5
2009	50.2	7	74.9	2	38.2	9	32.4	5	44.4	8	48.0	6
Variance	0.7		0.8		-5.3		-9.0		-7.5		-4.1	
Variance		-4		0		-2		-2		-4		-3
Quality		Advantage		Strength		Advantage		Strength		Advantage		Advantage

(1) With respect to overall ranking, United Kingdom's NIC ranked 6th among G20 nations in 2009, three places compared to 2001. Generally speaking, downward fluctuations were observed in the evaluation period.

(2) With respect to the points of indicators, United Kingdom's NIC scored 48 points in 2009, which is 35.7 points lower than the highest score and 11.2 points higher than the average score. Compared to 2001, United Kingdom's score dropped by 4.1 points,

narrowing its gap with the highest score in 2001 and the average score in 2001.

(3) With respect to the ranking sections, in 2009, among the 5 secondary indicators of United Kingdom's NIC, the competitiveness in innovation environment and the competitiveness in innovation output were strength indicators, while the competitiveness in innovation base, the competitiveness in innovation input and the competitiveness in innovation sustainability were advantage indicators. There w no weakness indicator.

(4) With respect to the variation tendency of indicator rankings, among the 5 secondary indicators, there was no rising indicator, but there were four dropping indicators (the competitiveness in innovation base, the competitiveness in innovation input, the competitiveness in innovation output, and the competitiveness in innovation sustainability), which were the main drivers of the decline in United Kingdom's NIC. Ranking of the competitiveness in innovation environment remained unchanged.

(5) With respect to the driver of such variations, no secondary indicator in ranking, while most secondary indicators experienced a drop in rankings. Due to the influence of dropping indicators, the overall ranking of United Kingdom's NIC dropped to 6th in 2009.

II. Dynamic Variations of All Levels of Indicators of United Kingdom's NIC

Dynamic variations of all levels indicators of United Kingdom's NIC and the structure there of during 2001-2009 are shown in Figure 18-3 and Table 18-2.

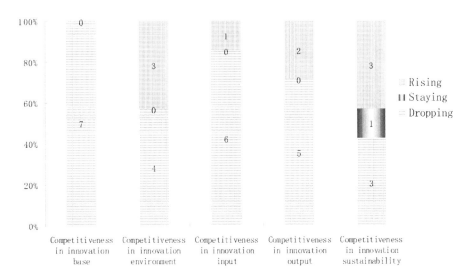

Figure 18-3   Dynamic Variation Structure of United Kingdom's NIC (2001-2009)

Table 18-2　Comparison of the Variations in Rankings of All Levels of Indicators of United Kingdom's NIC (2001-2009)

Secondary indicators	Number of tertiary indicators	Rising		Staying		Dropping		Variation tendency
		Number	Ratio (%)	Number	Ratio (%)	Number	Ratio (%)	
Innovation base	7	0	0.0	0	0.0	7	100.0	Dropping
Innovation environment	7	3	42.9	0	0.0	4	57.1	Staying
Innovation input	7	1	14.3	0	0.0	6	85.7	Dropping
Innovation output	7	2	28.6	0	0.0	5	71.4	Dropping
Innovation sustainability	7	3	42.9	1	14.3	3	42.9	Dropping
Total	35	9	25.7	1	2.9	25	71.4	Dropping

According to Figure 18-3, the number of rising tertiary indicators is less than the number of dropping ones, indicating that dropping indicators are dominating. The figures in Table 18-2 further demonstrate that, among the 35 tertiary indicators of United Kingdom's NIC, there are 9 rising indicators (25.7%), 1 staying indicators (2.9%) and 25 dropping indicators (71.4%). The rising is weaker than the dropping momentum. Therefore, the ranking of United Kingdom's NIC dropped three places to 6th among G20 nations in 2009.

III. Driver Analysis on the Variations of All Levels of Indicators of United Kingdom's NIC

Quality variations of all levels indicators of United Kingdom's NIC and the structure there of during 2001-2009 are shown in Table 18-3.

Table 18-3　Comparison of the Quality of All Levels of Indicators of United Kingdom's NIC (2001-2009)

Secondary indicators	Number of tertiary indicators	Strength		Advantage		Medium		Weakness		Quality
		Number	Ratio (%)	Number	Ratio (%)	Number	Ratio (%)	Number	Ratio (%)	
Innovation base	7	1	14.3	6	85.7	0	0.0	0	0.0	Advantage
Innovation environment	7	5	71.4	1	14.3	1	14.3	0	0.0	Strength
Innovation input	7	0	0.0	5	71.4	2	28.6	0	0.0	Advantage
Innovation output	7	5	71.4	2	28.6	0	0.0	0	0.0	Strength
Innovation sustainability	7	2	28.6	3	42.9	0	0.0	2	28.6	Advantage
Total	35	13	37.1	17	48.6	3	8.6	2	5.7	Advantage

According to Figure 18-3, among the 35 tertiary indicators of United Kingdom's NIC, there are 13 strength indicators (37.1%), 17 advantage indicators (48.6%), 3 medium indicators (8.6%), and 2 weakness indicators (5.7%). The sum of strength indicators and advantage indicators accounts for 85.7% of total indicators, which is greater than the sum of medium indicators and weakness indicators. Among secondary indicators, there are 2 strength indicator (40%), 3 advantage indicator (60%) and medium/weakness indicator. Since the indicator system is dominated by strength indicators and advantage indicators, United Kingdom's NIC was during 2001-2009.

Chapter 19

Evaluation and Analysis Report n the NIC of the United States

Situated in the middle of North America, United States faces Atlantic Ocean on east and Pacific Ocean on west, and borders Canada north and Mexico and the Gulf of Mexico south. The country covers a total area of 9.63 million square kilometers, with coastline extending 19,924 kilometers. As of late 2010, the gross population was 312.4 million, with GDP reaching USD 14,582.4 billion, up 2.83% year-on-year., United States maintain a leading position in terms of NIC. In 2001, the NIC of United States ranked 1st among G20 nations. In 2009, United States still ranked 1st. By analyzing the variations in the rankings of its NIC and respective elements there of among G20 nations 2001 2009, United States.

I. Summary of United States' NIC

The variations in the ranking and of United States' NIC are shown in Figure 19-1, and the variations in theof 5 secondary indicators are shown in Figure 19-2 and Table 19-2.

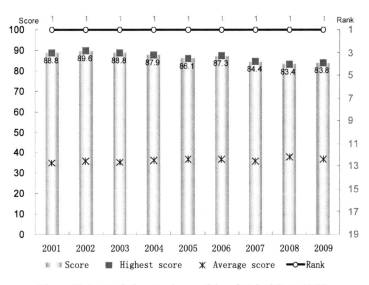

Figure 19-1   Variation Tendency of the of United States' NIC

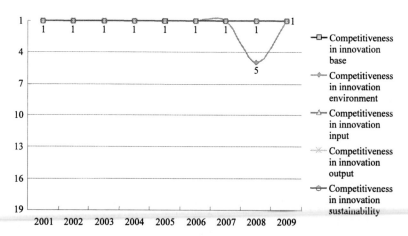

Figure 19-2   Variation Tendencies of the Rankings of the Secondary Indicators
of United States' NIC

Table 19-1   Scores and Rankings of the Secondary Indicators of United States' NIC

Item Year	Competitiveness in innovation base		Competitiveness in innovation environment		Competitiveness in innovation input		Competitiveness in innovation output		Competitiveness in innovation sustainability		Innovation competitiveness	
	Score	Rank	Score	Rank	Score	Rank	Score	Rank	Score	Rank	Score	Rank
2001	97.1	1	84.0	1	95.3	1	91.0	1	76.3	1	88.8	1
2002	98.5	1	84.6	1	94.5	1	92.0	1	78.6	1	89.6	1
2003	96.3	1	84.9	1	94.0	1	90.9	1	78.0	1	88.8	1
2004	95.1	1	85.0	1	92.8	1	90.1	1	76.8	1	87.9	1
2005	91.2	1	85.1	1	91.3	1	90.0	1	73.1	1	86.1	1
2006	95.6	1	84.8	1	91.3	1	88.1	1	76.7	1	87.3	1
2007	94.1	1	83.9	1	91.2	1	86.5	1	66.2	1	84.4	1
2008	91.3	1	70.5	5	92.7	1	85.6	1	76.9	1	83.4	1
2009	92.8	1	81.6	1	91.6	1	80.7	1	72.1	1	83.8	1
Variance	-4.3		-2.4		-3.7		-10.3		-4.2		-5.0	
Variance		0		0		0		0		0		0
Quality		Strength		Strength		Strength		Strength		Strength		Strength

(1) With respect to overall ranking, United States' NIC ranked 1st among G20 nations in 2009, remain unchanged compared to 2001. Generally speaking, top ranking was maintained in the evaluation period.

(2) With respect to the points of indicators, United States' NIC scored 83.8 points in 2009, which is the highest score and is 47 points higher than the average score. Compared to 2001, United States' score dropped by 5 points, narrowing its gap with the average score in 2001.

(3) With respect to the ranking sections, in 2009, among the 5 secondary indicators of United States' NIC, the competitiveness in innovation base, the competitiveness in innovation environment, the competitiveness in innovation input, the competitiveness in innovation output, and the competitiveness in innovation sustainability were all strength indicators.

(4) With respect to the variation tendency of indicator rankings, among the 5 secondary indicators, there was no rising indicator or dropping indicator. Rankings of all 5 secondary indicators remained unchanged.

(5) With respect to the driver of such variations, no secondary indicator in ranking. Due to the combined influence of these leading indicators, the overall ranking of United States' NIC remained unchanged in 2009 (1st).

II. Dynamic Variations of All Levels of Indicators of United States' NIC

Dynamic variations of all levels indicators of United States' NIC and the structure there of during 2001-2009 are shown in Figure 19-3 and Table 19-2.

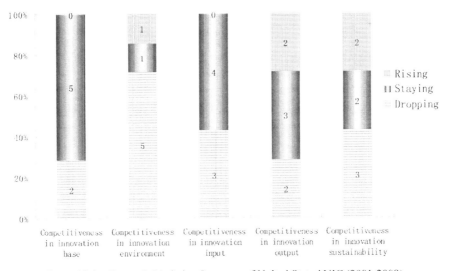

Figure 19-3   Dynamic Variation Structure of United States' NIC (2001-2009)

Table 19-2   Comparison of the Variations in Rankings of All Levels of Indicators of United States' NIC (2001-2009)

Secondary indicators	Number of tertiary indicators	Rising		Staying		Dropping		Variation tendency
		Number	Ratio (%)	Number	Ratio (%)	Number	Ratio (%)	
Innovation base	7	0	0.0	5	71.4	2	28.6	Staying
Innovation environment	7	1	14.3	1	14.3	5	71.4	Staying
Innovation input	7	0	0.0	4	57.1	3	42.9	Staying
Innovation output	7	2	28.6	3	42.9	2	28.6	Staying
Innovation sustainability	7	2	28.6	2	28.6	3	42.9	Staying
Total	35	5	14.3	15	42.9	15	42.9	Staying

According to Figure 19-3, the number of rising tertiary indicators is less than the number of dropping ones, indicating that dropping indicators are dominating. The figures in Table 19-2 further demonstrate that, among the 35 tertiary indicators of United States' NIC, there are 5 rising indicators (14.3%), 15 staying indicators (42.9%) and 15 dropping indicators (42.9%). The rising is weaker than the dropping momentum. However, due to the combined influence of external factors, the ranking of United States' NIC remained in 1st place among G20 nations in 2009.

III. Driver Analysis on the Variations of All Levels of Indicators of United States' NIC

Quality variations of all levels indicators of United States' NIC and the structure there of during 2001-2009 are shown in Table 19-3.

Table 19-3   Comparison of the Quality of All Levels of Indicators of United States' NIC (2001-2009)

Secondary indicators	Number of tertiary indicators	Strength		Advantage		Medium		Weakness		Quality
		Number	Ratio (%)	Number	Ratio (%)	Number	Ratio (%)	Number	Ratio (%)	
Innovation base	7	6	85.7	1	14.3	0	0.0	0	0.0	Strength
Innovation environment	7	4	57.1	3	42.9	0	0.0	0	0.0	Strength
Innovation input	7	7	100	0	0.0	0	0.0	0	0.0	Strength
Innovation output	7	6	85.7	1	14.3	0	0.0	0	0.0	Strength
Innovation sustainability	7	5	71.4	0	0.0	2	28.6	0	0.0	Strength
Total	35	28	80.0	5	14.3	2	5.7	0	0.0	Strength

According to Figure 19-3, among the 35 tertiary indicators of United States' NIC, there are 28 strength indicators (80.0%), 5 advantage indicators (14.3%), 2 medium indicators (5.7%), and   weakness indicator. The sum of strength indicators and advantage indicators accounts for 94.3% of total indicators, which is far greater than the sum of medium indicators and weakness indicators. Among secondary indicators, there are 5 strength indicators (100%) and   advantage/medium/weakness indicator. Since the indicator system is dominated by strength indicators, United States' NIC was during 2001-2009.

References

[1] Paul Blustein et al. *Recovery or Relapse: The Role of the G-20 in the Global Economy [R]* Global Economy and Development at BROOKINGS, June, 2010

[2] *Multipolarity: The New Global Economy [R]* 2011 The International Bank for Reconstruction and Development/The World Bank, 2011.

[3] Robert D. Atkinson and Scott M. Andes *The Atlantic Century: Benchmarking EU & U. S. Innovation and Competitiveness [R]* The Information Technology and Innovation Foundation, February, 2009.

[4] James P. Andrew et al. *The Information Technology and Innovation Foundation [R]* The Boston Consulting Group, February, 2009.

[5] Bengt-Åke Lundvall, Björn Johnson, Esben Sloth Andersen, Bent Dalum National systems of production, innovation and competence building *Research Policy*, 213-231.

[6] Bengt-Åke Lundvall National Systems of Innovation: Toward a Theory of Innovation and Interactive Learning [M] Anthem Press, 2010

[7] Bjørn T. Asheim and Arne Isaksen Regional Innovation Systems: The Integration of Local 'Sticky' and Global 'Ubiquitous' Knowledge *The Journal of Technology Transfer*, 77-86.

[8] Charles Edquist, Maureen McKelvey *Systems of nnovation: rowth, ompetitiveness and mployment [M]* Edward Elgar Publishing, 2000.

[9] Chun-Liang Chen, and Yi-Long Jaw Building global dynamic capabilities through innovation: A case study of Taiwan's cultural organizations *Journal of Engineering and Technology Management*, 247-263.

[10] David C. Mowery and Joanne E. Oxley Inward technology transfer and competitiveness: the role of national innovation systems *Cambridge Political Economy Society*, 1995: 67-93.

[11] David Soskice German technology policy, innovation, and national institutional frameworks *Industry & Innovation*, 1997: 75-96.

[12] Gabrijela Leskovar-Spacapan, and Majda Bastic Differences in organizations' innovation capability in transition economy: Internal aspect of the organizations' strategic orientation *Technovation*, 2007: 533-546.

[13] Jan Faber, and Anneloes Barbara Hesen Innovation capabilities of European nations: Cross-national analyses of patents and sales of product innovations *Research Policy*, 2004: 193-207.

[14] Jan Fagerberg, and Martin Srholec National innovation systems, capabilities and economic development *Research Policy*, 2008: 1417-1435.

[15] Jian Cheng Guan, Richard C.M. Yam, Chiu Kam Mok, and Ning Ma A study of the relationship between competitiveness and technology innovation capability based on DEA models *European Journal of Operational Research*, 2006: 971-986.

[16] Parimal Patel National Innovation Systems: Why They Are Important, And How They Might Be Measured And Compared *Economics of Innovation and New Technology*, 1994: 77-95.

[17] Patarapong Intarakumnerd, Pun-arj Chairatana, and Tipawan Tangchitpiboon. National innovation system in less successful developing countries: the case of Thailand *Research Policy*, 2002: 1445-1457.

[18] Pedro Conceição, Manuel V. Heitor and Bengt-Åke Lundvall. *Innovation, competence building, and social cohesion in Europe: towards a learning society* Edward Elgar Publishing, 2003.

[19] Pedro Conceição, Manuel V. Heitor Knowledge interaction towards inclusive learning: Promoting systems of

innovation and competence building *Technological Forecasting and Social Change,* 2002: 641-651.

[20] Pedro Conceição, Manuel V. HeitorSystems of Innovation and Competence Building Across Diversity: Learning from the Portuguese Path in the European Context *The International Handbook on Innovation,* 2003: 945-975.

[21] Phil Cooke Regionally asymmetric knowledge capabilities and open innovation: Exploring 'Globalisation 2'—A new model of industry *Research Policy,* 2005: 1128-1149.

[22] Prasada Reddy New trends in globalization of corporate R&D and implications for innovation capability in host countries: A survey from India *World Development,* 1997: 1821-1837.

Richard R. Nelson *National innovation systems: a comparative analysis* Oxford University Press, 1993.

[23] Walt Whitman Rostow *The Stages of Economic Growth* Beijing: The Commercial Press, 1962.

[24] Christopher Freeman *Japan: A New National System of Innovation?* Beijing: Economic Science Press, 1991.

[25] B. A. Lundvall *Innovation as an Interactive Process—from Userproducer Interaction to the National System of Innovation* Beijing: Economic Science Press, 1991.

[26] Philip Kotler *The Marketing of Nations* Beijing: Huaxia Publishing House, 1997.

[27] Jean Tirole *The Theory of Industrial Organization* Beijing: China Renmin University Press, 1999.

[28] Michael Porter *Competitive Advantage of Nations* Beijing: Huaxia Publishing House, 2002.

[29] Qi Jianguo Technology Innovation: Reform and Reorganization of National System Beijing: Social Sciences Academic Press, 1995.

[30] Wu Guisheng, Xiewei Elements, Function and Influence of National Innovation System 2nd China-Korea Workshop on Industrial and Technical Policies—Conference Papers on National Technology Innovation System for the 21st Century, 1997.

[31] Lu YongxiangInnovation and Future Beijing: Science Press, 1998.

[32] Liu Xielin Present Status Problems and Development Trends of China's National Innovation System *National Technology Innovation System Construction under Market Economy.* Subject Report, 1998.

[33] Wang Chunfa Technology Innovation Policy: Theoretical Basis and Tool Selection United States and Japan Beijing: Economic Science Press, 1998.

[34] Shi Dinghuan National Innovation System: Present and FutureBeijing: Economy & Management Publishing House, 1999.

[35] Feng Zhijun, Luo Weiummary of Theories and Policies Related to the National Innovation SystemBeijing: Qunyan Press, 1999.

[36] Hu Zhijian et al National Innovation System: Theoretical Analysis and International Comparison Beijing: Social Sciences Academic Press, 2000.

[37] Feng Zhijun. Outline of National Innovation System Studies Jinan: Shandong Education Press, 2000.

[38] Jin Bei Competitiveness Economics Guangzhou: Guangdong Economic Press, 2003.

[39] Du Dong, Pang QinghuaModern Comprehensive Evaluation Methods and Selected Cases Beijing: Tsinghua University Press, 2005.

[40] Chinese Group of Science and Technology for DevelopmentReport on China's Regional Innovation Capacity Beijing: Science Press, 2006.

[41] Ministry of Science and Technology, PRC: Technology Innovation Development Courses and Experiences of Major Innovative Countries Beijing: China Science and Technology Press, 2006.

[42] Song Yuhua, Wang Li omparative Institutional Study on Worldwide New Economic Developments Beijing: China Social Sciences Press, 2006.

[43] Zhao Zhongjian Innovation Leading the World—Innovation and Competitiveness Strategies of United States Shanghai: East China Normal University Press, 2007.

[44] Bu Lingge Focusing on Innovation Beijing: Science Press, 2007.

[45] Li Zhengfeng, Hu Yu Building An Innovative Country—A Key Choice for the Future Beijing: People's Publishing House, 2007.

[46] Chen Jin, Liu Xielin (Chief Editor) Independent Innovation and National Prosperity—Challenges in Building An Innovative Country with Chinese Features and the Corresponding Counter Measures Beijing: Science Press, 2008.

[47] Liu Fengchao et al Approach for Measuring National Innovation Capability and its Application Beijing: Science Press, 2009.

[48] Ni Pengfei (Chief Editor) Report on China's National Competitiveness—No.1 Beijing: Social Sciences Academic Press, 2010.

[49] Wang Chunfa Overall National Power Competition and National Innovation System *World Economy*, 1999: 4.

[50] Luo Shougui, Zhen Feng Evaluation Studies on Regional Innovation Capability *Journal of Nanjing University of Economics*, 2003: 3.

[51] Tong Xin, Wang Jici Local Innovation Network under the Background of Globalization *China Soft Science*, 2000: 9.

[52] Wang HaiyanFundamentals and Methods for the Operational Performance Evaluation of National Innovation System *Science and Technology Management Research*, 2001: 2.

[53] Ding Huanfeng Regional Innnovation System *Science Research Management*, 2001: 11.

[54] Shen Kunrong, Geng Qiang Direct Foreign Investment, Technology Spillover and Endogenous Economic Growth—Metrological Examination and Empirical Analysis of China's Data *Social Sciences in China*, 2001: 5.

[55] Wang Guojin, Wang Qifan New Progress in the Evaluation Studies on the Technology Innovation Capability of Enterprises *Science Research Management*, 2002: 4.

[56] Liu Xielin, Hu Zhijian Distribution of China's Regional Innovation Capability and the Corresponding Causes *Studies in Science of Science*, 2002.

[57] Liu Xielin How to Understand the Global Ranking of China's Competitiveness *Science of Science and Management of S. & T.* 2002: 10.

[58] Liu Xielin, Duan Xiaohua The Transforming National Innovation System of Russia *Studies in Science of Science*, 2003.

[59] Lu Feng, Mu Ling Local Innovation, Capacity Development and Competitive Advantage *Management World*, 2003: 12.

[60] Xiang Houjun National Competitive Advantage and National Innovation System—Comparative Analysis and Study *Studies in Science of Science*, 2004: 2.

[61] He Shuquan Framework, Challenges and Thoughts about China's National Innovation System *Forum on Science and Technology in China*, 2005: 3.

[62] Xie Yongqin Regional Innovation Network Construction in China's High-tech Industrial Park *Science and Technology Management Research*, 2005: 8

[63] Zhu Yong, Zhang Zongyi Study on the Regional Difference in Economic Growth Driven by Technological Innovation *China Soft Science*, 2005: 1.

[64] Zhang Haiyang Two Sides of R&D, Foreign Capital Movement and Industrial Productivity Growth in China *Economic Research*, 2005: 5.

[65] Shang YongEnhancing Independent Innovation Capability and Building an Innovative Country *China Soft Science*, 2005.

[66] Guan Jiancheng, He Ying DEA-based Regional Innovation System Evaluation *Studies in Science of Science*, 2002.

[67] Guan Jiancheng, Yu JinDEA-based National Innovation Capability Analysis *R&D Management*, 2005.

[68] Wang DachuanGermany's Innovation Course *Prospects of Global Sci-tech Economy*, 2005: 12.

[69] Sun Yutao, Yang ZhongkaiInteractive Analysis of Intellectual Property Protection and Economic Growth *Science and Technology Management Research*, 2005: 12.

[70] Yang Zhongkai, Sun Yutao Comparison between National Technology Strength Indexes Based on Patent

Citation *Science of Science and Management of S. & T.* 2005 10.

[71] Ju Hongyun, Chu Xuelin Study on the Dynamic Processes of Technology Innovation System *Studies in Science of Science*, 2006: 8.

[72] Xu Guanhua Constructing an Innovative Country and Following an Innovative Route with Chinese Features *Science & Technology Industry of China*, 2006: 1.

[73] Zhou Yong, Feng Congcong Indicator System for the Evaluation of An Innovative Country (Province/City) *Science-Technology and Management*, 2006: 3.

[74] Zhang Zhihe, Hu Shuhua and Jin Xin Building and Analysis of Industrial Innovation System Model *Science Research Management*, 2006: 2.

[75] Yang Zhongtai The Connection between Regional Innovation System and National Innovation System and the Principle of Construction *Forum on Science and Technology in China*, 2006: 9.

[76] Zhang Guoliang, Chen Hongmin Index-based Evaluation and Comparative Analysis of Domestic and International Technology Innovation Capability *Systems Engineering-Theory Methodology Application*, 2006: 5.

[77] Zhao Lingyunule of Innovative Country Formation and Revelation to China *Study Monthly*, 2006: 3.

[78] Zhao Lingyun Respecting the Rule of Innovative Country Formation and Propelling China's Innovative Country Construction *Studies on Mao Zedong and DengXiaoping Theories*, 2006: 7.

[79] Luo Ji, Wang DaijingCounter Measures for China to Build An Innovative Country *Economic Review*, 2006: 6.

[80] Wang MinxuanOutline of 10 Key Features of Major Overseas Innovative Countries *World Economy*, 2006: 7.

[81] Sun Hui Basic Features and Primary Advantages of Innovative Countries Like United States *Prospects of Global Sci-tech Economy*, 2006: 8.

[82] Wang Chengyun, Du Debin and Li YanPolicies and Route of Japan to Build An Innovative Country *Studies in Science of Science*, 2006 S1.

[83] Jia Genliang, Wang XiaorongSuccessful Experiences with the Building of An Innovative Country *Contemporary Economic Research*, 2006: 9.

[84] Li Anfang Experiences of South Korea in Building An Innovative Country and Revelation to China *World Economy Study*, 2006: 10.

[85] Xu GuanhuaSeveral Major Issues Related to Independent Innovation *China Soft Science*, 2006: 4.

[86] Zhang Yiliang, Zhang Yuzhe Study on the Indicator System for National Independent Innovation Capability Evaluation *Economist*, 2006: 6.

[87] Zhang Zhenzhen, Lin Xiaoyan International Comparison of Intellectual Property Protection and Technology Innovation Routes *China Soft Science*, 2006: 11.

[88] Zhou Li, Wu YumingRegional Innovation Capability in China: Factor Analysis and Clustering Study—And the Substitute for Factor Analysis of Regional Innovation Capability *China Soft Science*, 2006: 8.

[89] Gao Liang Independent Innovation Guideline and National Competitiveness Oriented Economic Development Strategy *Studies in International Technology and Economy*, 2007: 1.

[90] Qiu Junping, Tan Chunhui 50 Years of National Innovation Capability Evaluation *Evaluation and Management*, 2007: 4.

[91] Liu Weiping Revelation of France's "Pole of Competitiveness" Strategy to the Development of High-tech Industry in Bohai Economic Zone *Inquiry Into Economic Issues*, 2007: 11.

[92] Sun Wenjie, Shen Kunrong Technology Introduction and Independent Innovation of Chinese Enterprises: Quantile Regression Model Based Empirical Studies*World Economy*, 2007: 1.

[93] Mao Hao, Zhang Xianqiang and Zhang HongjiQuantity and Structure Based Quantitive Analysis of Service Invention's Patent Application by Foreigner-in-China*East China Economic Management*, 2007: 6.

[94] Pi Yonghua Regional Technology Innovation Diffusion and Economic Growth Convergence *Journal of Nanjing University of Finance and Economics*, 2008: 2.

[95] Liu Fengchao, Sun Yutao Review of Studies on Measuring National Innovation Capability *Studies in Science*

of Science, 2008: 4.

[96] Wan Yong, Wen Hao Study on the Economic Growth Effect of China's Inputs in Regional Technology Innovation *Social Scientist*, 2009: 5.

[97] Zhao Hailin, Wang Zhao Performance Appraisal of the Innovation Capability in South-west China *Technoeconomics & Management Research*, 2009: 6.

[98] Wan Yong, Wen Hao Study on the Indicator System for Evaluating China's Regional Innovation Capability *Journal of Central South University of Technology (Social Science)*, 2009 5.

[99] Gu Shengzu, Li Hua, et al Institutional Innovation and Business Technology Innovation during the Construction of An Innovative Country *Jianghai Academic Journal*, 2010: 6.

[100] Guo Shufen volution Process of China's National Innovation System *Studies In Dialectics of Nature*, 2010: 10.

[101] Liu Zhichun Concept & Structure of China's National Innovation System and the Present Status & Key Studies Related to Its Construction *Science and Technology Management Research*, 2010: 15.

[102] Cheng Siwei Construction of An Innovative Country *Theoretical References,* 2010: 5.

[103] Zhou Mi, Deng Xiangrong Route Selection for Transnforming into An Innovative Country *Theoretical References*, 2010: 5.

[104] Kong Jie Study on the National Innovation Policy Performance Evaluation Models Applied in Europe and America and the Revelation There of *Technology and Innovation Management*, 2010: 3.

[105] Gao LipingAnalysis and Revelation of the Innovation Policies in Developed Countries *Journal of Zhengzhou Institute of Aeronautical Industry Management (Social Science)*, 2010: 2.

[106] Xiao Haohui Building the Strategic Status of Innovative Country and Development Approach *Journal of Hunan University of Science & Technology (Social Science)*, 2010: 3.

[107] Liu Li, Li Zhengfeng, et al One Research Framework for the Internationalization of National Innovation System: Function-Phase Model *Journal of Hohai University (Philosophy and Social Sciences)*, 2010: 3.

[108] Feng Kaidong National Innovation System: From the Perspective of System and *Journal of National School of Administration*, 2011: 3.

[109] Zhao Junjie Construction of United States' National Innovation System *Prospects of Global Sci-tech Economy*, 2011: 4.

[110] Li Zhengfeng Knowledge, Innovation and National Innovation System *Journal of Shandong University of Sciences & Technology (Social Science)*, 2011: 1.

[111] Wu Xiaoyuan, Xu Mingxing, et al Evolutionary Economics Based Study on Hierarchies of National Innovation System *Technoeconomics & Management Research*, 2011: 7.

[112] Liu Fengchao, Feng Tingting System Dynamics Model Formed by National Innovation Capability: Regarding Invention Patent as Token Element of Capacity *Management Review*, 2011: 5.

[113] Zhong Jinsong Analysis and Revelation of Typical National Policies Supporting Independence Innovation—And the Future Trend of China's Innovation Policies *Theory and Reform*, 2011: 4.

[114] Cui Yonghua, Li Zhengfeng, et al Role of Cross-boundary Organizations in National Innovation System and Route Selection: Taking Association as the Example *Forum on Science and Technology in China*, 2011: 6.

[115] Chen QiBasic Elements and Framework of the National Innovation System of Great Powers *Journal of Hunan Business College*, 2011: 1.

[116] Chen Qiang, Bao Yuehua Comparative Study of the National Innovation Systems in German-Speaking Region *Comparative Economic and Social Systems*, 2011: 1.

[117] Li Taoya, Lin Weihua Model and Revelation of Japan's Innovative Country Construction *Macroeconomic Management*, 2011: 3.

[118] Li Jianping (Chief Editor) et alReport on the Development of China's Provincial Overall Economic Competitiveness (2005-2006) Beijing, Social Sciences Academic Press, 2007.

[119] Li Jianping (Chief Editor) et al Report on the Development of China's Provincial Overall Economic

Competitiveness (2006-2007) Beijing, Social Sciences Academic Press, 2008.

[120] Li Jianping (Chief Editor) et alReport on the Development of China's Provincinal Overall Economic Competitiveness (2007-2008) [M]. Beijing, Social Sciences Academic Press, 2009.

[121] Li Jianping (Chief Editor) et al Report on the Development of China's Provincinal Overall Economic Competitiveness (2008-2009) [M]. Beijing, Social Sciences Academic Press, 2010.

[122] Li Jianping (Chief Editor) et al Report on the Development of China's Provincinal Overall Economic Competitiveness (2009-2010) [M]. Beijing, Social Sciences Academic Press, 2011.

[123] Li Jianping, Hua Maoxing, et alReport on China's 60-Year Economic Development (1949-2009) Beijing, Economic Science Press, 2009.

[124] Li Jianping, Hua Maoxing, et al Report on the Development of China's Provincial Environmental Competitiveness (2005-2009) Beijing, Social Sciences Academic Press, 2011.

[125] Li Minrong, Li Jianping, Hua MaoxingReport on Predictive Studies on China's Provincial Overall Economic Competitiveness (2009-2012) Beijing, Social Sciences Academic Press, 2010.

[126] Li Minrong, Li Jianping, Hua Maoxing Evaluation and Predictive Studies of China's Provincial Overall Economic Competitiveness Beijing, Social Sciences Academic Press, 2007.

[127] Li Minrong Study Report on China's Provincial Overall Economic Competitiveness (1998-2004) Beijing, Social Sciences Academic Press, 2006.

[128] Li Jianping, Hua Maoxing, et al Scientific-technical Progress and Economic Growth—Theories and Practices Related to Fujian's Technology Development During the Comprehensive Construction of An Affluent Society Beijing, China Economic Publishing House, 2005.

[129] Huang Maoxin Technological Option and Economic Growth Beijing, Social Sciences Academic Press, 2010.

[130] Huang MaoxinTechnological Option and Industrial Structure UpgradeBeijing, Social Sciences Academic Press, 2007.

[131] Huang Maoxing et al Review of China's Economic Highlights during 30-year Reform and Opening-up and ProspectsBeijing, Social Sciences Academic Press, 2008.

[132] Huang Maoxing et al Study on the Economic Highlights in West Coast Economic Zone during the "12th Five Years" Beijing, China Social Sciences Press, 2010.

Postscript

This book is listed among the key research projects in 2012 of National Research Center for Overall Economic Competitiveness, 2012-2013 phased research result of the first Young Talents Development Program jointly launched by the Organization Department and Propaganda Department of CPC Central Committee,the major research results during 2011-2012 of the "Innovation Team of Fujian Normal University on Overall Competitiveness in Industrial and Regional Economy" funded by the Central Government (for supporting local universities/colleges to develop special projects), the major research results during 2011-2012 of the "Laboratory of Fujian Normal University on Overall Competitiveness in Regional Economy" (one of the advantageous-discipline laboratories jointly established by the Central Government and local government in universities/colleges), the current-stage research results of the general project of 2010 supported by National Social Science Fund (Project No. 10CJL006 and Project No. 10BJL046), the project supported by the Program 2010 for New Century Excellent Talents in University of the Ministry of Education (Project No.: NCET-10-0017), the project supported by 201 Fujian University/College Technology Innovation Team Nurturing Program (the current-stage research result of the Program for New Century Excellent Talents in University of Fujian Province (Project No.: JA10074S), and the final research result of the key research projects during 2011-2012 of the political economics of Fujian Normal University (as a provincial key discipline) and the key projects serving the construction of the West Coast of Taiwan Strait by Fujian provincial universities.

Nowadays, technology is playing increasingly prominent role as the primary productive force and the and source of echnology determines the well-being of people. In particular, with the substantial rise in the need for energy resources and the pressure of ecological environment and the booming development of economy/society, sustainable and development has become the common challenge faced by human, while technology innovation is exactly to address global challenges related to energy resource, ecological environment, natural disaster, and population healththe strong impetus driving economic growth. Experience show innovation has become the major to economic and social development, while innovation competitiveness has become the core factor of national competitiveness.

In recent years, an important platform for the international exchange and cooperation between developed countries and emerging market, is playing an increasingly important role. Since the of in 2008, G20 has convened multiple summits to discuss countermeasures, In the post-crisis era, the world is on the eve of new sci-tech revolution. countries are seeking for new ways of economic development and initiating a new round of competition occupy the commanding point of technological and industrial development. This will open up a new realm of productivity growth, create new social needs, and exert profound influence on people's production model, lifestyle and ways of thinking. In view of this, to deepen the research on the realities and levels of NIC and combithe new situations and requirements of innovation issues as global sci-tech development tide and new sci-tech revolution tendency, Fujian Normal University Sub-center of National Comprehensive Economic Competitiveness Research Center has, under the guidance and support of Social Sciences Academic Press of Chinese Academy of Social Sciences, established a research group since late 2009 for the "Report On the Group of Twenty (G20) NIC Development (2001-2010)" to discuss the evaluation and development of G20 NIC from the dimensions of theory, methodology and During the research, Professor Li Jianping, former president of Fujian Normal University and Fujian Normal University Sub-center of National Overall Economic Competitiveness Research Center, personally as the leader of the research group and one of the chief editors, directly instructed and participated in the research and review of the draft. Professor Li Minrong, one of the chief editor and secretary of the Party Leadership Group of Administration of Press and Publication (Copyright Bureau) of Fujian Province, directly instructed and participated in the research, modification and review of the draft. Research fellow Zhao Xinli, sci-tech counselor of China's Permanent Mission to UN and academician of International Academy of Sciences for Europe and Asia, offered guidance and great support for this book and served as one of the chief editors. Mr. Su Hongwen, Director of Competitiveness Division of "Management World" Development Research Center of the State Council, provided positive conditions for the successful completion of this book. Professor Li Jianjian, President of School of Economics, Fujian Normal University, provided guidance for the research work of this project.

Since December 2009, the Research Group has carried out all-around and in-depth research on the theoretical innovation and indicator evaluation system for G20 NIC, and traced the latest research dynamics and measurement indicator data, with research subjects covering 19 countries G20 and time span 10 years. This book contains more than 500,000 words. It arduous to acquire, input and analyze the miscellaneous data, including the collection and input of over 8,000 base data, calculation, collation and analysis of more than 40,000 data, and the preparation of over 300 diagrams, over 192 statistical tables and 18 competitiveness charts. For such a complicated and work, of the compilation team contributed a lot. Great gratitude is paid to the leaders of School of Economics, Fujian Normal University, and Dr. Li Junjun, Dr. Ye Qi, Dr. Lin Shoufu, Dr. Shen Neng, Dr. Chen Hongzhao, Dr. Wang Zhenzhen, Dr. Zheng Wei, Dr. Liu Xiaofeng, Dr. Chen Weixiong, Dr. Wang Ying, and Dr. Zhou Limei, as well as graduate students Chen Ling, Lin Qian, Zhang Baoying, Wu Yuning, Yang Xuexing, Yang Ting, Lei Xiaoqiu, Chen Xianlong, Guo Shaokang, Xiao Lei, and Wu Qimian. They worked for over 10 hours every day instead of taking vacation and holiday and contributed a lot for data acquisition and measurementthis research.

We also want to express our sincere gratitude to the authors of relevant literatures, with direct or indirect reference from which this book is therefore accomplished.

President Xie Shouguang of Social Sciences Academic Press, Director Wei Fei of Social Science Department and Chief Editor Cao Changxiang put forward many commendable modification opinions and made great efforts for this book. We also want to them our cordial thanks.

Given the limitations of time, there might be some omissions and defects in this book. Any comment or criticism is gratefully welcomed.

Editors

January 2012

This book is the result of a co-publication agreement between Social Sciences Academic Press (China) and Paths International Ltd.

The Competitiveness of G20 Nations
Report On the Group of Twenty (G20) National Innovation Competitiveness Development (2001-2010)

Chief Editors: Li Jianping, Li Minrong & Zhao Xinli
Deputy Chief Editors: Li Jianjian, Huang Maoxing & Su Hongwen

ISBN: 978-1-84464-142-0

CPSIA information can be obtained at www.ICGtesting.com
Printed in the USA
BVOW062121050213

312503BV00007B/36/P